DAVID BURKE'S
NEW AMERICAN
CLASSICS

DAVID BURKE'S
NEW AMERICAN
CLASSICS

DAVID BURKE

and

JUDITH CHOATE

Alfred A. Knopf   New York   2008

THIS IS A BORZOI BOOK
PUBLISHED BY ALFRED A. KNOPF

Copyright © 2006 by Dilcon, Ltd.

www.aaknopf.com

Library of Congress Cataloging-in-Publication Data

Burke, David, [date].
David Burke's new American classics / David Burke and Judith Choate.
p. cm.
ISBN 0-375-41231-X (alk. paper)
1. Cookery, American. I. Title: New American Classics.
II. Choate, Judith. III. Title.
TX715.B9533 2006
641.5973—dc22   2005044960

Manufactured in the United States of America
Published April 14, 2006
Reprinted One Time
Third Printing, June 2008

For Mom, Dad, Dillon, Connor & Madeline

Contents

Introduction   *xv*

BREAKFAST

BACON AND EGGS

Classic: Eggs Benedict with Hash Brown Potatoes and Oven-Dried Tomatoes   6
Contemporary: Canadian Bacon and Onion Potato Cake with Poached Eggs
and Spicy Tomato Salsa   10
Second Day Dish: Bacon, Potato, and Eggs Strudel   12

PANCAKES

Classic: Buttermilk Pancakes with Whipped Butter and Maple Syrup   14
Contemporary: Almond, Praline, and Banana Pancakes with Orange Syrup and Yogurt 16
Second Day Dish: Smoked Salmon Pancake Roll-Up with Onions and Capers   17

FRENCH TOAST

Classic: French Toast with Cinnamon-Brown Sugar and Apple Syrup   19
Contemporary: Titanic French Toast with Three Jams   21
Second Day Dish: French Toast with Bread Pudding Brûlée   22

DOUGHNUTS

Classic: Simple Sugar-and-Spice Doughnuts   26
Contemporary: Drunken Fortune Doughnuts   27
Second Day Dish: Stuffed Doughnuts with Whipped Cream and Berries   28

OATMEAL

Classic: Oatmeal with Cinnamon-Brown Sugar and Honey-Tossed
Berries and Raisins   30
Contemporary: Almond Oatmeal Crème Brûlée with Orange Essence   31
Second Day Dish: Oatmeal *Gougères*   33

APPETIZERS, SOUPS, AND SALADS

SHELLFISH COCKTAILS

Classic: Shrimp, Lobster, and Crab with Cocktail Sauce and Old Bay
Mayonnaise   40
Contemporary: Hot Shellfish Cocktail with Tomato-Roasted Garlic Aïoli   41
Second Day Dish: Chopped Seafood Salad with Tomato and Onion in Avocado Halves   43

SMOKED SALMON

Classic: Smoked Salmon with Horseradish Mousse and Corn Blini   46
Contemporary: Pastrami Salmon and Smoked Salmon with Potato
Pancakes, Honey Mustard Vinaigrette, and Apple Salad   47
Second Day Dish: Smoked Salmon Lollipops   50

CHOWDERS

Classic: New England Clam Chowder with Oyster Crackers   53
Contemporary: Two Soups—New England and Manhattan Clam
Chowders with Cheddar Biscuits   54
Second Day Dish: Clam Chowder Bread Pudding with Tomato and
Watercress Salad   56

COBB SALAD

Classic: Classic Cobb Salad   58
Contemporary: "Stacked" Chopped Cobb Salad with Chipotle Vinaigrette   60
Second Day Dish: Spiced Cobb Salad "Summer Roll" with Blue Cheese
Dipping Sauce   62

CHEF'S SALAD

Classic: Classic Chef's Salad Bowl   64
Contemporary: Carpaccio of Chef's Salad   65
Second Day Dish: Chef's Salad Bruschetta   66

CAESAR SALAD

Classic: The Famous Caesar Salad   68
Contemporary: Chopped Caesar Salad with Crab Cake Croutons   70
Second Day Dish: Spicy Spaghetti with Sausage and Caesar Sauce   71

POULTRY

Roast Chicken

Classic: Roast Chicken "Farmhouse Style" with Potatoes, Mushrooms,
Bacon, Onions, and Apple Cider Gravy 79
Contemporary: Seawater-Soaked Chicken with Thyme and Poppy Seed Gnocchi 80
Second Day Dish: Chicken-Potato Pancakes with Apple–Sour Cream Sauce 83

Fried Chicken

Classic: Southern Buttermilk-Fried Chicken, Coleslaw, Cornbread
Biscuits, Home-Style Green Beans, and Mashed Potatoes 86
Contemporary: Soy-Soaked Tempura Chicken with Vegetable Stir-Fry 89
Second Day Dish: Chicken and Cabbage Spring Rolls 91

Barbecued Chicken

Classic: Barbecued Chicken Parts with Corn on the Cob and Grilled
Vegetables 94
Contemporary: Pretzel-Onion Crusted Barbecued Chicken with Pretzel Latkes,
Corn, and Mustard 96
Second Day Dish: Barbecued Chicken Sticky Buns 99

Roast Long Island Duckling

Classic: Classic Roast Duck with Oranges 102
Contemporary: Soy-Honey Roast Duck 103
Second Day Dish: Duck Pithiviers 105

Roast Turkey

Classic: Traditional Roast Turkey with Condiments 109
Contemporary: Roast Half Turkey with Bread Pudding, Chestnut-Turkey
Cappuccino, and Candied Lemon Peel 113
Second Day Dish: Sweet Potato-Turkey Chowder 116

BEEF

Steak and Potatoes

Classic: Grilled Sirloin Steak with Garlicky Spinach 123

Contemporary:	Cracked Pepper Sirloin with Shrimp-Potato Pancakes and Roasted Asparagus	124
Second Day Dish:	Sirloin and Horseradish Knish with Mustard-Russian Sauce	126

Roast Prime Rib of Beef

Classic:	Roast Prime Rib with Gratin Potato	130
Contemporary:	Roasted Spice-Crusted Rib with Wild Mushroom-Vegetable Stew, Horseradish-Mustard Mousse, and Popovers	131
Second Day Dish:	Red Chili in a Potato Boat with Minced Crisp Onion	134

Pot Roast

Classic:	Yankee Pot Roast with Brown Bread Dumplings and Melted Vegetables	137
Contemporary:	Asian-Style Pot Roast	139
Second Day Dish:	Pot Roast Sloppy Joes	140

Meatloaf

Classic:	Not-So-Basic Meatloaf	142
Contemporary:	Meatloaf Bundt Cake	144
Second Day Dish:	Meatloaf Pancakes with Goat Cheese Salad and Fried Eggs	145

PORK

Fresh Ham

Classic:	Roast Fresh Ham with Pineapple Tarte Tatin	152
Contemporary:	Crackling Pork Shank with Firecracker Applesauce	154
Second Day Dish:	Barbecued Ham and Pineapple Kabobs	156

Pork Chops

Classic:	Grilled Pork Chops with Applesauce and Glazed Carrots	158
Contemporary:	Seared Pork with Chorizo and Garlicky Clams	159
Second Day Dish:	Sliced Pork Salad	161

Spareribs

Classic:	Barbecued Coffee Spareribs with Fixings	162
Contemporary:	Asparagus-Stuffed Spareribs with Corn Crêpes	165
Second Day Dish:	Barbecued Sparerib Home-Fries with Poached Eggs and Chili Corn Cakes	167

LAMB

Leg of Lamb

Classic: Roast Leg of Lamb, Stuffed Tomatoes, and Sliced Pan Potatoes   *173*

Contemporary: Boneless Leg of Lamb with Citrus-Mint Glaze   *175*

Second Day Dish: Lamb-Stuffed Shells with Tomato Broth   *176*

Lamb Chops

Classic: Rack of Lamb with Bouquet of Vegetables   *178*

Contemporary: Poached Rack of Lamb with *Fleur de Sel,* Tomato Couscous, and Garlic Pearls   *180*

Second Day Dish: Crisp Goat Cheese, Potato, and Lamb Sandwich   *182*

Lamb Stew

Classic: Lamb Stew with Root Vegetables and Honey-Thyme Croutons   *185*

Contemporary: Braised Lamb Shank with Cauliflower-Rosemary Purée   *187*

Second Day Dish: Tempura Lamb and Vegetables with Peanut Sauce   *189*

FISH AND SHELLFISH

Cod

Classic: Herb-Broiled Cod with Clams, Bacon, Cabbage, and Biscuits   *196*

Contemporary: Oh, My Cod!   *198*

Second Day Dish: Baked Potato with Cod and Red Pepper Coulis   *200*

Tuna

Classic: Tuna Steak Provençal   *204*

Contemporary: Tuna Steak au Moutarde with Miso Vinaigrette and Shiitake Dumplings   *205*

Second Day Dish: Tuna Niçoise Salad Hash   *208*

Salmon

Classic: Poached Salmon with Tomato-Herb Butter Sauce and Cucumber   *212*

Contemporary: Salmon Leaves Cooked on the Plate with Shrimp, Grapefruit, and Basil   *214*

Second Day Dish: Roasted Onion Stuffed with Salmon and Tomato Salad   *216*

Lobster

Classic: Boiled Lobster with Drawn Butter and Boiled Potatoes   *219*

Contemporary: Poached Lobster with Onion Rings and Basil Ranch Dressing   *220*

Second Day Dish: Mixed Green Salad with Tiny Potatoes Stuffed with Russian-Style
                     Lobster Salad   223
Classic: Grilled Lobster with Rosemary Oil, Asparagus, and Tomato-Garlic Aïoli 224
Contemporary: Angry Lobster with Lemon Rice and Crispy Basil   226
Second Day Dish: Lobster-Mango Rolls with Soy-Ginger Vinaigrette   228

Shrimp

Classic: Broiled Shrimp with Scampi Butter and Tomato-Rice Pilaf   231
Contemporary: Sautéed Shrimp with Spinach-Lasagna Roll and Crisp Spinach   233
Second Day Dish: Shrimp Fried Rice and Sausage   235

Crab

Classic: Crab Cakes with Baltimore-Spiced Tomato Vinaigrette   237
Contemporary: Chicken Breast Stuffed "Crab Francese"   239
Second Day Dish: Crab Clubs on Crackers   240

Soft-Shell Crabs

Classic: Soft-Shell Crabs with Olive-Tomato Tartar Sauce and Asparagus Salad 242
Contemporary: Grilled Soft-Shell Crabs with Curry-Yogurt Cream   244
Second Day Dish: Soft-Shell Crab Sandwich   245

MEATLESS MAIN COURSE

Macaroni and Cheese

Classic: Baked Horseradish-Cheddar Macaroni and Cheese   251
Contemporary: Macaroni and Cheese Tartlette with Mushroom and Truffle Oil   252
Second Day Dish: Macaroni and Cheese Fritters   254

DESSERTS

Chocolate Cake

Classic: Brooklyn Brownout Cake   258
Contemporary: Molten Chocolate Cake   261
Second Day Dish: Chocolate Cake "Truffles" in a Chocolate Bag   262

CHEESECAKE

Classic:	New York Cheesecake	264
Contemporary:	Grand Marnier Cheesecake Soufflés	266
Second Day Dish:	Coconut Cheesecake Beignets with Red Fruit Sorbet and Berries	267

APPLE PIE

Classic:	Flaky Apple Pie	270
Contemporary:	Apple Tart with Tahitian Vanilla Ice Cream	272
Second Day Dish:	Warm Apple-Blueberry Cobbler with Butterscotch Ice Cream	274

CHOCOLATE CHIP COOKIES

Classic:	All-American Chocolate Chip Cookies	276
Contemporary:	Chocolate Chip Taco with Chocolate Mousse	277
Second Day Dish:	Chocolate Chip UFOs	279

Mail Order and Web Site Sources	281
Acknowledgments	285
Index	287

Introduction

The classic recipes that so embody American cooking have their roots firmly planted in the hearty meals of our past. But because contemporary American cuisine has absorbed so many international influences, cooking here has moved far from its meat-and-potatoes heritage. And yet, whenever I want comfort and welcome at the table, I find myself returning to the simple and basic home cooking, such as the roast chicken, meatloaf, or apple pie that I first enjoyed at my mother's table. I admit, however, that I always put my own stamp on those tried-and-true classics.

Just as a chef must master the basics of French cuisine early in his or her career, it is necessary for the home cook to master these American classics before moving on to the more elaborate dishes of contemporary American cuisine. As I began this book, my aim was to revisit those classics and to imbue them with some contemporary flavor and zest. In doing so, however, it became clear to me that with further variations I could help you create haute cuisine. The basic recipe could be built into something a bit more special—a midweek dinner turned into great Saturday night dinner-party fare.

Along with creating these New American Classics, it seemed only right to devise some new methods of using the incumbent "leftovers." So I've created "Second Day Dishes" using some elements of a previous classic meal for a repast just as interesting and inviting as the dish from which it was derived.

Thus, throughout the book, I have offered what I hope are helpful hints for thinking about creating three meals from each classic. That should help you cut down on your time devoted to shopping, and in prep time as well—buying and roasting two chickens at once, one designated for a Second Day Dish, for example.

Some of my classic dishes in their initial stages, as I said, will remain much as they have always been, with minimal innovation like my recipe for Roast Chicken "Farmhouse Style" (see page 79). On the other hand, my Not-So-Basic Meatloaf (see page 142) incorporates new flavors and presentation that are designed to help you create a new classic.

I have tried here to elicit the essence of each classic dish. I have looked at the beginnings and the evolution of the classic American repertoire. When I introduce a new note into a time-honored recipe, I always remain faithful to its basic conception. Of course, changing times and tastes are also reflected in the natural progression of a recipe so that ingredients and methods once unavailable or misunderstood are now easily incorporated into the classic style. Health concerns, the availability of international ingredients, both fresh and processed, and modern kitchen appliances have each played a part in the transformation of a classic into a New American Kitchen Classic. And, all of these components assist in the transformation of a classic into contemporary fine dining and then into a Second Day Dish—all, I hope, New American Classics.

DAVID BURKE
2005

DAVID BURKE'S
NEW AMERICAN
CLASSICS

BREAKFAST

Not so very long ago, for many people, labor was hard and demanding, with work beginning at dawn, so that a hearty, nourishing meal was a necessary beginning to difficult twelve- or fifteen-hour days. Meat and starch were featured with fruit, dairy, and sometimes even vegetables as side dishes. The foods were often grown, raised, or created by those who consumed them with only a few items purchased to fill out the larder. That was certainly a long, long way from an Egg McMuffin and a Styrofoam container of coffee to go.

So much convenience has replaced the slow-cooked and lovingly prepared breakfasts of the past. Oatmeal and other hot cereals are now either in ready-to-eat packets or are instant preparations. Juice is either frozen or in ready-to-pour cardboard containers. Potatoes come precut, precooked, or preseasoned. Eggs and typical breakfast meats are considered taboo by many because of cholesterol and fat concerns. In addition, every fast-food stop, convenience store, gas station, and corner deli features its own version of a quick-and-easy breakfast. Health concerns quickly get lost in all of this convenience.

For me, a quietly eaten, balanced breakfast offering some protein, fiber, and carbohydrates with a little fat and cholesterol is far better for your health and mental state than a doughnut and coffee on the run. It always stays with you for a better part of the day with no midmorning hunger pangs leading you to a quick fix at a snack bar.

Unfortunately, nowadays, about the only time a good, solid breakfast is eaten is late in the morning on weekends when it's no longer called breakfast. Either at home or in a restaurant, brunch has become a very social occasion with hearty main courses and, often, an appetizer and dessert added to make a many-course meal. The food is often preceded by light cocktails, whereas the farmer of yore might have ended his hearty breakfast with a stiff shot of whiskey or brandy to warm his body before going out to work.

For me, nothing is better than a hearty meal early in the morning with my children. Many of the recipes that follow come from just such times. My boys have enormous appetites, and I'm always trying to think of new ways to satisfy them. And I often make more than necessary because many Second Day Dishes have evolved from my own, at-home, breakfast repertoire.

BACON AND EGGS

I've gathered some pretty basic and familiar ingredients to create my first breakfast classics. One of my favorites, Eggs Benedict, has been on American menus for almost one hundred years. To me, it perfectly combines American ingenuity with some fine, French touches. In France, I never saw hollandaise sauce in the morning, nor did I see English muffins on those magnificent hotel buffets in Great Britain. Somehow, an American chef—legend says it was a chef at the grand, turn-of-the-century Delmonico's Restaurant—devised the dish for a demanding client named Mrs. Benedict and pulled many ordinary components together to make a delicious, now-classic, breakfast-brunch dish.

The egg is, to me, a perfect food. A total meal in its own container. Eggs are high in cholesterol, fat, and sodium, so they have come in for much criticism. I personally feel that they can be enjoyed on an occasional morning. As with all things in life, moderation is the key.

The evolution of the Contemporary and Second Day Dishes becomes pretty clear when you think of the way we now eat. The Contemporary Dish brings together the elements of Eggs Benedict in an up-to-date fashion and then adds a little ethnic splash with a Latino salsa. The Second Day Dish uses a bit from both dishes to make an easy but very *au courant* meal.

CLASSIC

Eggs Benedict with Hash Brown Potatoes and Oven-Dried Tomatoes

SERVES 6

For perfect Eggs Benedict, featuring eggs with tender whites and runny yolks, you must gently poach the eggs in just barely simmering water. They should never be cooked at a hard simmer or boil, or the whites will become tough and the yolks firm. Since there is now much concern about the safety of lightly cooked eggs, I barely poach the eggs and then hold them in a saucepan of very warm water (130 degrees) for 15 minutes. This method allows the cook to prepare the remaining ingredients as the eggs warm and cook.

How could any breakfast be more delicious than slightly salty, meaty, Canadian bacon; a runny, gently poached egg; and rich, barely tart, easy-to-make hollandaise all piled on top of a crisp, just-a-hint of sweet, English muffin with some zesty potatoes at the side? A great cup of steaming hot café au lait would complete this wonderful meal for me.

1 tablespoon white vinegar	12 slices Canadian bacon
12 very fresh, large eggs (see Note)	6 English muffins, split
3 very fresh, large egg yolks	3 tablespoons salted butter, softened
1 tablespoon fresh lemon juice, strained	12 slices black truffle, optional
About ¾ teaspoon coarse salt	¼ cup chopped fresh flat-leaf parsley
½ teaspoon Tabasco sauce	Hash Brown Potatoes (recipe follows)
½ cup very hot, clarified, unsalted butter	Oven-Dried Tomatoes (recipe follows)
(see Note)	

NOTE: The fresher the eggs the less likely that you will have a problem with bacteria. You will want to buy refrigerated eggs that are less than 1 week old with clean, blemish-free shells. Do not use dirty eggs or those that have cracks. If you have any question about the safety of your eggs, cook them to at least 140 degrees and do not use raw eggs as for hollandaise.

Clarified butter is the clear liquid that appears when the butterfat separates from the water and milks solids in slowly melted butter. To make clarified butter, cut 1 pound of unsalted butter into cubes and place it in a medium saucepan over very low heat. Cook, without stirring and without the butter bubbling and browning, for 20 minutes. Strain the yellow liquid that rises to the top into a clean container and discard all of the solids. Cool to room temperature; then cover and refrigerate for up to 1 week, or freeze for up to 6 months. Reheat the clarified butter as needed. For hollandaise sauce, you will want the butter to be just below the boiling point so that its heat will help to kill any bacteria in the raw egg yolks.

Preheat the oven to 275 degrees.

Heat about 3 inches of water in a large, shallow saucepan (a rondeau works well) over medium heat until bubbles form around the edge. Add the vinegar.

In another saucepan of similar size, heat 3 inches of water to 130 degrees on a candy thermometer. Remove from the heat but keep in a warm spot to maintain the temperature.

Carefully break the eggs, a few at a time, into small custard-type cups and then gently slide the eggs, one at a time, into the barely simmering vinegar-water. Cook for about 2 minutes, or until the egg whites are just set but the yolks are still very loose. Using a slotted spoon, carefully lift the eggs, one at a time, and place them into the 150-degree water. Cover the eggs and let them rest for 15 minutes. From time to time, you should check the temperature of the water. If it falls below 130 degrees, slowly add enough boiling water to bring the temperature back up as desired.

To make the hollandaise sauce, place the egg yolks, lemon juice, salt, and Tabasco in a blender and process the mixture on medium speed for 45 seconds. With the blender running, add the hot, clarified butter in a very slow, steady stream and process the mixture until it is very smooth and slightly thickened. Scrape the sauce from the blender into the top half of a double boiler placed over very hot water and keep it warm.

Place six serving plates in the preheated oven to warm.

Place the Canadian bacon in a large nonstick frying pan over medium-high heat and fry, turning it occasionally, for about 4 minutes, or until it is just lightly browned around the edges; you may have to do this in batches. Remove the bacon as it browns and place it on a baking sheet in the preheated oven to keep it warm.

Toast the English muffin halves and, as they are toasted, butter them lightly with the softened salted butter; then place on a baking sheet in the preheated oven to keep them warm.

Remove the plates from the oven. Place two English muffin halves on each plate. Cover each muffin half with a slice of Canadian bacon. Using a slotted spoon, lift the poached eggs, one at a time, from the water and pat them gently with a clean kitchen towel to remove excess water. Place an egg on top of the bacon on each muffin. (If the edges of the eggs are a bit ragged, carefully trim them with a small knife or with kitchen scissors.) Spoon equal portions of the reserved hollandaise sauce on top of each egg. If using the truffles, place a truffle slice on top of each egg and sprinkle chopped parsley over the plate. Serve immediately with Hash Brown Potatoes on one side of the plate and Oven-Dried Tomatoes on the other.

Hash Brown Potatoes

8 medium Yukon Gold potatoes or other all-purpose potatoes, boiled
3 tablespoons canola oil
1 cup finely diced red onion

½ cup finely diced red bell pepper
½ teaspoon chili powder or paprika
Coarse salt and freshly ground black pepper
¼ cup chopped scallions

Peel the boiled potatoes and cut them into small cubes. Set aside.

Heat the oil in a large, heavy-bottomed frying pan (a cast-iron skillet works well) over medium-high heat. Add the onions and bell pepper and sauté for about 3 minutes, or until they just begin to soften. Add the reserved potatoes and stir to combine. Sprinkle in the chili powder (or paprika) and salt and pepper to taste. Press the mixture down into the pan using the back of a spatula. Lower the heat to medium, cover, and cook the potatoes for about 20 minutes, or until the bottom is brown and crusty. Carefully turn the potatoes in large chunks. Cover and cook them for an additional 10 minutes, or until they are well browned. Uncover the potatoes and toss in the scallions. Taste and, if necessary, adjust the seasoning with additional salt and pepper. Serve hot.

Oven-Dried Tomatoes

3 pounds very ripe, plum tomatoes
¼ cup olive oil
Coarse salt

Preheat the oven to 300 degrees.

Line two cookie sheets with parchment paper.

Cut the tomatoes in half lengthwise. Using a teaspoon, scrape the seeds from the tomato halves and discard them. Place the tomatoes in a bowl and drizzle them with the olive oil. Season to taste with salt and toss to coat well.

Lay the tomato halves, cut side down, on the prepared cookie sheets. Place the sheets in the preheated oven and bake the tomatoes for about 90 minutes, or until they are quite dry but remain soft to the touch. Remove from the oven and allow to cool.

Place the cooled tomato halves in a nonreactive container. You can store them, covered and refrigerated, for up to 1 week. If desired, reheat in a low oven or microwave before using.

Canadian Bacon and Onion Potato Cake with Poached Eggs and Spicy Tomato Salsa

SERVES 6

This is a great breakfast or brunch dish. (For a lunch or late-night supper dish, you might want to add a green salad and some garlic bread.) This dish has its origins in the classic French galette and the peasant Swiss *rösti* potato pancake, but it owes more to an old-fashioned crispy potato cake. Here we start with raw potatoes, so that they can cook a bit longer and get a bit browner and crispier than they do when precooked. However, if you have leftover cooked potatoes (even mashed), you can also use them. Just watch the frying cake closely, so that it browns but does not burn. I've used bacon fat as the oil in this recipe as it adds so much flavor to the potato cake, but, by all means, use whatever oil you prefer. Keep in mind, though, that mild vegetable oils will add little flavor and aromatic oils such as extra virgin olive oil will add a distinctive taste to the dish. The Canadian bacon can be replaced with any fine-quality ham (Serrano, Westphalian, country ham, tasso), and the onion can be replaced with scallions and a hint of garlic. If poached eggs seem too time-consuming, substitute big, beautifully runny, sunnyside-up eggs.

6 large Idaho potatoes, peeled and patted dry
1 large sweet onion such as Vidalia
1 pound Canadian bacon, chopped
Coarse salt and freshly ground pepper
3 tablespoons bacon fat, vegetable oil,
    or olive oil

6 large Poached Eggs (see page 8)
Spicy Tomato Salsa (recipe follows)
Sour cream, optional

Using a box grater or a food processor fitted with the shredding blade, shred the potatoes and the onion. Place the grated potatoes and onion in a clean kitchen towel. Fold the towel over the mixture and twist to wring out as much of the liquid as possible.

Place the potato mixture in a bowl and toss in the bacon. Season to taste with salt and pepper.

Preheat the oven to 375 degrees.

Heat the fat in a large, heavy-bottomed frying pan (cast iron is the absolute best) over medium-high heat. Add the potato mixture and, using the back of a spatula, press it down into the pan in a smooth layer. Lower the heat and cook for about 20 minutes, or until the bottom of the potato cake is brown and crisp. Slide the potato cake onto a plate and then slide it, browned side up, back into the pan. Place it in the preheated oven and bake for about 20 minutes, or until the interior is well cooked and the bottom is crisp and brown.

Remove the potato cake from the oven and cut it into 6 equal wedges. Place a warm poached egg on top of each wedge, and spoon some Spicy Tomato Salsa over the top and around the edge of each plate. Garnish with a dollop of sour cream, if desired.

Spicy Tomato Salsa

4 large, ripe tomatoes
½ cup finely diced red onion
¼ cup finely chopped fresh cilantro
2 teaspoons chopped, canned chipotles in adobo (see Note)
1 teaspoon Roasted Garlic Purée (recipe follows)

1 teaspoon minced serrano chili
1 tablespoon fresh lime juice
1 tablespoon fresh orange juice
Coarse salt and cracked black pepper

NOTE: Chipotles in adobo are canned chilies in a vinegar-based sauce, which are available in Hispanic food shops, specialty food stores, and some supermarkets.

Preheat the broiler or a grill.

Place the tomatoes on a pan under the preheated broiler or on the preheated grill. Cook, turning the tomatoes occasionally, for about 5 minutes, or until the skin has blackened and the flesh is slightly soft. Remove the tomatoes from the heat and allow them to cool slightly.

When the tomatoes are cool, remove and discard the core. Place the tomatoes in a food processor fitted with the metal blade. Process to a slightly chunky purée. Place the tomato purée in a medium bowl and set aside.

Add the onion, cilantro, chipotles in adobo, garlic purée, and serrano chili. Stir to combine. Stir in the lime and orange juices and salt and cracked black pepper to taste. Taste and adjust the seasoning with more juice, salt, and/or pepper, if needed. Cover and store the salsa, refrigerated, until you are ready to use it. Serve at room temperature.

Roasted Garlic Purée

>   6 heads garlic
>   ½ cup olive oil

Preheat the oven to 350 degrees.

Pull the garlic heads apart. Combine the garlic cloves with the olive oil in a baking pan, spreading them out to form a single layer. Place them in the preheated oven and roast them for about 30 minutes, or until the garlic is very tender. Remove them from the oven and allow to cool.

When the garlic is cool enough to handle, using your fingertips, push the soft garlic pulp from the skins. Place the pulp in the small bowl of a food processor fitted with the metal blade and process to a smooth purée. Transfer it to a nonreactive container. Cover and refrigerate it for up to 1 week, or freeze for up to 3 months.

Bacon, Potato, and Eggs Strudel

SERVES 2

In this dish, everything gets chopped up and rolled inside a crisp phyllo crust, so nobody will know that they are eating "leftovers." This inspiration came from a strudel that I created for the Sunday brunch menu when I was working at the Park Avenue Café in New York City. A little bit from the classic dish and a little from the contemporary one are combined here, but you can always visit the supermarket, too. If you are planning a cocktail get-together, make tiny strudels (freeze them if the party is days or weeks in the future) and bake and serve them as hors d'oeuvres on the day of your festivities.

1 package frozen phyllo dough, thawed according to the manufacturer's directions
Approximately ½ cup clarified butter (see page 7)
4 large eggs, scrambled
4 slices cooked Canadian bacon or fine-quality, regular bacon

Approximately ½ cup chopped Hash Brown Potatoes (see page 9) or Canadian Bacon and Onion-Potato Cake (see page 10)
2 tablespoons chopped scallions
1 tablespoon chopped fresh flat-leaf parsley
Coarse salt and freshly ground black pepper
Spicy Tomato Salsa (see page 11) or catsup, chutney, or commercial salsa

Unwrap the phyllo sheets and carefully lift off approximately 12 sheets. (I know that it is hard to lift an exact number.) Tightly rewrap the remaining phyllo dough in plastic wrap and then in freezer wrap. Label and date it and return it to the freezer.

Quickly place the 12 sheets, in a stack, on a clean surface. Cover them with parchment (or waxed) paper and then with a clean, damp, kitchen towel, taking care that the towel does not come in direct contact with the phyllo, as the dampness will cause the dough to melt. Using a sharp knife, trim the phyllo sheets to an even rectangle. You must work rapidly, as uncovered phyllo will dry out quickly.

Separate 1 sheet of phyllo from the layer and, using a pastry brush, lightly coat it with clarified butter. Top it with another sheet of phyllo and brush it with butter. Continue making layers until you have used all of the phyllo and are ending with a buttered top. If a sheet tears, just put it back together as best you can.

Combine the scrambled eggs, bacon, potatoes, scallions, and parsley in a medium mixing bowl. Season with salt and pepper to taste. Set aside.

Preheat the oven to 375 degrees.

Line a baking sheet with parchment paper. Lightly coat the parchment with nonstick vegetable spray. Set aside.

Place the egg mixture along the longer part of the phyllo rectangle, leaving approximately a 3-inch edge. Fold the edge up and over the egg mixture and roll to form a log shape and completely enfold the egg mixture. Carefully transfer the log to the prepared baking sheet. Lightly brush the top of the log with any remaining clarified butter. Place it in the preheated oven and bake for about 25 minutes, or until the phyllo is golden brown and crisp.

Remove the strudel from the oven and let it stand for 5 minutes. Using a serrated knife, cut it crosswise into sushi-like pieces. Place an equal portion, cut side up, on each of two luncheon plates along with a bowl of Spicy Tomato Salsa or other condiment as a dipping sauce. Serve hot.

PANCAKES

Since time immemorial (whenever that was), people all over the world were probably making some sort of pancake if they had a flat surface, some heat, and a bit of grain. What began as a very basic form of nourishment has, through culinary evolution, become crêpes, blinis, blintzes, and a myriad of other flat cakes. Some, such as Ethiopia's enjera, are more bread like and are, in fact, an integral part of a culture's cuisine. Others remain special-occasion treats such as the deliciously aromatic blini topped with caviar.

In almost every culture, except America's, these cakes are eaten with savory toppings or fillings. Here, we mound the butter and pour on sugary syrup with reckless abandon and, occasionally, add some fresh fruit or other fruit-based sweet topping. So beloved are pancakes here that a restaurant chain, International House of Pancakes (more familiarly and lovingly known as IHOP), has devoted its menu to them.

In my repertoire, pancakes are basic as well as extravagant as well as both sweet and savory. At home, for the most part, they remain a breakfast treat. However, I always freeze leftover pancakes; then when I get home late and haven't eaten, I pop a couple of them in the microwave and roll them around some smoked salmon, cheese, or whatever I've got in the fridge. I also use them to make a really delicious Second Day turkey or chicken sandwich. Pancakes can serve up much, much more than a breakfast stack.

CLASSIC

Buttermilk Pancakes with Whipped Butter and Maple Syrup

SERVES 6

To me, buttermilk pancakes are the absolute best: light and fluffy, tender, and slightly tart. Although this recipe is for the basic pancake, you can, with enthusiasm, add a little cornmeal or other flour, dried or fresh fruit (about one half cup is adequate), chopped bacon or ham, spices or herbs, and when the kids are really demanding your creativity in the kitchen, a chocolate chip addition will always win them over. I have a couple of my own unbreakable rules when I serve buttermilk pancakes—I use only whipped, salted butter for its slightly foamy texture and always pure maple syrup for its pure taste. Sometimes I flavor it, but the mix always has to begin this way.

This recipe can easily be doubled for making extra pancakes for a Second Day Dish, bigger crowds, or healthier appetites.

2¼ cups buttermilk	2 teaspoons baking powder
¼ cup (½ stick) melted unsalted butter	¾ teaspoon baking soda
3 large eggs, separated	½ teaspoon salt
2¼ cups all-purpose flour	1 cup whipped salted butter (see Note)
¼ cup sugar	Approximately 2 cups pure maple syrup

NOTE: You can buy whipped, salted butter at most supermarkets. However, if you can't find it, place room-temperature butter in a food processor fitted with the metal blade and process for about 2 minutes, or until the butter is light and fluffy. Use immediately or store, covered and refrigerated (or frozen), just as you would regular butter.

Preheat the oven to 200 degrees.

Line a baking sheet with parchment paper. Set aside.

In a medium mixing bowl, beat together the buttermilk and melted butter. When they are well combined, whisk in the egg yolks. Set aside.

Combine the flour, sugar, baking powder, baking soda, and salt in another mixing bowl. Set aside.

Using an electric mixer, beat the egg whites until soft peaks form. Pour the buttermilk mixture into the dry ingredients and mix them together to just blend. Do not overbeat. Using a rubber spatula, gently fold in the egg whites to just incorporate.

Heat a nonstick griddle over medium heat. Spoon the batter, about ¼ cup at a time, onto the hot griddle to make neat circles. Cook it for about 3 minutes, or until the top is filled with bursting bubbles and the bottom is golden. Turn and cook the remaining side. Place the cooked pancakes on the prepared baking sheet and into the preheated oven to keep them warm while you continue making pancakes.

Serve hot, at least three per person, with a teaspoon of whipped, salted butter on the top of each pancake and warm maple syrup passed alongside.

Almond, Praline, and Banana Pancakes with Orange Syrup and Yogurt

SERVES 6

This is a rather fancy and very rich brunch-style take on pancakes. If time does not allow, you could serve them with plain maple syrup, but if you've gone to the trouble to get the ingredients for the pancakes you might as well go the distance and make the Orange Syrup. These would be marvelous preceded by a toast with refreshing champagne cocktails, Mimosas, or Bellinis.

3 navel oranges

2 cups pure maple syrup

1 cup fresh orange juice

1 recipe Buttermilk Pancakes (see page 14)

½ cup praline paste (see Note)

1 large firm banana, peeled and diced

1 cup sliced almonds, toasted

1 cup plain yogurt

1 tablespoon chopped fresh mint leaves

6 sprigs fresh mint

NOTE: Praline paste is available at some supermarkets and at most specialty food stores. If you can't find it, try substituting smooth peanut butter. It will create a different and not as exotic flavor, but the pancakes will still be delicious.

Preheat the oven to 200 degrees.

Line a baking sheet with parchment paper. Set aside.

Zest the oranges to make 1 teaspoon of grated rind. Set the grated rind aside. Using a sharp paring knife, peel the oranges, taking care to remove all of the rind and white pith. Working over a bowl, carefully section each orange by cutting between the membrane surrounding each section. Drain the juice from the orange sections and use the juice to make up part of the 1 cup of orange juice called for in the recipe.

Combine the maple syrup, orange juice, and grated rind in a small saucepan over medium heat and bring the mixture to a simmer. Add the reserved orange sections, lower the heat, and gently simmer the mixture for 5 minutes. Remove it from the heat and keep it warm. (You can make the syrup a day or two ahead and store it, covered and refrigerated. Reheat it before serving.)

Add the praline paste and banana to the Buttermilk Pancake Batter, stirring to combine well.

Heat a nonstick griddle over medium heat. Spoon the batter, about 3 tablespoons at a time, onto the hot griddle to form neat circles. Cook the pancakes for about 3 minutes, or until the top is filled with bursting bubbles and the bottom is golden. Sprinkle a few toasted almonds on top and quickly turn and cook the remaining side. Place the cooked pancakes on the prepared baking sheet and into the preheated oven to keep them warm while you continue making pancakes.

Place the yogurt in a small mixing bowl and whisk vigorously to loosen.

Stir the chopped mint into the warm orange syrup. Place three pancakes on each of six serving plates. Spoon some of the warm syrup over the top of the pancakes, and drizzle yogurt over the top and around the edge of each plate. Garnish with a mint sprig and serve.

Smoked Salmon Pancake Roll-up with Onions and Capers

SERVES 2

If you have frozen those leftover pancakes, then this dish is a breeze to put together. If not, it really doesn't take too long to make up a fresh batch. This is a very tasty preparation that works well for lunch, brunch, or even a light supper. You could also cut the roll-ups into sushi-size pieces, fasten with toothpicks, and serve as hors d'oeuvres. If you don't like smoked salmon, you could substitute some very thinly sliced, flavorful ham (such as prosciutto or Westphalian) and a creamy, rich cheese such as Pont-l'Évêque, or an herbed goat cheese.

⅓ cup whipped cream cheese

2 tablespoons minced onion

1 teaspoon well drained capers

Freshly ground black pepper

4 cooked Buttermilk Pancakes
(see page 15)

⅓ pound thinly sliced smoked salmon

1½ tablespoons chopped fresh chives

Place the cream cheese in a mixing bowl. Add the onions, capers, and black pepper to taste and beat to combine.

Place the pancakes in a single layer on a clean, flat surface. Using a spatula, lightly coat each pancake with the cream-cheese mixture. Lay a single layer of salmon on top of the cream cheese on each pancake. Sprinkle some chopped chives about ¼ inch in from the edge that you will begin rolling. Fold the ¼-inch edge up and over the chives, and continue rolling to make a neat, firm wrap. Trim off the uneven ends, and cut the rolls, on the bias, through the center, into two pieces.

Place two cut roll-ups on each of two luncheon plates—two pieces seam side down and two pieces standing upright against them. Grind some black pepper over each plate and serve.

FRENCH TOAST

Pain perdu was one of my favorite simple, home-style desserts when I was a young chef working in France. It is not much different than our French toast, but it is always served as a dessert with a dusting of confectioners' sugar and perhaps some jam or sliced fresh fruit. I always use brioche (or other eggy bread), but you can use almost any type of bread that suits your fancy. I've even had croissant French toast, but I found it a bit over-the-top. Whole-grain breads, baguettes, Italian loaves, and rich wheat breads will also make very distinctive French toast. Just as with pancakes, I always serve French toast with salted butter and pure maple syrup.

You can also use the basic principles of making French toast to create absolutely marvelous sandwiches. Pull together whatever filling you find interesting—ham and cheese; bacon, avocado, and tomato; or grilled vegetables. Place the filling between two slices of bread and firmly press the bread into the filling. Holding the sandwich together, dip the entire sandwich into the same egg-milk bath you used to make French toast. Fry the sandwich just as you would French toast and serve it piping hot.

CLASSIC

French Toast with Cinnamon-Brown Sugar and Apple Syrup

SERVES 6

This is my very special version of everyday French toast. Of course, you can also serve it with butter and syrup, but the hint of cinnamon and the sweet-tart flavor of the apples make it a breakfast apart. To make the Second Day Dish of French Toast with Bread Pudding Brûlée, make six extra slices of French toast from this recipe.

4 large Granny Smith apples

3 tablespoons unsalted butter

½ cup firmly packed light brown sugar

2 cups apple cider or juice

1 tablespoon plus 1 teaspoon ground
cinnamon

1 teaspoon fresh lemon juice

2 cups heavy cream

½ cup milk

6 large eggs

¼ cup granulated sugar

1 teaspoon pure vanilla extract

Pinch of salt

Approximately 1 cup clarified butter
(see page 7)

18 thick slices brioche or other egg
bread

½ cup confectioners' sugar

Preheat the oven to 200 degrees.

Line a baking sheet with parchment paper. Set aside.

Peel, core, and slice each apple into 12 wedges. Heat the butter in a large sauté pan over medium heat and add the apple wedges. Sprinkle with the brown sugar and sauté for about 5 minutes, or just until the apples are beginning to soften and the sugar is beginning to glaze. Pour in the apple cider (or juice) and stir to deglaze the pan. Stir in 1 tablespoon of the cinnamon and cook for about 10 minutes, or until the mixture is syrupy. Remove from the heat and stir in the lemon juice. Keep warm. (You can make this syrup a day or two in advance and store, covered and refrigerated. Reheat before serving.)

Whisk together the cream, milk, eggs, granulated sugar, vanilla, and salt with the remaining teaspoon of cinnamon in a large, shallow bowl.

Heat about 2 tablespoons of the clarified butter in a nonstick griddle or frying pan. One at a time, dip the bread slices into the cream mixture until they are nicely soaked but not soggy and disintegrating. Place them on the griddle, without crowding, and cook, turning once, for about 4 minutes, or until both sides are golden brown. Place the cooked French toast on the prepared baking sheet and into the preheated oven to keep it warm while you continue to make French toast, using additional clarified butter to fry each batch. (If the butter gets too brown on the griddle, wipe the griddle clean with some paper towels and use fresh butter to continue frying.)

When ready to serve, place three pieces of French toast on each of six serving plates. Spoon warm apple syrup over each serving. Place the confectioners' sugar in a fine sieve and tap gently against the edge of the sieve, holding it over each plate, to dust the plate with sugar. Serve immediately.

Titanic French Toast with Three Jams

SERVES 6

I was sitting in a chair facing the ocean trying to come up with a very special wedding brunch menu for some friends, when a cruise ship steamed by. Somehow, the three smokestacks triggered my imagination to create this extravagant French toast recipe. Since the movie *Titanic* had just hit the theatres, I decided to add a bit of drama to the recipe title.

Although the recipe calls for whole loaves of bread, you could also cut very thick (about 2 inches) slices of home-style bread to make smaller versions of the Titanic. In my restaurant, we bake our own *tuiles* to make the smokestacks on the loaves, but I thought I'd give you a break and just call for prepared cookies. For an extra hit, blend a bit of an appropriate liqueur into each jam. If the jams are too sweet for your taste, replace them with three different fresh fruits, chopped or puréed (to which you could also add liqueur), or barely sweetened whipped cream.

6 small loaves home-style bread or brioche
4 cups heavy cream
½ cup fresh orange juice
¼ cup Grand Marnier
6 large eggs
1 cup granulated sugar
1 teaspoon ground cinnamon
¼ teaspoon freshly grated nutmeg
Approximately 6 cups vegetable oil
18 Pirouettes or other commercially
   prepared, rolled, crisp cookie (see Note)

½ cup orange marmalade
½ cup raspberry or strawberry jam
½ cup apricot jam
Approximately ¼ cup confectioners' sugar
Approximately 2 cups fresh berries (all of
   one kind or a mixture), hulled or
   stemmed
Approximately 1½ cups strawberry or
   raspberry syrup, optional (see Note)

NOTE: Pirouettes are either plain or chocolate-tinged rolled cookies made by the Sara Lee company. They are available in most supermarkets.

Fruit syrups, such as raspberry, blueberry, or strawberry, are available in most supermarkets and specialty food stores.

Preheat the oven to 200 degrees.

Line a baking sheet with parchment paper. Set aside.

Using a bread knife, trim the crust off of each loaf of bread, leaving a neat rectangle about 6 inches long. Using an apple corer or a small sharp knife, make 3 holes in the top of each loaf equidistant from each other. Set aside.

Whisk together the cream, orange juice, and Grand Marnier in a deep bowl. Add the eggs and whisk to combine. Add the granulated sugar, cinnamon, and nutmeg and continue whisking until the sugar has dissolved. One at a time, dip the loaves into the cream mixture to soak well. Place the loaves on a platter or baking sheet.

Heat the vegetable oil in a deep-fat fryer over medium-high heat to 360 degrees on a candy thermometer.

One at a time, place the soaked loaves into the hot fat and fry, making sure that the loaf is submerged in the fat, for about 4 minutes, or until the outside is crisp and golden. Remove from the fat and place on a triple layer of paper towels to drain. Place the fried loaf on the prepared baking sheet and into the preheated oven to keep it warm while you continue frying the remaining loaves.

When ready to serve, place a loaf on each of six serving plates. Place a Pirouette into each of the three holes on top of each loaf. Fill each cookie with a different jam or fruit. Place the confectioners' sugar in a fine sieve and tap gently against the edge of the sieve, holding it over each plate, to dust the plate with sugar. Sprinkle berries around the edge of each plate, and serve immediately with optional fruit syrup passed on the side, if desired.

French Toast with Bread Pudding Brûlée

SERVES 6

I hope that you will find this a great take on the now almost ordinary crème brûlée, the classic French dessert that became the apple pie of the 1980s restaurant boom. Every restaurant, by popular demand, now has to have one on their menu, and pastry chefs are challenged to keep inventing new flavors and finishes. This is my easy-to-make contribution.

4 slices brioche French toast (see page 19)
1½ cups half-and-half
Approximately ¾ cup sugar
1 vanilla bean, split

6 large egg yolks
1 cup very cold, heavy cream
Approximately 1 cup fresh raspberries

> NOTE: Handheld propane torches made especially for kitchen use are available at kitchenware and baker's supply shops, many specialty food stores, and some hardware stores. If you don't have one, preheat the broiler and place the ramekins under the hot broiler for less than 1 minute, or just until the sugar has caramelized. Take care not to heat the custard as the whole point of this dessert is to have a crackling hot sugar coating over a well-chilled custard.

Preheat the oven to 350 degrees.

Trim and discard the crusts from the French toast. Cut the trimmed toast into small cubes. Set aside.

Combine the half-and-half with ½ cup of sugar and the vanilla bean in a medium saucepan over medium heat. Cook, stirring frequently, for about 4 minutes, or until the mixture is quite hot and the sugar has dissolved. Remove the mixture from the heat and allow it to infuse for 10 minutes.

Place the egg yolks in a medium mixing bowl and whisk until well blended. Remove the vanilla bean from the warm half-and-half and, whisking constantly, slowly pour the liquid into the egg yolks. Whisk until the eggs are completely incorporated into the half-and-half.

Pour the cold heavy cream into a mixing bowl. Pour the half-and-half mixture into the heavy cream through a fine sieve, stirring to combine. Stir in the reserved French toast cubes. Spoon the mixture into six 5- to 6-ounce ramekins, crème brûlée dishes, or custard cups. Nestle a few raspberries into the top. Place the filled ramekins into a baking dish and carefully fill with enough warm water to come halfway up the sides of the ramekins. Tightly cover the entire dish with aluminum foil; then carefully place the baking dish into the preheated oven. Bake for 30 minutes.

Remove the foil and check for doneness. The custards should jiggle slightly when the baking dish is moved and the very center should be slightly runny. If the custards are not done, replace the foil and cook for an additional 5 minutes, taking care not to overcook, or the custards will be tough. Remove them from the oven and the water bath and place them on a wire rack to cool. When cool, refrigerate, uncovered, for 1 hour or up to 8 hours to chill them through.

When ready to serve, using the remaining ¼ cup of sugar, sprinkle the top of each custard with a smooth coating of sugar. Using a handheld propane torch (see Note), carefully caramelize the sugar coating by running the flame over the sugar in quick, even strokes. Serve chilled.

DOUGHNUTS

In America, culinary historians think that doughnuts are almost as old as the country itself. Some I've picked out from under a plastic dome on road trips taste like it. No matter what you hear about the latest, greatest doughnut—whether from a chain or a local bakery—I guarantee you that it is nothing like one fresh from your own kitchen.

It is said that doughnuts were introduced into the American food chain with the arrival of the early Dutch settlers who brought with them the traditional Dutch fried cake called an *olie koechen.* There are now many types of fried dough to be had, ranging from Dunkin's to Krispy's to Pennsylvania fried dough at county fairs to the French-influenced beignets of New Orleans. They can be yeast-raised or baking powder–leavened; they can be iced, dipped into sugar (granulated, confectioners', or cinnamon); filled with jellies or creams; and dunked or eaten with a dainty pinky raised in the air à la Ralph Cramden.

Over the years, I've used doughnuts both as a garnish and as a featured dessert, in part because I love them and primarily because they cause such surprise and delight in diners. The effort of making them is well worth it.

At home, simple cake doughnuts are so easy to make (if a bit messy) that you really have no excuse to buy the commercially prepared ones. Once you have made Simple Sugar-and-Spice Doughnuts (see page 26), I can guarantee that you will make them time and again, for your family, for friends, and to dunk into your morning coffee.

When making doughnuts, place about a half cup of cinnamon-scented sugar in a small pan in the oven. This will fill the house with a wonderful, sweet-spicy smell that will let everyone know that you are in the kitchen working your magic. This is an old baker's trick to lure customers into the shop. It still works.

Simple Sugar-and-Spice Doughnuts

MAKES ABOUT 3 DOZEN

It can't get any simpler than this: a soft, easy-to-make, easy-to-roll-out dough that is quickly deep-fried in bubbling, hot, fresh peanut oil. It's fun to watch the circles turn golden brown as they float around the top of the pan. A speedy flip, and in minutes a golden-brown and tender, warm doughnut is yours. A fast drain on paper towels and a quick toss in cinnamon-sugar, and you have the perfect accompaniment to a steaming cup of coffee or tea or a cold glass of milk.

3½ cups all-purpose flour plus more
    for rolling
1 tablespoon baking powder
1 teaspoon freshly grated nutmeg
½ teaspoon salt
2 tablespoons ground cinnamon

3½ cups sugar
2 tablespoons unsalted butter, at room
    temperature
3 large eggs, beaten
½ cup milk
Approximately 6 cups peanut oil

Combine the flour, baking powder, nutmeg, and salt. Set aside.

Combine the cinnamon with 2 cups of the sugar in a resealable plastic bag. Set aside.

Place the butter in the large bowl of an electric mixer and begin beating. Add the remaining sugar and continue beating until the mixture is well combined. Add the eggs and continue beating. When well incorporated, begin adding the reserved flour mixture, alternately with the milk. Beat until a soft dough forms.

Lightly flour a clean, flat surface. Transfer the dough to the floured surface and lightly sprinkle the top with additional flour. Either pat the dough down or gently roll it out with a rolling pin to a thickness of about ½ inch. Using a doughnut cutter (a round cutter with a removable disk in the center to create the hole) or a biscuit cutter (if you use a biscuit cutter, you will have to carefully hand cut the center holes), cut out circles, reserving the "holes." Gather up any remaining dough along with the "holes" and, again, pat or roll out the dough and cut out circles. Don't discard any dough, as the bits and pieces of the leftover dough can be fried to make oddly shaped doughnuts.

Place a thick layer of paper towels on a flat surface.

Heat the oil in a deep-fat fryer to 360 degrees on a candy thermometer. Add the doughnuts, a few at a time, and fry, turning occasionally with a slotted spoon, until the doughnuts have risen and are golden brown. Using the slotted spoon, gently lift the doughnuts to the paper towels to drain for just a few seconds. Then, transfer the doughnuts to the cinnamon-sugar mixture in the plastic bag and gently toss to coat them well. Remove the doughnuts from the cinnamon-sugar mixture and place them on a serving platter.

CONTEMPORARY

Drunken Fortune Doughnuts

MAKES ABOUT 2½ DOZEN

This might be called the hardworking man's version of the classic New Orleans breakfast of warm beignets and café au lait. In the "Big Easy," beignets are not just consumed at breakfast but are also indulged throughout the day, coated in confectioners' sugar, piping hot, and puffy. Made from a rich choux paste, the New Orleans classic is crisper than my filled, raised doughnut, which I first created as a steak house dessert.

Drunken doughnuts, especially with the hidden fortune, are fun, rich, sweet, and intoxicating. When serving children, obviously you should omit the liqueur flavoring, but never the fortunes. When making the fortunes, try to re-create the look of the paper fortunes found in Chinese fortune cookies, and have fun with what you write.

1½ cups fine-quality raspberry jam
¼ cup framboise
1 cup warm water (about 120 degrees)
1 cup warm milk (about 120 degrees)
1 ounce yeast
2 large eggs, at room temperature
½ cup canola oil
2 pounds all-purpose flour

¾ cups granulated sugar
2 teaspoons salt
1 tablespoon ground cinnamon
1 teaspoon ground cloves
½ teaspoon freshly grated nutmeg
Approximately 6 cups peanut oil
30 handmade paper fortunes, optional
Approximately 1 cup confectioners' sugar

Combine the raspberry jam and frambroise in a small bowl, stirring to blend well. Set aside.

Combine the water, milk, and yeast in a large mixing bowl, stirring until the yeast has dissolved. Whisk in the eggs and oil until well combined. Using a wooden spoon, beat in 1½ pounds of the flour. If the dough becomes too stiff to mix with a wooden spoon, use your hands to knead the dough together. When the flour is well incorporated into the dough, cover the bowl with a clean kitchen towel and place the dough in a warm spot to rest until doubled in size. This should take about 90 minutes.

While the dough is rising, mix the remaining flour with the granulated sugar, salt, cinnamon, cloves, and nutmeg. When the dough has doubled in size, knead in the spiced flour mixture, kneading until the mixture is smooth. Place into a large, clean bowl and again place in a warm spot to rest until doubled in size.

Lightly flour a clean, flat surface. Pat the dough out on the floured surface. Sprinkle the top with additional flour and gently roll out the dough to a thickness of about ½-inch. Using a biscuit cutter, cut out circles until you have used all of the dough.

Heat the oil in a deep-fat fryer to 360 degrees on a candy thermometer. Add the doughnuts, a few at a time, and fry, turning occasionally with a slotted spoon, until the doughnuts have risen to the top and are golden. Transfer them to wire racks to cool slightly.

When just cool enough to handle, using a small, sharp knife, cut a small opening in one side of each doughnut and a tiny opening in the opposite side. Using a teaspoon, stuff a bit of the jam-liqueur mixture into the larger opening in each doughnut and tuck a fortune into the smaller opening. Place the doughnuts on a serving platter.

Place the confectioners' sugar in a fine sieve and, holding the sieve over the platter, tap gently against the edge of the sieve to dust the doughnuts. Serve immediately.

SECOND DAY DISH

Stuffed Doughnuts with Whipped Cream and Berries

SERVES 6

This is a very simple and very delicious Second Day Dish. The cream and berries soak into the day-old doughnuts and create a fantastic dessert. I thought of the wonderful French dessert, Paris-Brest, when I created this easy sweet. Traditionally, a Paris-Brest is a baked ring of almond-crusted choux paste that is split and filled with a praline cream. Using yesterday's doughnuts and fragrant berries and sweet cream, this is a lot simpler to put together.

1 cup cold water
1 cup granulated sugar
1 cup heavy cream
1 teaspoon pure vanilla extract
1 cup blanched sliced almonds
6 day-old Simple Sugar-and-Spice

Doughnuts (see page 26) or other
   plain doughnuts
¼ cup plus 3 tablespoons confectioners'
   sugar
1 pint raspberries

Combine the water and granulated sugar in a medium saucepan over high heat and bring to a boil. Cook for about 2 minutes, or until the sugar has dissolved. Remove the simple syrup from the heat and allow it to cool.

Combine the cream and vanilla in a mixing bowl. Cover and refrigerate the mixture until you are ready to use it.

Preheat the oven to 350 degrees.

Line a baking sheet with parchment paper and set it aside.

Place the almonds on a clean plate.

Using a bread knife, slice each doughnut in half crosswise. Dip both sides of each half into the cooled simple syrup to just dampen. Place the browned part of the top half into the almonds to coat evenly. Place the doughnut halves, split side down, on the prepared baking sheet and into the preheated oven, and bake for 12 minutes, or until the almonds are golden and the doughnuts are slightly crisp on the outside but warm and moist on the inside. Remove them from the oven and allow them to cool.

Remove the chilled cream from the refrigerator and, using an electric mixer, beat for 1 minute. Add the 3 tablespoons of confectioners' sugar and continue to beat until soft peaks form.

Place the doughnut bottoms, split side up, on a flat surface. Using a spatula, generously coat each bottom with some of the whipped cream. Nestle some raspberries into the cream on each doughnut. Using the spatula, lightly coat the split side of the doughnut tops with whipped cream. Gently place the top half onto the bottom, almond-coated side up. Place each doughnut onto a dessert plate. Sprinkle some raspberries around the edge of the plate. Place the remaining ¼ cup of confectioners' sugar into a fine sieve and, holding the sieve over each plate, tap gently on the edge of the sieve to lightly dust the entire plate. Serve immediately.

OATMEAL

Americans have almost forgotten what real oatmeal tastes like given the availability of all the instant, flavored versions, ready-to-eat with the addition of hot water or milk. Soft, pudding-like, and almost tasteless oatmeal except for the added flavor or sweetener is now the norm. Old-fashioned steel-cut or Irish oatmeal (also known as oat groats), on the other hand, is earthy, nutty, slightly crunchy, chewy, and extremely healthy. It does, without question, stick to your ribs and is the perfect way to start a cold winter's day.

Oatmeal has been shown to lower cholesterol, regulate blood sugar, cleanse the skin, and serve as a great source of B vitamins, calcium, and fiber. And perhaps the most amazing attribute of oats is their ability to enhance vitality, most particularly in men. Those old sayings, "feeling your oats" and "sowing your oats" are based on truth as recent studies have shown that oats contain exsativa, which enhances male sexuality.

I only use steel-cut oats. Health-food stores are usually the best source of this nutritious grain, but McCann's, an Irish company, distributes its very distinctive metal tin filled to the brim with steel-cut oats to supermarkets and specialty food stores across the country.

CLASSIC

Oatmeal with Cinnamon-Brown Sugar and Honey-Tossed Berries and Raisins

SERVES 6

This is the best winter breakfast. Hearty, filling, and energy-building, it will keep you moving the whole day through. If you are pressed for time, or have a hard time getting started in the morning, soak the oats in 4 cups of water the night before and they will cook in about 20 minutes or in just enough time for you to jump in the shower and wake up. Also, you don't have to make the Honey-Tossed Berries and Raisins on a workday morning—just toss a few berries and raisins on top and pour some cream (or for you calorie-conscious types, skim milk) over it all.

4 cups cold water
½ teaspoon coarse salt
1 cup steel-cut oats
¾ cup firmly packed light brown sugar
1 teaspoon ground cinnamon
3 tablespoons unsalted butter
1½ cups sliced strawberries or whole

blueberries or raspberries, hulled or stemmed
½ cup golden raisins
2 tablespoons honey
1½ cups warm heavy cream, half-and-half, or milk

Place the water and salt in a medium saucepan over high heat and bring to a boil. Stir the oats into the boiling water; then lower the heat to a bare simmer. Cook, stirring occasionally, for about 1 hour, or until the water has been absorbed and the oatmeal is very thick.

While the oatmeal is cooking, combine the brown sugar and cinnamon in a small mixing bowl, making sure to blend it well. Set aside.

Melt the butter in a medium sauté pan over medium heat. Add the berries and raisins and cook, stirring frequently, for about 3 minutes, or just until the fruit begins to soften and let off some juice. Drizzle in the honey and stir to combine. Remove from the heat and cover loosely to keep warm.

Pour equal portions of the oatmeal into each of six shallow bowls. Sprinkle the top with the cinnamon-brown sugar mixture. Spoon some honey-tossed berries and raisins over the oatmeal, and pour warm cream over the top. Serve immediately.

CONTEMPORARY

Almond Oatmeal Crème Brûlée with Orange Essence

SERVES 6

This is a far stretch from the traditional French dessert, but I think that it works beautifully. I serve it in a hollow egg shell—it's a surprise to dig in and find crunchy, orange-flavored oatmeal hidden under the crackling sugar and rich custard. This is a great way to get the kids to eat their breakfast!

1 cup leftover oatmeal (see page 30)

2 tablespoons light brown sugar

2 teaspoons freshly grated orange zest

2 cups heavy cream

Approximately ¾ cups granulated sugar

1 cup toasted almonds, chopped

6 large egg yolks, beaten

Preheat the oven to 325 degrees.

Lightly butter the bottoms of six 5-ounce ceramic ramekins or crème brûlée dishes.

Combine the oatmeal and brown sugar with 1 teaspoon of the orange zest. Spoon equal portions of the flavored oatmeal into the bottom of each buttered ramekin, carefully smoothing the tops with a small spatula. Set aside.

Combine the cream with ½ cup of the granulated sugar, the chopped almonds, and the remaining orange zest in a medium saucepan over medium heat. Cook, stirring frequently, for about 4 minutes, or until the mixture is quite hot and the sugar has dissolved. Remove from the heat and allow to rest for 10 minutes.

Place the egg yolks in a medium mixing bowl and whisk until well blended. Whisking constantly, slowly pour the warm cream through a fine sieve into the eggs. Whisk until the eggs are completely incorporated into the cream. Pour the custard over the oatmeal in the prepared ramekins. Place the filled ramekins into a baking dish and carefully fill with enough warm water to come halfway up the sides of the ramekins. Tightly cover the entire dish with aluminum foil; then carefully place the baking dish into the preheated oven. Bake for 30 minutes. Remove the foil and check for doneness. The custards should jiggle slightly when the baking dish is moved, and the very center should be slightly runny. If not done, replace the foil and cook for an additional 5 minutes, taking care not to overcook the custard, or it will be tough. Remove the crème brûlées from the oven and the water bath and place them on a wire rack to cool. Refrigerate for 1 hour or up to 8 hours to chill through.

When ready to serve, sprinkle the top of each ramekin with a smooth coating of the remaining sugar. Using a handheld propane torch (see page 23), carefully caramelize the sugar coating by running the flame over the sugar in quick, even strokes. Serve chilled.

Oatmeal Gougères

SERVES 6

Gougères are tasty little cheese puffs that are a traditional hors d'oeuvres from Burgundy. They are light as air and the classic French accompaniment to a glass of champagne. In this recipe, the addition of a little cooked oatmeal creates a heartier flavor and a little crunch, but the outcome is the same—a perfectly elegant hors d'oeuvre to serve at cocktail time.

½ cup cooked oatmeal (see page 30)	½ teaspoon coarse salt
½ cup water	1 cup sifted all-purpose flour
½ cup milk	4 large eggs
1 cup (1 stick) unsalted butter	1¾ cups grated fine-quality Cheddar cheese

Preheat the oven to 275 degrees.

Spread the oatmeal out on a baking sheet and place it in the preheated oven for about 12 minutes, or until quite dry and the grains can be loosened. Remove from the heat and allow to cool. When cool, rub the oatmeal between the palms of your hands to further separate the grains. Don't overrub the grains, or they will adhere to one another.

Raise the oven temperature to 400 degrees.

Line two baking sheets with parchment paper and set aside. (If you have nonstick, silicone, baking-sheet liners, they work extremely well when baking *gougères*.)

Heat the water, milk, butter, and salt in a heavy-bottomed saucepan over medium-high heat. Bring to a rapid boil. Add the flour all at once and, using a wooden spoon, immediately beat it in until a thick paste forms. Continue cooking and beating for about 2 minutes, or just long enough to eliminate some of the moisture. Remove from the heat and transfer to the bowl of an electric mixer fitted with the paddle attachment. Add the reserved oatmeal and beat on high for about 2 minutes, scraping down the sides of the bowl from time to time.

With the mixer running, add the eggs, one at a time, and continue beating and scraping down the sides of the bowl for about 1 minute, or until the eggs are well incorporated into the flour mixture. The batter should form a soft peak when it is lifted. Using a wooden spoon, beat in 1 cup of the cheese until blended. (If you are not using the dough immediately, it can be covered and refrigerated for up to 2 days.)

Scoop the dough into a pastry bag fitted with a ½-inch-plain tip. Squeeze the dough out onto the prepared baking sheets into 1½-inch rounds, taking care to allow room for the puffs to rise. Lightly sprinkle the tops with some of the remaining cheese. Place in the preheated oven and bake for 15 minutes. Lower the temperature to 350 degrees, and continue baking for an additional 10 minutes, or until the puffs have risen and are golden brown and quite firm. Remove from the heat and serve warm.

APPETIZERS, SOUPS, AND SALADS

Appetizers are meant to be just what they sound like—appetite teasers! They can be an extremely elaborate or quite simple beginning to a meal. Soups can be (and often are) served as an appetizer course, but salads usually are a course served on their own later in the meal. Yet all of them can be turned into a meal that stands on its own.

I focus here on two classic appetizers. A shrimp cocktail is, for most people, the first grown-up appetizer they experience. The zesty cocktail sauce served with it covers all bases—it can mask the tastelessness of shrimp that has been frozen too long and it can excite the flavor of the most sweet, succulent, and tender of shrimp. I've pretty much kept the classic shellfish preparation as it deserves to be while giving some extra play on the Contemporary and Second Day versions.

And then there is Smoked Salmon, which I adore. My Pastrami Salmon has been much-imitated (I'm flattered) since I introduced it to the market some years ago. It has great flavor and can easily be made at home. Unlike traditional smoked salmon, it is based on the cured gravlax (raw salmon that is cured in a sugar-salt-dill combination) that I came to love when I cooked in Norway as a young chef. Working with the freshest fish imaginable, I learned how to create the delicate balance between the sweet salmon and the aromatic cure. When I returned to America, I added some spice and heat to make this classic my own.

Traditional smoked salmon is created by one of two methods: hot smoking when the fish is smoked at temperatures ranging from 120 degrees to 180 degrees for up to 12 hours, or cold smoking where the fish is cured at low smoke temperatures ranging from 70 degrees to 90 degrees from 1 to 20 days. The size of the fish will determine the heat and the time. Premium salmon is generally Atlantic salmon known as "Scotch," but it is interesting to note that this export from the British Isles has evolved out of London's early-twentieth-century, Jewish immigrant community. Today, one of the most prestigious purveyors of Scottish smoked salmon remains a small London company run by the descendents of an early, emigrant fish smoker. I use the fine-smoked salmon sold by Perona Farms (see Sources) when I am not making my own. There is nothing more delicious served as an appetizer, as a late-night snack, for brunch or lunch—you name the time, and it is always right for a bite of this delicately smoked fish.

Clam Chowder is the classic soup I've chosen to include. Cobb and Caesar are the salads. As I see it, they are the classics that most lend themselves to reinterpretation at the contemporary table. Chowder can be served equally well as both a first course and an entrée. Cobb Salad is almost always an entrée, but you could easily take elements of it to create a salad course. And, of course, everywhere you turn you will find a Caesar Salad, sometimes as a first course and just as often as an entrée served with grilled chicken or seafood. Only infrequently is the dressing still freshly made, tableside, as it was originally, but as long as it has the sweet crunch of romaine lettuce, the piquancy of lemon and anchovy, and the creaminess of Parmesan all is right in the world.

SHELLFISH COCKTAILS

I've done a bit of research, but I have yet to discover who first had the idea to serve chilled shellfish, usually shrimp, with a slightly spicy, tomato ketchup or chili sauce–based dressing for dipping. Whoever it was certainly struck a culinary note as shrimp cocktails have starred on restaurant menus for generations. No other dish, except perhaps a mound of caviar or a slice of foie gras, automatically marks a special occasion at the table.

Since I was born and raised on the New Jersey shore, to me a shellfish cocktail means freshly shucked clams and oysters eaten right from the shell outdoors on a picnic table or sitting on the sand. Man, could we gobble up those fresh-from-the-ocean tidbits! When I was a kid, my friends and I would all gather in our dirty shorts and high rubber boots to shuck. The juices would run down our arms, saturate our shorts, and dribble down our legs into our boots; by the end of an afternoon, our feet would be swimming inside them.

In France, I was introduced to the classic *fruits de mer,* a combination of shellfish nestled into shaved ice and served on terraced, metal trays. (I always watched the shuckers to see if the juice was finding its way to the inside of their boots. Inevitably it did.) I can close my eyes and see these magnificent presentations displayed on the street in front of a neighborhood bistro in Paris or at the water's edge in Brittany or along the Mediterranean in the south. The glorious panorama of lobster, shrimp, langoustines, crab, clams, oysters and, perhaps, sea urchin, periwinkles, and whelk is the lure that draws the diner into the restaurant with the promise of a beautifully fresh and perfectly prepared meal.

Over the years, as fresh seafood has become more widely available and tastes have changed, the waters have brought Florida stone crab claws and Alaskan king crab to our tables. Pristine shellfish, such as diver scallops and day boat shrimp, is now served raw, either as a component of a shellfish presentation or alone, garnished with Latin or Asian condiments and spices. So, the basic shellfish cocktail, as delicious as it can be, has been brought to new heights and flavor thrills.

Shrimp, Lobster, and Crab with Cocktail Sauce and Old Bay Mayonnaise

SERVES 6

This is my version of the standard shrimp cocktail. All of the basic elements are here, but I've added some extra ingredients. I've added more luxury with lobster and crab and used some zesty mayo for a change from a delicious cocktail sauce. I haven't given instructions for individual plating simply because the presentation works best on a huge platter with everybody sharing the bounty. However, if individual plates suit your plans, by all means make them. In that case, you might want to line the plates with chopped lettuces, seaweed, or watercress. If fresh crab and lobster aren't available locally, they can easily be ordered (see Sources) with early morning delivery, ensuring a perfectly fresh cocktail. Since I've striven for an extra-special presentation, it could, I think, very nicely serve as a luncheon main course.

2 pounds supercolossal (12 to a pound) shrimp, cooked, peeled, and deveined, tails intact

3 1½ pound lobsters, steamed

3 Dungeness crabs, steamed and split in half lengthwise (or 12 cooked stone crab claws,

6 cooked king crab legs, or 18 cooked langoustines)

Cocktail Sauce (recipe follows)

Old Bay Mayonnaise (recipe follows)

Approximately 3 lemons, quartered

Line a huge platter with shaved or chopped ice. Place two martini glasses into the ice in the center of the platter. Mound the shrimp around the bottom of the martini glasses. Place three lobsters at each end of the platter and the split crab on the sides. Nestle some lemon quarters around the shellfish. Place some Cocktail Sauce in one martini glass and some Old Bay Mayonnaise in the other, and serve immediately with bibs and lobster crackers.

Cocktail Sauce

1 cup prepared chili sauce
½ cup prepared horseradish, well drained
1 tablespoon fresh lemon juice plus more
to taste

1 teaspoon Tabasco sauce
½ teaspoon Worcestershire sauce
Coarse salt

Combine the chili and horseradish sauces in a small nonreactive mixing bowl. Whisk in the lemon juice, Tabasco, and Worcestershire sauces. Taste and adjust the seasoning with salt and, if desired, additional lemon juice. If the sauce seems a bit thick, loosen it with cold water, ½ teaspoon at a time. Store, covered and refrigerated, for up to 1 week.

Old Bay Mayonnaise

2 cups fine-quality mayonnaise
1 tablespoon Old Bay Seasoning
2 teaspoons fresh lemon juice

Combine the mayonnaise, seasoning, and lemon juice in a small mixing bowl, whisking to blend well.

If not using it immediately, cover and refrigerate it for up to 1 week.

CONTEMPORARY

Hot Shellfish Cocktail with Tomato-Roasted Garlic Aïoli

SERVES 6

For this dish you can use any type of shellfish you like or whatever is readily available in the market. Almost every supermarket sells bags of mussels and clams. I like to use a combination of clams, mussels, and oysters that I quickly cook on the grill, but, for the home cook, I think it is easier to bake them. The shellfish is ready in a snap but the aïoli takes a little more time; however, it can be made in advance.

Approximately 2 pounds mussels, cleaned, scrubbed, beards removed
2 dozen clams, cleaned and scrubbed
2 pounds shrimp, shelled with their tails on
1 cup olive oil
2 tablespoons minced flat-leaf parsley
1 tablespoon minced fresh chives
1 teaspoon minced fresh tarragon
1 teaspoon minced fresh chervil
Coarse salt and freshly ground black pepper
Tomato-Roasted Garlic Aïoli (recipe follows)

Preheat the oven to 450 degrees.

Place the mussels, clams, and shrimp in a large roasting pan. Add the olive oil, parsley, chives, tarragon, chervil, and salt and pepper to taste. Toss the mixture to coat the seafood well. Place the shellfish in the preheated oven and roast it for about 10 minutes, or until the shells open, the juices are running, and the shrimp has turned bright pink and curled. Remove it from the oven.

Place equal portions of the shellfish into each of six large, shallow bowls. Spoon some of the pan juices into each bowl. Serve immediately with the aïoli on the side.

Tomato-Roasted Garlic Aïoli

1 large head garlic
3 tablespoons olive oil
1 medium onion, diced
1 teaspoon minced garlic
1 teaspoon hot red pepper flakes
1 cup chopped canned plum tomatoes
Coarse salt and freshly ground black pepper, if needed
1½ cups fine-quality mayonnaise
1 teaspoon fresh lemon juice

Preheat the oven to 325 degrees.

Separate the garlic into cloves and place the cloves in a small baking dish. Add 2 tablespoons of the olive oil and toss the garlic to coat it. Place the garlic in the preheated oven and roast it, turning occasionally, for about 20 minutes, or until the cloves are very soft. Remove the garlic from the oven and set it aside until cool enough to handle.

When the garlic cloves have cooled, using a small paring knife, slit the skin open and pop each clove from its skin. Place the soft garlic in a small shallow bowl and, using the back of a spoon, press it into a paste. Set aside.

Place the remaining tablespoon of olive oil in a sauté pan over medium heat. Add the onions and sauté for about 5 minutes, or until they are quite soft and translucent. Stir in the minced garlic and red pepper flakes and cook, stirring constantly, for 1 minute. Stir in the tomatoes along with their juices and season the mixture with salt and pepper to taste. Bring it to a simmer and then lower the heat and cook, stirring occasionally, at a bare simmer for 30 minutes. Remove from the heat and set aside to cool slightly.

Place the cooled tomato mixture in a blender and process for about 30 seconds, or until smooth. Pour it into a mixing bowl. Add the mayonnaise, lemon juice, and reserved garlic paste, whisking to combine. Taste and, if necessary, adjust the seasoning with salt and pepper.

If you are not using the aïoli immediately, cover and refrigerate it for up to 1 week. Bring to room temperature before using.

Chopped Seafood Salad with Tomato and Onion in Avocado Halves

Serves 2

This is a great recipe for any remaining seafood, shellfish, or otherwise. It is so simple to pull together that you might want to make it a "first day" dish using ingredients especially purchased to make it. It's really a fancy version of the everyday, New England lobster roll, featuring my crisp, down-home hot dog rolls.

2 hot dog rolls
½ tablespoon olive oil
1 cup chopped cooked seafood such as shrimp, lobster, or clams, or any fish
⅓ cup peeled, cored, seeded, and diced very ripe tomatoes
1 tablespoon finely diced, Vidalia (or other sweet) onion
2 teaspoons minced mixed fresh herbs

(such as parsley, chives, marjoram, cilantro, and/or mint) (see Note)
Approximately ¾ cup Old Bay Mayonnaise (see page 41)
Coarse salt and freshly ground black pepper
1 ripe avocado, halved
Juice of 1 lime
2 cups chopped lettuce

NOTE: Use any combination of herbs that appeals to your taste. If you prefer using something simple like parsley or chives, fine, but don't omit the hint of fresh green from the salad.

If you have a bit of Tomato-Horseradish Mousse in the fridge, put a dollop on top of each salad and stick the herb sprig into it.

Preheat the oven to 375 degrees.

Line a baking sheet with parchment paper. Set aside.

Open up the hot dogs rolls and split each one in half on the fold. Place the halves on a clean, flat work surface. Using a rolling pin and working with 1 piece at a time, roll the pieces out to very thin waferlike disks. Using a pastry brush, lightly coat both sides of each disk with olive oil. Place the disks on the prepared baking sheet and into the preheated oven. Bake for about 4 minutes, or until the bread is golden but still pliable. Remove the disks from the oven and, working quickly, gently place each warm, pliable disk over a bottle placed on its side to mold a curved circle. Set the molded disks on a wire rack to cool.

Place the seafood in a mixing bowl along with the tomatoes, onions, and minced herbs. Toss to combine. Add the Old Bay Mayonnaise and gently mix. Taste and adjust the seasoning with salt and pepper. Set aside.

Cut each avocado in half lengthwise. Stick a knifepoint into each seed and give a quick pull to remove the seed. Sprinkle the cut sides with lime juice to keep the avocado from discoloring. Heap the seafood mixture into the cavity of each avocado. Place an equal portion of shredded lettuce in the center of each of two luncheon plates. Center an avocado half on each plate and stick two crisp hot dog roll disks on each side. Serve immediately.

SMOKED SALMON

I first immersed myself in curing meats and fish when I was a young chef in France. I was fascinated with the flavors you could ignite with brining, smoking, and curing. The basics I learned then have become an essential part of my cooking techniques. The Pastrami Salmon I developed is simply a quirky extension of the cured salmon I learned to love in Norway and the delicately smoked version I prepared in France.

As I said earlier, salmon can be either hot or cold smoked or cured. It is an exceptionally good fish to smoke or cure because it has such a high-fat content and rich flavor. It almost never dries out or loses flavor during the curing process. In addition, its flavor is often enhanced by the herbs or spices or the wood used in the process.

People have been curing fish for about as long as they have been catching and eating it. Hot smoke cooks the fish as it deeply flavors it with the aromatic wood smoke. Ultimately the smoking serves as a preservative. The home cook can purchase a home smoker made specifically for this purpose and can also use a basic covered grill or the stove top to hot smoke salmon nicely.

Cold smoke penetrates the fish at a very low temperature that does not actually cook the fish. Consequently, the fish must first be brined or cured with salt and/or sugar before it enters the smoking stage. It is this method that most often applies to smoked salmon. Cold smoking is infrequently done at home except by the most avid fans of smoked fish. The curing process takes a couple of days, and then the smoking, which takes quite a few hours, must be done under very controlled conditions.

My Pastrami Salmon (see page 47) is cured much in the manner of gravlax (literally translated as burned fish). It came about because I used so much salmon in the restaurant kitchen that I needed to find a use for the salmon bellies that remained after I had filleted the whole fish. It is substantially spicier than the Scandinavian gravlax. I named it as I did because it made me think about the spice-cured meat of New York deli fame. It is quite easy to make at home as you will see.

Smoked salmon has, traditionally, been cut paper-thin and served with aromatic accompaniments because, in the beginning, it was usually extremely salty. This is no longer the case as both the quality and the curing and smoking techniques have improved greatly. Start with great fish, give it a light cure and a quick smoke, and you will have a delicately delicious appetizer. However, tradition will probably rule since almost everyone looks for the classic presentation that follows.

CLASSIC

Smoked Salmon with Horseradish Mousse and Corn Blini

SERVES 6

For this classic, I've just improved on the sour cream with a little Horseradish Mousse, but the remaining accompaniments are traditional. In the manner of the Tsars, blinis are usually made with buckwheat flour. I've Americanized them by replacing the buckwheat with corn-meal, which adds some subtle sweetness to the succulent salmon.

1 cup crème fraîche
½ cup prepared horseradish, well drained
1 teaspoon coarse salt plus more to taste
3 large hard-boiled eggs
¾ cup sifted all-purpose flour
⅔ cup yellow cornmeal
2 tablespoons sugar
2 packets Rapid-Rise yeast

1½ cups warm (about 115 degrees) milk
¼ cup (½ stick) melted, unsalted butter
3 large eggs, beaten
24 very thin slices (about 3 pounds) fine-quality smoked salmon
1 cup finely diced, white onion
½ cup well-drained capers

> NOTE: Feel free to make simple breakfast pancakes instead of blinis. They are not quite as authentic but still very tasty!

Using an electric mixer, beat the crème fraîche until soft peaks form. Fold in the horseradish and season to taste with salt. Cover and refrigerate until ready to use.

Peel the hard-boiled eggs and cut them in half. Separate the whites from the yolks. Using a chef's knife, separately chop the egg whites and yolks. Place each separately in small containers. Cover and refrigerate until ready to use.

Combine the flour, cornmeal, sugar, yeast, and 1 teaspoon of salt in a medium mixing bowl. Add the warm milk and butter and stir to just combine. Scrape down the sides of the bowl with a spatula; then, cover and set the mixture in a warm spot for about 30 minutes, or until the batter has doubled in size.

Preheat the oven to 200 degrees.

Line a baking sheet with parchment paper and set aside.

Using a wooden spoon, stir the batter. Add the beaten eggs and stir to combine.

Preheat a griddle or a heavy-duty nonstick skillet. If necessary, lightly grease the griddle or coat it with nonstick vegetable spray.

Spoon about 2 tablespoons of batter per blini onto the hot griddle. Cook for about 2 minutes, or until the top is filled with bursting bubbles and the bottom is golden brown. Turn the blinis and cook for another minute, or until they are cooked through. As the blinis are cooked, place them on the prepared baking sheet and into the preheated oven to keep warm. Make 24 blinis.

Place four blinis on each of six luncheon plates. Lay a generous slice of salmon over each blini. Garnish each plate with a small mound of chopped egg yolk and egg white, onion, and capers. Dollop a small amount of Horseradish Mousse on each piece of salmon and serve immediately.

CONTEMPORARY

Pastrami Salmon and Smoked Salmon with Potato Pancakes, Honey-Mustard Vinaigrette, and Apple Salad

SERVES 6

If you don't want to make Pastrami Salmon, you can order mine from Perona Farms (see Sources). However, it is quite easy to prepare, so I think you should give it a try. The salad to serve with it combines all of the elements I love with salmon, crisp and slightly oily yet succulent potato pancakes, hot yet sweet vinaigrette, and the touch of tartness from the apples.

4 large, Idaho potatoes, peeled
5 large shallots, peeled
2 large eggs
Coarse salt and freshly ground black pepper
Approximately ¼ cup olive oil
18 slices smoked salmon

18 slices Pastrami Salmon (recipe follows)
3 large Granny Smith apples, peeled, cored, and julienned
1 cup red onion slivers
3 cups watercress leaves
Honey-Mustard Vinaigrette (recipe follows)

Preheat the oven to 200 degrees.

Line a baking sheet with parchment paper and set aside.

Using a food processor fitted with the shredding disk (or using a handheld grater), shred the potatoes and shallots. Transfer the potato-shallot mixture to a medium mixing bowl, and stir in the egg along with salt and pepper to taste.

Heat about 1 tablespoon of the oil in a nonstick skillet or sauté pan over medium-high heat. Spoon about 2 tablespoons of the potato-shallot mixture into the hot pan to make a small, neat pancake. Cook for about 3 minutes, or until the bottom of the pancake is golden. Lower the heat, turn and cook for an additional 4 minutes, or until the potatoes are cooked and the pancakes are crisp and golden. As each pancake is cooked, place it on the prepared baking sheet and into the preheated oven to keep warm while you continue to make pancakes. You will need 18 pancakes.

Roll each piece of smoked salmon and Pastrami Salmon, cigar-fashion, into neat rolls. (This can be done early in the day. Cover the rolls and refrigerate them until ready to use.)

Combine the apple, onion, and watercress in a mixing bowl. Add about ½ cup of the Honey-Mustard Vinaigrette and toss to combine.

Slightly overlap three warm pancakes down the center of each of six dinner plates. Place a smoked salmon and a Pastrami Salmon roll on top of each pancake. Spoon equal portions of the apple salad on each side and drizzle some of the vinaigrette around the edge of the plate. Serve immediately.

Pastrami Salmon

1 cup coarse salt
½ cup sugar
2 bunches fresh cilantro
1 bunch fresh flat-leaf parsley, well-washed
½ pound shallots, peeled and chopped
1 2- to 2½-pound side salmon, skin and
    bones removed

½ cup molasses
2 tablespoons cayenne pepper
5 bay leaves
¼ cup paprika
¼ cup ground coriander
¼ cup freshly ground black pepper
¼ cup cracked black pepper

Combine the salt and sugar in a small mixing bowl.

Place the cilantro, parsley, and shallots in the bowl of a food processor fitted with the metal blade and process to a smooth purée.

Place the salmon on a platter and generously season both sides with the salt-sugar mixture. When well seasoned, coat each side with a generous layer of the purée. Cover the platter with plastic wrap. Place the salmon in the refrigerator and allow it to marinate for 3 days.

When the salmon has cured for 3 days, combine the molasses, cayenne, and bay leaves in a small saucepan over medium heat. Bring to a boil; then lower the heat and simmer for 1 minute. Remove the mixture from the heat and allow it to cool.

Combine the paprika and coriander with the black peppers in a small bowl.

Remove the salmon from the refrigerator and, using a spatula, scrape off and discard all of the seasoning from the fish. Using a pastry brush, lightly coat both sides of the salmon with the cooled molasses mixture. Sprinkle the spice mixture on both sides of the salmon to lightly coat it. Place the salmon on a clean platter and cover it with plastic wrap. Refrigerate for 24 hours. Pastrami Salmon will keep, covered and refrigerated, for 1 week.

When you are ready to serve the salmon, unwrap it and cut it, on the bias, into thin slices.

Honey-Mustard Vinaigrette

1 cup olive oil
¾ cup extra virgin olive oil
1 tablespoon mustard oil (see Note)
¼ cup tarragon vinegar
¼ cup sherry wine vinegar

2 tablespoons honey
2 tablespoons Dijon mustard
1 teaspoon freshly ground black pepper
Coarse salt

Combine the olive oils and mustard oil in a small mixing bowl. Whisk in the tarragon and sherry wine vinegars. Add the honey, mustard, pepper, and salt and whisk vigorously for about 2 minutes, or until the mixture is emulsified.

This will make more vinaigrette than you will need for the salmon. The remainder may be stored, covered and refrigerated, for up to 1 week.

SECOND DAY DISH

Smoked Salmon Lollipops

SERVES 6

I first created these pops after making chocolate lollipops with my kids. Since that day, I have gone on to develop a packaged version that I now market through specialty food stores across the country (see page 281). The line has been extended to include savory foie gras and goat cheese pops as well. If you want to make these at home, you will need twelve lollipop sticks, available from pastry supply stores and some craft stores. Since these lollipops freeze and thaw extremely well, making them is a good rainy day project, leaving you with a great hors d'oeuvre for spur-of-the-moment entertaining.

¼ cup poppy seeds
4 ounces chopped smoked salmon
4 ounces cream cheese
2 tablespoons minced scallions, with some
   green parts

1 tablespoon capers, well drained
1 tablespoon fresh lemon zest
Coarse salt and freshly ground white
   pepper
4 ounces thinly sliced smoked salmon

Line a small baking sheet with parchment paper. Set aside.

Place the poppy seeds in a small bowl and set aside.

Combine the chopped salmon, cream cheese, scallions, capers, and lemon zest in the bowl of a food processor fitted with the metal blade and process to combine well. Taste and adjust the seasoning with salt and pepper. Scrape the mixture into a pastry bag fitted with a medium, plain, round tip. Pipe 12 small rounds onto the prepared baking sheet and place the sheet in the refrigerator for 30 minutes, or until the rounds are firm to the touch.

Working quickly, roll each round in the palm of your hands to make a smooth ball and immediately wrap a smoked salmon slice around the ball to enclose it. (If the round gets too soft, return it to the refrigerator to firm up.) Place a lollipop stick in the center of each salmon-covered round. Dip each lollipop into the reserved bowl of poppy seeds. Return the lollipops to the parchment-lined baking sheet and refrigerate until ready to serve. (You may also freeze the lollipops. Place the pops, sticks straight up, in a single layer in the freezer and freeze for about 2 hours, or until hard. Once hard, you can store the pops, in layers separated by freezer paper, if necessary, on their side in a freezer-proof container. When ready to serve, thaw the pops in a single layer, sticks straight up.)

CHOWDERS

Once a very basic, warming meal made from kitchen staples like salt pork and bread and whatever neighborhood fish or shellfish was available, chowders are now often exotic, first-course extravaganzas. In fact, on today's menus, the name chowder is often used to describe any rich, thick, chunky soup, with or without fish or shellfish. I've gone straight back to the original with my New England and Manhattan Clam Chowders, only the garnish brings them up to the contemporary table.

The name chowder derives from the French word *chaudière,* a type of large cauldron used by fishermen to prepare their fresh-from-the-sea meal. I would imagine that the early versions were made from whatever fish or shellfish was on hand, water, a bit of seasoning, and very little else. In fact, most historical cookbooks list the ingredients as water seasoned with salt or salt pork and fish, with stale bread or biscuits as the thickening agent. Potatoes, onions, and other vegetables were introduced as thickeners in the nineteenth century. Then came cream and milk to enrich the soup. Much later, fresh and/or dried corn was used as both a thickener and as enrichment.

Most people think that the main ingredient for a great chowder has to be a chowder clam. These large, meaty clams, about 3 to 4 inches in diameter, are also known as quahogs or, simply, large clams. They are usually chopped into small pieces, both to tenderize them and to make them easier to incorporate into a thick soup. However, almost any clam can be used to make chowder. If you are using small, sweet clams, it is best to cook them in their shells in the chowder.

For years, on the East Coast, there has been a running argument over the merits of New England Clam Chowder as opposed to those of Manhattan Clam Chowder. I don't find one better than the other. Sometimes I'm in the mood for the rich, creamy New England chowder and sometimes the tomatoey Manhattan chowder fits the bill. And, when I can't make up my mind, I put them both together (see page 54).

CLASSIC

New England Clam Chowder with Oyster Crackers

SERVES 6

New England is *the* place for chowder. So much so that once upon a time each Yankee town had a chowder master whose job was to prepare huge batches of the creamy brew for all town functions and celebrations. My chowder is thick and rich with both potatoes and cream. I thought about developing a recipe for oyster crackers, but I couldn't think of anything better than reaching into that big, store-bought, crinkly bag of tiny, slightly salty disks and tumbling them into a steaming bowl of homemade chowder.

3 pounds cherrystone or littleneck clams,
    cleaned and scrubbed
3 strips bacon, finely diced
1 large Idaho potato, peeled and cubed
¾ cup minced onion
¼ cup minced celery
1 clove garlic, minced
1 bay leaf

2 cups chicken stock (see page 110)
2 Russet potatoes, peeled and diced
2 stalks celery, diced
Coarse salt and freshly ground black
    pepper
1 cup heavy cream
2 tablespoons minced fresh chives
Oyster Crackers

Using a stiff-bristled vegetable brush, scrub the clams under cool running water to remove all of the sand and grit. Set aside.

Place the bacon in a large saucepan over medium heat and fry, stirring frequently, for about 5 minutes, or until the bacon is crisp and the fat has rendered out. Using a slotted spoon, remove half of the cooked bacon and place it on some paper towels to drain. Set the drained bacon aside.

Add the cubed potato to the saucepan along with the minced onion, celery, and garlic. Cook, stirring constantly, for 2 minutes. Add the bay leaf and the reserved clams. Cover and steam for about 10 minutes, or until all of the clams have opened. Using a slotted spoon, remove all of the clams from the saucepan and discard any that have not opened. Set aside.

Add the chicken stock to the saucepan and bring it to a simmer. Lower the heat and cover.

Simmer for 10 minutes; then remove the stock from the heat. Remove and discard the bay leaf.

While the chicken stock mixture is simmering, remove the meat from one half of the clams and cut each piece in half. Discard the empty shells and reserve the remaining clams and the meat.

Using a food processor fitted with the metal blade, process the chicken stock mixture to a smooth purée. Transfer the purée to a clean saucepan. Add the diced potatoes and celery and place over medium heat. Season to taste with salt and pepper and bring to a simmer. Cover and simmer for 10 minutes, or until the potatoes are almost tender. Stir in the cream and again bring to a simmer. Cover and simmer for 5 minutes. Add the reserved bacon and clam meat along with 1 tablespoon of the chives and cook for an additional minute or two, or until the soup is very hot.

Pour equal portions of the clams in their shells into each of six shallow soup bowls. Ladle the hot soup over the top. Garnish the top with the remaining chives, and serve piping hot with oyster crackers.

Two Soups—New England and Manhattan Clam Chowders with Cheddar Biscuits

SERVES 6

I once visited a well-known Chinese chef in his kitchen. After showing me his exquisite and quick fold for *dim sum,* he began to talk about his particular take on yin and yang—the art of juxtaposing male and female characteristics in cooking, as in life. There is sweet and sour, he said, as well as bitter and spice. He then drew me a picture of the yin-yang symbol; two curved apostrophe-like bodies that nestle together as one or neatly separate into two complete designs. His inspiration helped me create this chowder dish—two distinct but similar soups nestled together in a shallow bowl to create one unified taste. In this dish, the Manhattan Chowder is slightly lighter than the New England variety, which allows it to keep suspended beside the other thicker soup. However, don't be upset if they begin to mingle. The Cheddar Biscuits are not necessary, but they do complement the soups beautifully.

34 fresh cherrystone or little neck clams, cleaned and scrubbed

3 strips bacon, finely diced

4 cloves garlic, peeled and minced

2 large Idaho potatoes, peeled and diced

1 stalk celery, peeled and diced

1 medium onion, peeled and diced

1 red bell pepper, cored, seeded, and diced

1 tablespoon minced fresh thyme

1 bay leaf

2 cups canned, crushed tomatoes with juice

2 cups tomato juice

6 cups New England Clam Chowder (see page 53)

1 tablespoon salted butter, at room temperature

Coarse salt and freshly ground black pepper

Tabasco sauce to taste

Cheddar Biscuits, optional (recipe follows)

Scrub the clams thoroughly under cold running water to remove all sand and grit. Set aside.

Place the bacon in a large saucepan over medium heat. Cook the bacon bits, stirring frequently, for about 5 minutes, or until they are crisp and all of the fat has rendered out.

Add the garlic, potatoes, celery, onion, bell pepper, thyme, and bay leaf. Cook, stirring constantly, for 1 minute. Add the clams. Cover and allow to steam for about 15 minutes, or until all of the clams have opened. Using a slotted spoon, transfer the clams from the saucepan to a large platter, discarding any that have not opened.

Add the tomatoes and tomato juice to the saucepan and bring to a simmer. Lower the heat and simmer for 10 minutes. Remove and discard the bay leaf.

While the soup is cooking, remove and chop the meat from 16 of the clams. Discard the shells and reserve the chopped meat. Reserve the remaining whole clams.

Place the New England Clam Chowder in a saucepan over medium heat and bring it to a simmer. Lower the heat to just keep warm.

Stir the butter into the Manhattan Clam Chowder. Add the chopped clams and season to taste with salt, pepper, and Tabasco. Cook for about 2 minutes, or until the soup is very hot.

Working with one bowl at a time, lift the bowl to slightly elevate one side. Carefully place one ladleful (about 1 cup) of New England Clam Chowder into the lower side of the bowl. Working quickly, carefully place a ladleful of Manhattan Clam Chowder into the opposite side, gently lowering the bowl to allow the two soups to meet in the middle. Place three clams in their shells in the center where the soups meet, and serve piping hot with Cheddar Biscuits, if using, passed on the side.

Cheddar Biscuits

2 cups bread flour

1½ cups all-purpose flour

1 package Rapid-Rise yeast

3 tablespoons sugar

1 teaspoon sea salt

1¼ cups milk

6 tablespoons unsalted butter

2 large eggs

¾ cup grated Cheddar cheese

2 tablespoons poppy seeds

Preheat the oven to 350 degrees.

Line a baking sheet with parchment paper. Set aside.

Combine the flours with the yeast, sugar, and salt in the large mixing bowl of an electric mixer fitted with the dough hook.

Combine the milk and butter in a small saucepan over medium heat. Cook for about 1 minute, or until the liquid is 115 degrees on an instant-read thermometer. Pour the liquid into the dry mixture and begin beating on low. Add 1 egg, raise the speed to medium, and continue beating until the mixture is smooth and elastic.

Add the Cheddar cheese and beat until well incorporated into the dough.

Pinch the dough into ½-ounce balls and place on the prepared baking sheet, leaving room for the dough balls to rise.

Place the remaining egg in a small bowl and beat lightly. Using a pastry brush, lightly coat each biscuit with the egg wash. Sprinkle the top of each roll with poppy seeds.

Place the baking sheet in the preheated oven and bake for 15 minutes, or until the biscuits have risen and are golden brown. Serve hot.

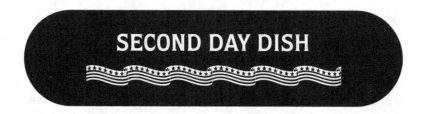

SECOND DAY DISH

Clam Chowder Bread Pudding with Tomato and Watercress Salad

SERVES 2

This makes an absolutely terrific luncheon dish served at room temperature. Add a big pitcher of ice-cold beer and great company, and it will be as good as an old-fashioned clambake. There are many variations on this theme to keep Second Day Dishes coming: Try lining the soufflé dish or ramekins with thin slices of zucchini, sprinkle grated Parmesan cheese in the buttered dishes, top the puddings with grated cheese, or toss the croutons in Old Bay Seasoning.

1 cup fresh, French bread croutons
1 large egg
¼ cup milk
1 cup New England or Manhattan Clam
  Chowder (see pages 53 or 54)

½ teaspoon minced fresh rosemary needles
  or basil leaves
¼ teaspoon fresh lemon juice
Coarse salt and freshly ground pepper
Tomato and Watercress Salad (recipe follows)

Preheat the oven to 350 degrees.

Lightly butter two 6-ounce soufflé dishes or ramekins or one 4-cup soufflé or baking dish. Evenly divide the croutons among the prepared dishes. Set aside.

Combine the egg and milk in a large mixing bowl. Add the chowder, rosemary or basil, and lemon juice and stir to combine. Season with salt and pepper. Pour the chowder mixture over the croutons in the prepared dishes.

Place the puddings in a baking pan large enough to hold them without the edges touching. Carefully add cold water to the baking pan until it measures ½ inch deep. Place the entire pan in the preheated oven and bake for about 20 minutes, or until the puddings have puffed slightly, are set in the middle, and are golden brown. Remove them from the oven and serve immediately in the individual dishes with salad on the side of the plate. If baked in one large dish, spoon out portions onto serving plates and garnish the plate with the salad.

Tomato and Watercress Salad

⅓ cup olive oil
¼ cup extra virgin olive oil
1 teaspoon mustard oil (see page 50)
1½ tablespoons tarragon vinegar
1½ tablespoons sherry wine vinegar

Coarse salt and freshly ground black pepper
1 bunch watercress, well washed and dried,
  tough stems removed
2 very ripe plum tomatoes, peeled, cored,
  seeded, and julienned

Combine the olive oils with the mustard oil. Whisk in the vinegars. When well emulsified, season to taste with salt and pepper. (The vinaigrette may be made up to 3 days in advance and stored, covered and refrigerated. Bring it to room temperature before using.)

When ready to serve, toss the watercress and tomato julienne together in a mixing bowl. Spoon the vinaigrette over the salad and toss to combine. Taste and adjust seasoning with salt and pepper.

COBB SALAD

Legend has it that Cobb Salad was invented by Bob Cobb, the owner of the world-famous (and now defunct) Brown Derby restaurant in Los Angeles. The restaurant was evocative of the California love of kitschy architecture as it was shaped like a derby, and the wait staff was outfitted in period costumes topped off with brown derby hats. It was a celebrity haunt from the late 1920s to the 1950s, and even through the sixties it remained a place to be seen. It is said that the salad came about when Mr. Cobb needed to make a special presentation to a regular diner who had demanded "something made just for me." Apparently, the kitchen had bits and pieces of cooked chicken and bacon, avocado, and Roquefort cheese along with the necessary salad makings, and Cobb used his artistry to put them together in a unique way. Obviously, the salad made a hit, as it remained on the menu and then made its way onto the menus of "classy" restaurants all across the country.

After years of being *the* salad, Cobb Salad seemed to disappear from restaurant menus while all kinds of new and exotic salads made their mark. In fact, the Niçoise Salad and all of its variations became the Cobb Salad of the eighties. Then, suddenly, the Cobb Salad was back in favor. I've seen Lobster Cobb Salad, Southwestern Bean Cobb Salad, Blackened Catfish Cobb Salad—well, you get the picture.

The classic vinaigrette for the salad is a light, creamy mixture of oil and lemon juice, but I think that a great Roquefort dressing is the perfect match for the rich mix.

CLASSIC

Classic Cobb Salad

SERVES 6

Here is the classic. I like to serve the salad in a glass bowl. The ingredients are so colorful that I think seeing them through the glass only makes the salad more appetizing. And, by the way, don't use mesclun or any fancy greens for a Cobb Salad—you need the heft and crunch of iceberg or romaine to give the correct balance to the finished salad.

8 cups (about 1½ pounds) chopped iceberg
or romaine lettuce

3 whole grilled (or poached) boneless,
skinless chicken breasts, diced

6 large hard-boiled eggs, peeled and chopped

1 pound fine-quality, thick-sliced bacon,
fried, drained, and crumbled

2 large, ripe, beefsteak tomatoes, peeled,
cored, seeded, and chopped

3 medium Haas avocados, peeled and
chopped (see Note)

½ cup pitted Niçoise olives

1 cup crumbled fine-quality blue cheese
such as Maytag blue

2 cups Roquefort Dressing (recipe follows)

¼ cup chopped fresh chives

> NOTE: Toss the avocado with a bit of fresh lime or lemon juice or a bit of vinegar to keep it from discoloring.

Place the salad greens in the bottom of a large glass bowl. Make a line of diced chicken down the center. Neatly make a line of hard-boiled egg along one side of the chicken and a line of crumbled bacon down the other side. Place a line of chopped tomatoes next to the egg and a line of avocado next to the bacon. Place the olives around the edge of the bowl, and sprinkle the crumbled cheese over the top. Drizzle about one-half of the dressing over the top and sprinkle the chives over the dressing. Pass the remaining dressing on the side.

Roquefort Dressing

½ pound Roquefort or other fine-quality
blue cheese, crumbled

½ cup heavy cream

½ cup buttermilk

12 tablespoons champagne vinegar

½ cup peanut oil

¼ teaspoon paprika

Coarse salt and freshly ground white pepper

Place the cheese in a fine sieve and, using a rubber spatula, push the it through the sieve into a nonreactive bowl. Add the cream and buttermilk to the cheese and, using a wooden spoon, stir to combine. Beat in the vinegar and then the oil. Add the paprika and salt and pepper to taste. If the dressing seems too thick, add additional cream and/or buttermilk, a tablespoonful at a time. Store, covered and refrigerated, for up to 3 days.

"Stacked" Chopped Cobb Salad with Chipotle Vinaigrette

SERVES 6

This is a dramatic and very architectural version of a Cobb Salad. More interesting than the regular salad but still containing all of the basic elements, it makes a spectacular luncheon dish. Since almost everything can be prepared in advance, leaving just the final put-together for the last moment, this is a terrific salad for at-home entertaining. If you want to make the Second Day Dish, buy additional avocados, tomatoes, and olives, make some extra vinaigrette, and grill at least six extra pieces of chicken.

2 tablespoons chipotle chilies in adobo (see page 11)
1 cup Basic Vinaigrette (recipe follows)
12 cherry tomatoes
12 pitted Niçoise olives (see Note)
Standard 6-inch-long bamboo skewers
6 boneless, skinless chicken breast halves, rinsed and patted dry
1 tablespoons olive oil

Coarse salt and freshly ground black pepper
1 tablespoon canola oil
2 large sweet onions, thinly sliced crosswise
½ pound mesclun or other soft salad greens
1 cup crumbled blue cheese
6 slices homemade-style white bread, toasted
6 ¼-inch-thick slices beefsteak tomatoes
12 slices crisp bacon

NOTE: Niçoise olives are available from gourmet markets, specialty food stores, and some supermarkets.

To make the Chipotle Vinaigrette, place the chipotle chilies in the bowl of a food processor fitted with the metal blade and process to a smooth purée. Whisk the purée into the Basic Vinaigrette and set aside.

Alternately, push 2 cherry tomatoes and 2 Niçoise olives onto each of 6 bamboo skewers. Set aside.

Oil and preheat a grill or stove-top grill pan.

Place the chicken breasts on a flat surface between two pieces of waxed, butcher, or parchment paper. Using a heavy frying pan or mallet, pound each piece to a thickness of about a ¼ inch. Lightly coat the chicken with the olive oil and season with salt and pepper. Place the chicken on the preheated grill (or stove-top grill). Grill, turning occasionally, for about 10 minutes, or until golden and the juices run clear.

While the chicken is grilling, heat the canola oil in a medium sauté pan over medium heat. Add the onions and cook, stirring frequently, for about 10 minutes, or until they are very soft and aromatic and lightly browned. Remove from the heat and tent lightly with aluminum foil to keep warm.

Toss the greens with the blue cheese with just enough of the reserved vinaigrette to lightly coat them. Set aside.

Place a piece of toast in the center of each of six dinner plates. Top each piece of toast with a tomato slice. Top it with a mound of sautéed onions followed by a chicken breast. Cover each chicken breast with a loose mound of the reserved dressed greens; then crisscross two slices of bacon on top. Push one of the reserved skewers into each "sandwich" to hold it together. Drizzle some of the leftover vinaigrette around the edge of the plate and serve immediately.

Basic Vinaigrette

1 cup olive oil
½ cup extra virgin olive oil
1 tablespoon mustard oil (see page 50)
¼ cup tarragon vinegar

¼ cup sherry wine vinegar
Coarse salt
1 teaspoon freshly ground black pepper

Combine the olive oils with the mustard oil in a small mixing bowl. Add the tarragon and sherry vinegars, whisking to blend well. Season with salt and pepper to taste.

The vinaigrette will keep, covered and refrigerated, for up to 3 days. Bring to room temperature before using.

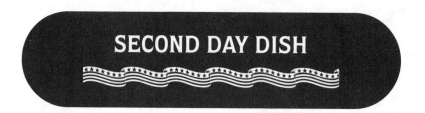

Spiced Cobb Salad "Summer Roll" with Blue Cheese Dipping Sauce

SERVES 2

These are great for lunch, brunch, or cocktails by the pool. I was inspired by light Vietnamese summer rolls, but these chicken and blue cheese combos are a bit more substantial. All of the flavors of the traditional Cobb are here, put together a bit differently.

2 pieces grilled chicken, chopped

2 slices crisp bacon, chopped

1 avocado, peeled and chopped

½ cup peeled, seeded, and chopped
   beefsteak tomato

1 tablespoon chopped Niçoise olives

3 tablespoons Chipotle Vinaigrette (see
   page 60)

2 cups chopped mixed lettuce (iceberg,
   romaine, mesclun)

2 tablespoons crumbled blue cheese

3 tablespoons fine-quality mayonnaise

2 sheets flat bread or 2 flour tortillas

NOTE: If you have made the Cobb Salad, you should have some Roquefort Dressing that can be used as a dipping sauce in place of the blue cheese–mayonnaise mixture.

Lay a clean kitchen towel out on a flat surface.

Combine the chicken with the bacon, avocado, tomato, and olives in a mixing bowl. Add just enough vinaigrette to lightly coat. Add the lettuce and toss to combine.

Press the cheese through a fine sieve into a small mixing bowl. Add the mayonnaise and stir to combine. Set aside. (See Note.)

Place a heaping mound of the salad mixture in the center of each flat bread or tortilla. Fold the sides up and over the filling and roll it up, cigar-fashion.

Slice each roll on the bias crosswise. Set one-half of the roll upwards in the center of each of two plates and lay the other half next to it. Place an equal amount of the leftover salad on each plate with a small container (a tiny soufflé dish works well) of the blue cheese dipping sauce on the plate.

CHEF'S SALAD

I have not found any real history of the Chef's Salad, so I just have to guess about its origins. One theory is that composed or combination salads came into being in health-conscious California, but I have found no proof of this. I would assume that it probably grew out of hotel and country-club dining where all of the elements were always on hand, and the salad could be prepared easily and quickly.

In French cooking, the classic *salades composées* are divided into several categories. A combination of cooked vegetables put together in a simple salad is the most basic. Another version is composed with a variety of ingredients, including meat, cheese, and vegetables and put together in a simple but eye-appealing pattern. The most expansive of these are often served as a cold entrée with, perhaps, a base of vegetables (something as simple as chopped lettuce) and a topping of another mayonnaise-based mixture such as a chicken salad. And, finally there are salads with numerous ingredients that are brought together in an elaborate presentation in accompaniment to classic *chaudfroid* or meat or poultry mousses. If you put all of the classic *composées* together, you will certainly find the genesis for the all-American Chef's Salad.

In looking through old cookbooks for a classic Chef's Salad recipe, I have not found any hard-and-fast rules. Some call for Russian Dressing, others for blue cheese, while others simply say whatever dressing you like. Some call for roast beef, others roast poultry, while some type of ham always seems to play a role. The cheese can be Swiss, Gruyère, or any other hard cheese. What it comes down to is that this is a salad for which you can use a combination of whatever meats, poultry, and cheese you have on hand, and then arrange them in an attractive pattern and garnish with hard-boiled eggs, olives, tomatoes, or whatever else strikes your fancy. It seems that no matter what you pull together, you will have created the perfect Chef's Salad.

CLASSIC

Classic Chef's Salad Bowl

Chef's Salad and a club sandwich were the test dishes I got to create when I was working in my first restaurant kitchen, as a teenager, and aspired to be a chef. Chef's Salad was a steady seller, one of the most popular items on the menu, so I got a lot of practice. I took a lot of pride in cutting the meat slices just so and making sure that the egg quarters were perfectly formed. In fact, I did so well that I worked my way out of dishwashing and into making all of the Chef's Salads and club sandwiches.

With so many more "sophisticated" salads gaining popularity, Chef's Salad is no longer a popular dish in most restaurants, but it remains standard diner fare. And with good reason. If you want to make the Second Day bruschetta, make sure that you buy enough ingredients to create this really tasty snack.

1 pound crisp lettuce (such as romaine or iceberg), roughly chopped
Approximately 1 cup Basic Vinaigrette (see page 61)
½ pound Black Forest ham, julienned
½ pound rare roast beef, julienned
½ pound turkey breast, julienned
¼ pound Swiss cheese, julienned

¼ pound Cheddar cheese, julienned
3 large hard-boiled eggs, peeled and quartered
6 plum tomatoes, peeled, cored, and thinly sliced crosswise
¼ cup thinly sliced red radish
1 large red onion, thinly sliced crosswise
2 cups croutons

Toss the lettuce with about ¾ cup of the vinaigrette in a large wooden salad bowl; the lettuce should just be lightly coated with the dressing. Place the ham in a circle around the edge of the salad bowl. Then make a circle of roast beef followed by a circle of turkey. Place the two cheeses in the center of the ring of meats. Evenly space the egg quarters around the edge of the ham. Place a circle of tomato between the ham and roast beef and a circle of radish in between the roast beef and turkey. Pull the onion slices apart, and place the rings over the top of the salad. Sprinkle over the croutons and drizzle the remaining vinaigrette over all. Serve immediately.

Carpaccio of Chef's Salad

SERVES 6

This is a great dish to prepare in advance for casual entertaining. The plates can be prepared in advance, covered with plastic wrap, and refrigerated. The greens can be put together, the dressing made, and the quail eggs boiled and peeled. At the last minute, dress the greens, pop them on the plates, and serve. A basket of warm breads and a great glass of wine will help make a perfect meal.

1 cup aged balsamic vinegar
2 tablespoons minced shallots
1 cup olive oil
Coarse salt and freshly ground black pepper
12 quail eggs
1 pound beef tenderloin, sliced paper-thin against the grain (see Note)
4 ounces smoked turkey, sliced paper-thin against the grain
4 ounces Black Forest ham, sliced paper-thin against the grain

4 ounces Swiss cheese, sliced paper-thin
4 ounces Cheddar cheese, sliced paper-thin
12 cups (about 1½ pounds) chopped mixed salad greens
3 bunches arugula, well-washed, tough stems removed, and chopped
3 tablespoons fresh fines herbes (see Note)
1 cup halved cherry tomatoes

NOTE: The meats are most easily cut on an electric meat slicer or a mandoline. However, if you don't have either, place the tenderloin in the freezer for about 20 minutes to firm it enough to facilitate slicing with a very sharp chef's knife. The turkey and ham shouldn't be frozen, but they should be quite cold.

Fines herbes are a classic French mixture of equal parts of chopped fresh chervil, parsley, chives, and tarragon. However, you can use whatever fresh herbs appeal to you. Savory or marjoram work well in combination with parsley and chives. Just don't use dried fines herbes in this recipe since what you really need is the zesty, pungent taste of the fresh.

Combine the balsamic vinegar and shallots in a small bowl. Whisk in the olive oil and season to taste with salt and pepper. Set aside.

Place the quail eggs in a small saucepan over high heat in enough cold water to cover them by 1 inch. Bring to a boil; then lower the heat and simmer for 4 minutes. Remove the eggs from the heat and drain well. Place them in cold water to cover for about 5 minutes, or until cooled. Carefully peel the eggs and cut them lengthwise in half. Set aside.

Place the tenderloin, turkey, ham, Swiss cheese, and Cheddar cheese in slightly overlapping, alternating slices around the edge of six plates, using a slice of tenderloin between each of the other meats and cheeses.

Combine the salad greens, arugula, and fines herbes in a large mixing bowl. Add the tomatoes and quail eggs and just enough of the reserved vinaigrette to lightly coat it all. Gently toss to combine. Place the salad in a loose mound in the center of each of the meat-and-cheese–covered plates. Drizzle some of the remaining vinaigrette over the entire plate and serve.

SECOND DAY DISH

Chef's Salad Bruschetta

SERVES 6

This is a great football-watching snack or a light lunch, and you can actually make it with almost anything you have on hand. Leftover club sandwich makings, Cobb Salad remains— you name it, you can make a bruschetta from it. This recipe also works well as an hors d'oeuvre if you can find very thin baguettes that can be cut into almost bite-size rounds.

2 French baguettes
½ cup extra virgin olive oil
6 ounces Black Forest ham or smoked turkey, finely diced
6 ounces Swiss or Cheddar cheese, finely diced

6 plum tomatoes, peeled, cored, seeded, and diced
2 cloves garlic, peeled and minced
Coarse salt and freshly ground black pepper
¼ cup fresh basil chiffonade

NOTE: The chiffonade cut is made by cutting leaves into thin strips or ribbons. This is most easily done by stacking a group of leaves, rolling them up cigar-fashion, and then cutting them crosswise into thin pieces. Once pulled apart, you will have a tangle of thin strips.

Cut the baguettes into eighteen 2-inch-thick rounds. Hollow out the center of each round, leaving just a thin layer of bread at the bottom. (Save all of the excess to dry for bread crumbs.) Using a pastry brush, lightly coat the cut sides with a bit of the olive oil. Place the bread in a nonstick pan over medium heat and cook, turning occasionally, for about 4 minutes, or until golden brown. Remove from the heat and set aside.

Combine the ham or turkey and the cheese with the tomatoes and garlic. Add the remaining olive oil along with salt and pepper to taste.

Place equal portions of the ham mixture into the hollowed-out bread rounds. Place three filled rounds on each of six plates. Garnish with the basil and serve.

CAESAR SALAD

There are all kinds of stories about the origin of Caesar Salad. Some say it was a hastily put together, Sunday-night improvisation. Others say it was a planned salad created to wow diners with a big show and little substance. Some say the original had anchovies and Worcestershire sauce, others say not. Was it made with only the tiny, inner leaves of the lettuce, or was it chopped pieces? Was it made to be eaten with a knife and fork, or to be eaten with fingers? The one thing that everyone agrees upon is that it was created by a Tijuana restaurateur, Caesar Cardini, for his Hollywood clientele on the Fourth of July in 1924. His restaurant, Caesar's Place, was frequented by movie stars who, in the early twenties and thirties, often found their R & R and free-wheeling nightlife south of the border. Prepared tableside, a coddled egg the pièce de résistance in the creation of a creamy, stick-to-your-ribs dressing, the show came with the shaving of the cheese, the mashing of the anchovies, and the breaking of the egg over the crisp romaine leaves. However it came about, and with whatever intent, it's now a classic salad. I use romaine hearts, anchovies, and barely cooked eggs for my version and invite you to improvise your own.

CLASSIC

The Famous Caesar Salad

SERVES 6

Almost no one makes a "real" Caesar Salad anymore. Too many people dislike anchovies or feel it is too much trouble or fear using raw eggs. Obviously, I'm not among them. So get out that old wooden salad bowl and let's get started.

1 large clove garlic, peeled
¼ teaspoon dry mustard
Coarse salt and freshly ground black pepper
4 anchovy fillets
6 tablespoons olive oil

Juice of 2 lemons
2 large eggs
3 large romaine hearts, nicely chilled
¼ pound Parmesan cheese
2 cups very crisp croutons

NOTE: To have enough dressing for the contemporary Caesar Salad recipe, you will want to double the amount of mustard and anchovy mixtures and whisk them together before adding them to the salad greens.

Cut the garlic clove in half and vigorously rub the inside of a wooden salad bowl with the cut sides.

Combine the mustard with the salt and pepper to taste in a small bowl, keeping in mind that both the anchovies and the cheese will add salt to the salad.

Place the anchovy fillets in a small bowl and mash them to a pulp with a fork. Add the olive oil and lemon juice and, using the fork, beat to emulsify. Set aside.

Place the eggs in a small saucepan and cover them with cold water. Place over high heat and bring to a boil. Boil for exactly 1 minute.

While the eggs are cooking, place the greens into the prepared bowl and toss in the cheese. Toss in the reserved mustard mixture along with the anchovy mixture (see Note). Immediately break the eggs over the greens, using a teaspoon to clean out the shells, if necessary, and toss to just combine. Add the croutons and briefly toss to mix. Serve immediately.

Chopped Caesar Salad with Crab Cake Croutons

SERVES 6

This is a more contemporary take on Caesar Cardini's original salad. I love the melding of flavors and textures with the sweet, crisp crab cakes, the crunchy lettuce, and the lemony dressing. If crab is not available, you could make salmon or cod cakes. Chicken croquettes would even make a great statement combining two old traditions in a fresh new way.

1¼ pounds lump crabmeat, picked of all shell and cartilage

1 shallot, peeled and minced

2½ cups fresh bread crumbs

½ cup mayonnaise

1½ tablespoons chopped fresh tarragon

1½ tablespoons chopped fresh chervil

1½ tablespoons chopped fresh chives

1 tablespoon Dijon mustard

½ tablespoon minced cornichons

½ tablespoon Old Bay Seasoning

½ tablespoon minced capers

3 dashes Worcestershire sauce

3 dashes Tabasco sauce

¼ teaspoon fresh lemon zest

Juice of ½ lemon

Coarse salt and freshly ground black pepper

1 cup Wondra flour (see Note)

2 large eggs

¼ cup water

¼ cup clarified butter (see page 7)

24 cups (about 3 pounds) ½-inch pieces romaine lettuce, nicely chilled

2 cups croutons

3 tablespoons Roasted Garlic Purée (see page 12)

Caesar salad vinaigrette (see page 69)

12 lemon wedges

NOTE: Wondra flour, an extremely fine flour that dissolves instantly and does not clump together, is available in most supermarkets and some specialty food stores, usually in the baking section.

Combine the crabmeat with the shallot, ½ cup of the bread crumbs, mayonnaise, tarragon, chervil, chives, mustard, cornichons, Old Bay, capers, Worcestershire sauce, Tabasco sauce, lemon zest and juice. Season to taste with salt and pepper. Do not overmix. Form the crab mixture into 12 hockey puck–size disks. Set aside.

Place the Wondra flour in 1 large shallow dish and the remaining 2 cups of bread crumbs in another. Whisk the eggs and water together in a third, large, shallow bowl. Dip the crab cakes into the flour, shaking off any excess. Then dip each cake into the egg mixture. Finally, lightly coat each cake in the bread crumbs.

Heat the butter in a large sauté pan over medium heat. Add the crab cakes and fry, turning once, for about 4 minutes, or until golden. Using a slotted spatula, lift the crab cakes from the pan and place on a double layer of paper towels to drain.

Place the lettuce in a large mixing bowl. Toss the croutons with the roasted garlic purée and then into the lettuce. Add the vinaigrette and toss to combine. Season with salt and pepper to taste. Place equal portions of the salad onto each of six serving plates. Place three crab cakes on top of each salad. Garnish the plates with lemon wedges and serve.

SECOND DAY DISH

Spicy Spaghetti with Sausage and Caesar Sauce

SERVES 6

Caesar Salad and spaghetti? Yes, I got the idea when I noticed that so many people ordered a Caesar Salad followed by a dish of pasta. What would happen if you put them together? I tried it and it worked—so well, in fact, that I often make it as a first day dish!

½ pound dry spaghetti
½ cup olive oil
4 sausages, spicy Italian or spicy breakfast
Approximately 4 cups Caesar Salad with any remaining vinaigrette (see page 68 and Note)

Coarse salt and freshly ground black pepper
Freshly grated Parmesan cheese
Lemon wedges

Bring a large pot of salted water to a boil over high heat. When boiling, add the spaghetti and cook it according to the package directions for al dente.

While the pasta is cooking, heat the olive oil in a medium sauté pan over medium heat. Cut the sausages into thin round circles and add to the hot oil. Cook, stirring frequently, for about 6 minutes, or until the sausage is golden brown.

Drain the pasta well and transfer it to a warm serving bowl. Scrape the sausage and oil into the pasta and toss to blend. Add the salad and vinaigrette and toss again to coat. Taste and, if necessary, season with salt and pepper. Sprinkle with cheese and serve hot with lemon wedges on the side.

POULTRY

All of the domestic poultry that we eat today, with the exception of turkey, was served in Roman times. Everything from chicken to peacock made its way to the table. The Egyptians and the Greeks both had special preparations that were fit for kings.

Although poultry played a role in the development of national cuisines and political loyalties (Henri IV wished every home in France a *poule au pot* and in recent American history, its citizens were promised a chicken in every pot), it was not until after World War II that poultry became a featured component of the daily diet in many parts of the world. Ducks were the first to be farmed, beginning in China over 4,000 years ago, but it has only been in recent years that farming chickens and turkeys has become a major industry in the United States.

At the outset, most fowl raised for food was found on farms, left to its own devices to peck nourishment from the ground with an infrequent toss of table scraps and an even more infrequent handful of grain to fatten it. Only the fowl not needed for the farm-family's table was sent to the market. These birds were not the fattest, healthiest birds that would bring top dollar in the marketplace, which led farmers to an increased interest in raising a more economically reliable fowl.

Geese, pheasant, quail, guinea fowl, and other birds were usually taken from the wild, so the first attempts at large-scale, poultry farming in America were with chickens. Chicken farming became so successful that a couple of the major food companies in the United States are now chicken processors. Of course, the rise in fast-food chains serving chicken "nuggets" and sandwiches has certainly helped the industry to explode.

It was in France that I learned much about the preparation of fowl. In fact, it is the *poulets de Bresse* (Bresse chickens) that are the measure of a great chicken. These beautiful and expensive birds with sparkling white plumage, a bright red wattle, and distinctive blue-gray legs truly live the life of Riley. No prince or princess is better treated. For the first 12 weeks of their lives, Bresse chickens live freely, in the pristine out-of-doors, eating whatever strikes their fancy. Then, just before they are sent to market, they are fattened up on a diet rich in corn and milk for about 2 weeks. They are ready to go at about 3½ months, fat and sassy with a glorious slightly yellow flesh ready to be roasted to perfection. The fatter and much more expensive *poulardes de Bresse* and even more expensive *chapons de Bresse* receive the royal treatment for 2 to 3 months longer. We have nothing quite like these birds in America although some years ago an adventurous poultry farmer tried his hand at raising them. Unfortunately, he found the cost too prohibitive for the marketplace to bear and went out of business.

The rules for selecting any type of poultry are the same. You want to find a bird that is free of hormones and blemishes, and a bit thin-skinned. It should have some fat around the cavity, the breastbone should be slightly flexible, and the weight should be compatible with the size. In America, chickens are now marketed at about nine weeks and since the consumer doesn't have any real notion of where the birds come from, it is vitally important that chickens are purchased from a fine-quality butcher. I try to avoid prepackaged, plastic-wrapped, and sorted chickens, but I realize that is a chef's luxury.

It is now impossible to get anything other than a chicken labeled "fryer" or "roaster" unless you live in an area with a live poultry market at hand. In these small, owner-operated markets, you can usually find roosters (imperative for the classic *coq au vin*), stewing hens (essential for great chicken soup), or a fattened pullet ready for the fire. These markets are an anachronism in consumer marketing and can usually be found only in metropolitan areas where there is a large Asian population. Of course, if you live in a rural area, it might still be possible to barter with a local farmer, but even small farms do not always keep chickens since most farmer's wives (who used to tend the chickens) work, and supermarkets offer such a wide selection of processed birds.

Turkey is now available all year, frozen, whole, and fresh in parts. Big, fat, fresh birds still only seem to come to the market at Thanksgiving and Christmas. The marketing of turkey has made us think of it as a low-fat, nutritious alternative to meat. However, unless you are eating the breast meat or ground turkey made entirely of skinless breast, the fat and cholesterol are not all that low. I use turkey mainly for its versatility and its ability to absorb other more intense flavors.

With their heavier carcass, thicker skin, and bountiful layer of fat, pound for pound ducks offer much less meat than chicken. Ducklings, those about two months old, are usually the ones we roast. Larger ducks are usually broken down into parts with the breasts sold separately and the legs made into confit. In the United States, the most recognizable duck is the Long Island variety, and in France it is that from Rouen. It is in China, however, that the duck reigns supreme. The ancient Chinese recipe for lacquered duck is still the measure for many of the contemporary "fusion" recipes now featured in restaurants across America.

I have had one of my most interesting culinary adventures working with duck in restaurants. Wherever I cooked, we used lots of duck breasts, which left us with lots of unused duck meat. Only so much confit of duck legs could be prepared, so I began playing with new ideas for an unusual but tasty duck presentation. One day, thinking back to my childhood (as I often do in the kitchen when looking for inspiration), I thought about the street game of "Duck, Duck, Goose" that we frequently played. And from there came the melding together of the ingredients for what became my Duck Meatloaf, which is now sold nationally through D'Artagnan, the fine meat and game company.

One of the strangest poultry preparations I have eaten is the now infamous turducken of Louisiana's Cajun country (where, by the way, the method of deep-fat frying turkey also got its start). A chicken, a duck, and a turkey are deboned and a savory stuffing is made. The interior of the duck and turkey are lined with stuffing while the chicken is filled with the stuffing. The chicken is held together and placed inside the duck. The duck is then held together around the chicken, and the bundle is placed inside the turkey. The whole thing is tied together and roasted to perfection. I must admit that it is a little hard to keep the turkey moist and juicy while trying to cook the interior of the chicken, but the whole thing makes a pretty spectacular presentation (one much easier to eat than to carve).

In America, most other fowl is served only on special occasions, or if a family member is a hunter. Goose, pheasant, partridge, quail, guinea fowl, squab, and pigeon are, for the most part, farm raised, but it is still possible to obtain birds that have been taken in the wild. In fact, some of the most expensive fowl is flown in, overnight, from Scotland where bird hunting is an art.

I would guess that poultry is going to continue to grow in popularity. Its health benefits measured against red meat remain an attraction to the diet conscious, the breast meat is easy to prepare in a myriad number of ways, a simple roast always works for a family meal or for entertaining, and almost everybody likes it. Hopefully, the availability of birds other than chicken and turkey will increase, and more diners will acquire a taste for the most interesting textures and flavors offered by ducks, partridge, pheasant, and quail.

ROAST CHICKEN

They say that the true test of a great chef is a roast chicken. It seems like such a simple dish, but a great one is not all that easy to prepare. This is, in part, because the breast meat cooks so much quicker than the thigh meat and is, to begin with, much less fatty, so that often, when the breast meat is beautifully cooked, the thigh meat still needs some time in the oven. By the time the thigh meat is beautifully cooked, the breast meat has often become dry and stringy. Plus, there is a very fine line between buttery-golden, crisp skin and skin that is dry and charred. Trial and error is probably the best teacher, although every chef has a secret method. Some soak the chicken in brine, others roast breast-side-down, some baste, others tent, some truss, others don't, some use high heat, others low. And each believe that their method sets the standard.

In today's markets, most chickens weigh in from two to four-and-a-half pounds. The smaller birds usually find their way to restaurants and the mid-range size end up in the supermarket meat section. Large birds, those weighing from 5 to 7 pounds, are usually labeled roaster. All of the birds have a similar, relatively bland taste with their size dictating their use. You will also find very small Rock Cornish game hens (which taste just like chicken) and extremely large capons weighing eight to ten pounds (which are castrated male birds) to roast throughout the year. Whatever weight you opt for, I recommend buying fine-quality, free-range or kosher chickens simply because I think they taste better. If you purchase a kosher chicken, remember it has already been salted in the koshering process.

I always truss my roasting birds. This binds the wings and legs to the body and makes a neat package for the roasting pan and a pulled-together bird for carving. It is not obligatory, but I've always found that my birds look and taste better with a neat trussing.

Probably the most difficult thing for the home cook to gauge is when the bird is done. To facilitate this step, I suggest that you buy and use an accurate instant-read thermometer. This simple implement can be inserted into the thickest part of the breast (it is a good idea to insert it so that it runs the length of the breast as near as possible to the bone without touching it) to get an accurate internal temperature. You will need to have this area register 160 degrees. Test the degree of doneness of the legs by inserting the instant-read thermometer

French Toast with
Cinnamon-Brown Sugar
and Apple Syrup
(Classic)

Two Soups—New England
and Manhattan Clam Chowders
with Cheddar Biscuits
(Contemporary)

Classic Cobb Salad

"Stacked" Chopped Cobb Salad
with Chipotle Vinaigrette
(Contemporary)

Spiced Cobb Salad "Summer Roll"
with Blue Cheese Dipping Sauce
(Second Day Dish)

Roast Chicken "Farmhouse Style" with Potatoes, Mushrooms, Bacon, Onions, and Apple Cider Gravy (Classic)

Pretzel-Onion Crusted Barbecued Chicken with Pretzel Latkes, Corn, and Mustard (Contemporary)

Barbecued Chicken Sticky Buns (Second Day Dish)

Soy-Honey Roast Duck
(Contemporary)

Duck Pithiviers
(Second Day Dish)

into the thickest part of the thigh, taking care not to touch the bone. The thermometer should register 170 degrees for a correctly cooked leg-thigh area. At these temperatures, the meat should still be moist and there should be a slightly pink tinge around the bones. If you roast the bird to higher temperatures, the pinkness will disappear, but the breast meat will probably be dry and stringy.

Always roast more chicken than you need. There is nothing more convenient to have on hand than ready-to-eat roast chicken. It is great for salads, sandwiches, hash, croquettes, and old-fashioned casseroles. Plus, the carcass can be the basis for a big pot of chicken soup. In true French fashion, nothing should go to waste!

CLASSIC

Roast Chicken "Farmhouse Style" with Potatoes, Mushrooms, Bacon, Onions, and Apple Cider Gravy

Serves 6

This is the homiest version of an old-fashioned, farmhouse roast chicken that I can imagine. Endless times I have roasted a chicken in the most straightforward way, just as my mom would have done when I was a kid. And after all these years, the flavors still sing of pure, home-cooked goodness.

Two 3-pound free-range, roasting chickens, thoroughly rinsed and patted dry
Coarse salt and freshly ground black pepper to taste
4 large Idaho potatoes, scrubbed and quartered
2 large onions, diced

1 pound button mushrooms, wiped clean and stems trimmed
1 pound slab bacon, diced
¼ cup vegetable oil
2 cups apple cider
3 tablespoons Wondra flour (see page 70) dissolved in 3 tablespoons chicken broth

Preheat the oven to 450 degrees.

Season the chickens, inside and out, with salt and pepper. Truss the chickens and place them on a rack in a roasting pan.

Combine the potatoes, onions, mushrooms, and bacon in a mixing bowl. Add the vegetable oil and season with salt and pepper. Toss to coat well. Transfer the nicely oiled vegetables and bacon to the roasting pan. Place the pan in the preheated oven and roast for 15 minutes. Reduce the heat to 375 degrees and continue to roast, turning the vegetables and bacon pieces occasionally, for about 30 minutes, or until an instant-read thermometer inserted into the thickest part of the chicken (between the thigh and the breast) reads 160 degrees. Remove the pan from the oven and transfer the chickens and vegetables to a serving platter. Tent them lightly with aluminum foil and allow them to rest for 10 minutes before carving the chickens into serving pieces. (The carving should be done at the table.)

Remove the rack from the roasting pan. Place the roasting pan on top of the stove over high heat. Add the apple cider and bring the mixture to a boil, frequently scraping the bottom of the pan with a wooden spoon to release all of the browned bits. Boil for about 5 minutes, or until the cider has reduced slightly. Reduce the heat to medium and whisk in the flour-chicken broth mixture. Season to taste with salt and pepper. Cook, whisking constantly, for about 5 minutes, or until the gravy has thickened slightly and the raw flour taste has cooked out. Pour the gravy into a sauceboat and keep it warm until ready to serve.

Carve the chickens into large serving pieces, home-style, and serve directly from the platter along with the roasted vegetables and crisp bacon bits.

CONTEMPORARY

Seawater-Soaked Chicken with Thyme and Poppy Seed Gnocchi

SERVES 6

This method of brining the chicken takes a bit more time, but the end result is perfection. This is a very old technique that I have recently rediscovered. It will ensure that a chicken comes out of the oven tender, sweet, and juicy. I add some sugar to the saltwater brine to help with the caramelization of the natural sugars in the skin and to balance the retention of salt throughout.

Brining is not at all difficult to do, but it does require the allotment of some additional time (I suggest 12 hours, but you can cut the time down to 6 hours with little loss of quality) and a refrigerated space large enough to hold the stockpot in which you have placed the chickens. It is worth the effort, as I think you will find that you will have produced the juiciest, sweetest-tasting bird you have ever roasted.

2 4-pound free-range roasting chickens, thoroughly rinsed and patted dry
2 gallons cold water
2½ cups sea salt plus more to taste
1½ cups sugar
2 sheets nori or ½ pound common seaweed
1 cup (2 sticks) fine-quality, unsalted butter, softened

2 tablespoons fresh lemon juice
1½ tablespoons freshly grated lemon zest
1 tablespoon finely chopped fresh thyme leaves
Freshly ground black pepper to taste
2 tablespoons clarified butter (see page 7)
Thyme and Poppy Seed Gnocchi (recipe follows)

Using a boning knife, remove the first two sections of the wing bone from each chicken. Set aside.

Combine the water with the sea salt, sugar, and seaweed in a deep stockpot or dish large enough to hold the two chickens. Allow to sit, stirring occasionally, for about 15 minutes, or until the salt and sugar have dissolved. Place the chickens in the stockpot or dish, making sure that each chicken is covered with brine. Put it in the refrigerator and allow to brine for 6 hours.

Place the softened butter in a small mixing bowl. Add the lemon juice and zest along with the chopped thyme and, using a spatula, blend them into the butter until well-incorporated. Place the butter mixture into the center of an 8-inch × 10-inch sheet of plastic wrap. Fold the wrap up and over the butter, folding in the ends to make a 1-inch-thick log shape. If necessary, gently roll the butter back and forth to form a log. Refrigerate for about 1 hour (or up to 24 hours), or until firm. (The lemon-thyme butter may be made up to a week in advance and frozen. Thaw it before using.)

Preheat the oven to 450 degrees.

Remove the chickens from the brine and pat them dry. Using a boning knife, cut each chicken in half by cutting along the breastbone. Leaving the drumstick intact, debone each chicken half and, using the boning knife, scrape all of the flesh from the remaining wing bone. Season the chicken with freshly ground black pepper. *Do not use salt!* Place the chicken halves on a baking sheet with sides. Place the baking sheet in the preheated oven and roast the chicken for 20 minutes.

While the chicken is baking, cook the gnocchi as directed in the recipe.

Once the gnocchi has been cooked and drained, heat the clarified butter in a large sauté pan over medium heat. Add the gnocchi and sauté them for about 4 minutes, or until they are heated through and lightly colored. Season to taste with salt and pepper and remove them from the heat.

Place the chicken in the center of a large serving platter; then place the gnocchi around the edge. Slice 4½-inch-thick disks of the lemon-thyme butter and place them on top of the chicken. Take the platter to the table and cut the chicken in serving pieces.

Thyme and Poppy Seed Gnocchi

2½ pounds Idaho potatoes, scrubbed

½ cup freshly grated Parmesan cheese

¼ cup fresh thyme leaves

2 tablespoons poppy seeds

1 large egg

1¼ cups cake flour

¾ cup bread flour

Approximately 2 tablespoons olive oil

Approximately ½ cup Wondra flour, if
   necessary (see page 70)

Preheat the oven to 375 degrees.

Place the potatoes in the preheated oven and bake for about 45 minutes, or until their centers are tender when pierced with the point of a sharp knife. Remove the potatoes from the oven and immediately cut them in half lengthwise and scrape out the pulp. Push the pulp through a potato ricer into a mixing bowl. Allow to cool for 15 minutes.

Line two baking sheets with parchment paper. Set aside.

Using a wooden spoon, mix the cheese, thyme, and poppy seeds with the cooled potatoes. Add the egg and beat to mix well.

Combine the cake and bread flours, whisking gently to blend. Slowly stir the blended flours into the potato mixture until combined well enough to begin to knead by hand. Scrape the dough onto a clean surface and knead for about 5 minutes, or until the dough is a smooth, moist ball that does not stick to your hands. Shape the dough into a large meatloaf-like shape; then cut the loaf into breadlike slices.

Working with 1 slice at a time, roll each slice into a ½-inch-thick rope. If the dough is sticky, lightly flour your work surface with the Wondra flour. Cut each rope, on the bias, into 1-inch squares. Place the squares on the parchment-lined baking sheets. (This can be done early in the day. Cover with plastic wrap and refrigerate the squares until ready to use. Or store them, frozen, for up to 1 month. You can cook them, directly from the freezer, allowing a few more minutes cooking time.)

When ready to cook, fill a large bowl with ice and water. Set aside. Bring a large pot of salted water to a boil over high heat. Add the gnocchi squares and allow them to boil for about 4 minutes, or until the gnocchi float to the top. Using a slotted spoon, lift the gnocchi from the boiling water and place them in the ice water to immediately stop the cooking. Drain them on paper towels. Transfer them to a clean bowl and toss them with just enough olive oil to keep them from sticking together. (This cooking and chilling process may have to be done in batches.) Cover them with plastic wrap and let them stand at room temperature until you are ready to finish the cooking as directed in the main recipe.

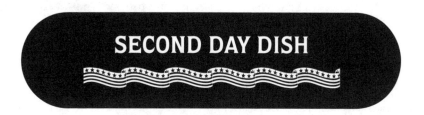

Chicken-Potato Pancakes with Apple–Sour Cream Sauce

SERVES 2

The inspiration for this dish comes from my very good friend and colleague, Charlie Palmer, who has made Sea Scallop Sandwiches a signature dish at his Manhattan restaurant, Aureole. Charlie's sandwiches are an appetizer show-stopper that encase tender, sweet sea scallops in a robe of crusty, buttery potato strands. In my version I use leftover roast chicken to make the filling. Since the longer you can make the potato shreds the better the pancakes will hold together, I suggest that you use either a mandoline or a Japanese vegetable slicer to cut them into long, even shreds. Once fried to a golden crunch, you should try to serve them quickly so that they retain their crispness.

½ cup sour cream
2 tablespoons fine-quality applesauce
1 teaspoon fresh lemon juice
Tabasco sauce
Coarse salt and freshly ground black pepper
2 large Idaho potatoes, peeled and shredded

Approximately ¼ cup clarified butter (see page 7) or vegetable oil
1½ cups julienned roast chicken
2 cups mesclun or baby salad greens
2 tablespoons Basic Vinaigrette (see page 61)

NOTE: These pancakes would also be delicious served with a lightly poached or sunny side-up egg perched on the top.

Combine the sour cream, applesauce, and lemon juice with Tabasco to taste in a nonreactive container. Season to taste with salt and pepper. Cover and refrigerate until ready to use.

Place the potatoes in a bowl of cold water and allow them to soak for about 15 minutes. Using a slotted spoon, scoop the potatoes from the water, leaving the starch in the bottom of the bowl. Transfer the potatoes to a clean kitchen towel, and twist the towel around them to dry thoroughly. You may have to do this a couple of times, using a clean, dry towel each time, to ensure that you have extracted all of the water. Place the potatoes in a clean bowl and season to taste with salt and pepper. Divide the potatoes into four mounds of equal size.

Preheat the oven to 200 degrees.

Line a baking sheet with parchment paper and set aside.

Heat 1 tablespoon of the clarified butter (or vegetable oil) in a crêpe-style pan over medium-high heat until almost smoking. Place 1 mound of potatoes into the pan, pressing down with a spatula to pack the potatoes into the pan. Cover with a layer of chicken and then with another layer of potato. Cook for about 6 minutes, carefully lifting the edge of the pancake with a flexible spatula from time to time to check the color, until the bottom is golden brown. Carefully flip the pancake over. (If you have trouble flipping, place a plate over the pan and turn the pan upside down onto the plate. The pancake will flop out, and you can then slide the uncooked side back into the pan.) If necessary, add a bit more butter (or oil) and continue cooking, pressing down on the top from time to time to pack the pancake into the pan, for an additional 6 minutes, or until very crisp. Place the cooked pancake on paper towels to drain. Transfer it to the parchment-lined baking sheet and place it in the oven to keep warm while you continue making the second pancake.

Place one pancake on each of two luncheon plates. Drizzle the Apple-Sour Cream Sauce mixture over the pancakes and around the edge of the plate. Place the greens in a medium mixing bowl and toss with the vinaigrette. Garnish the top of each pancake with a small mound of greens and serve immediately.

FRIED CHICKEN

Fortunes have been made on fried chicken. Look at Colonel Sanders, a good ole southern gent, who earned his title for his contributions to Kentucky cookin' not for his military service. Long past retirement age and with meager funds, Harland Sanders, going door-to-door with a cache of his blended spice mixture and a pressure cooker, sold his "secret" recipe to restaurants in exchange for a royalty on every chicken sold. It took just eight years for him to collect over six-hundred franchises and sales of over $37 million. By the time he went on to the big chicken shack in the sky, Kentucky Fried Chicken franchises were grossing over $2 billion a year.

I always use a flavorless oil like canola or peanut to fry chicken. However, you can use almost any fat you like. Originally, lard was used, but many people now choose solid vegetable shortening as its replacement. Of course, nothing tastes quite like rich, nutty lard but, for health considerations, most cooks now bypass a bit of flavor for better nutrition. If you prefer a richer taste, you can add a bit of clarified butter to your oil or use olive oil.

Many southern cooks marinate the chicken in buttermilk for a couple of hours before preparing it. It is said that the buttermilk tenderizes the chicken and ensures that the meat stays juicy after it is subjected to high heat. Since I consider them to be the experts, I follow the lead with my version. However, lots of cooks just give the chicken a good flour coating and put it straight into the frying pan. Some of the best fried chicken I have ever eaten is prepared at Charles' Southern-Style Kitchen on Eighth Avenue between 151st and 152nd Streets in New York City's Harlem. Charles brines his chicken and then fries it up with a golden brown, crispy coating hiding succulent, moist meat.

Although the name would indicate that fried chicken is prepared on top of the stove in a large frying pan, it really has come to mean the result rather than the method. Fried chicken is prepared in pressure cookers, deep-fat fryers, or in the oven. Whatever method you use has to give you a crisp, crackling, golden-brown skin that is greasefree and a tender, juicy interior.

Contemporary takes on fried chicken have introduced tempura coatings, Japanese panko, bread crumb coatings, corn flake or other cereal coatings, cornmeal batter crusts, and cheese-flavored crusts. I pay tribute to the southern style as well as the Asian in the following recipes.

CLASSIC

Southern Buttermilk-Fried Chicken, Coleslaw, Cornbread Biscuits, Home-Style Green Beans, and Mashed Potatoes

SERVES 6

I have learned all about southern fried chicken in my monthly visits to my daughter who lives in Nashville. Crisp and crunchy and slightly salty on the outside, and tender and juicy inside, there is nothing quite like it. We Northerners try and try, but somehow the best fried chicken still seems to be made down south. I think this is because Southerners rely on tradition and don't give much thought to contemporary health concerns when it comes to their fried chicken. If Grandma threw lots of fat in the pan and a ton of salt and pepper in the flour, that's how the chicken still gets fried. The main consideration is to keep the fat as near 365 degrees as you can, from the moment you place the chicken in the pan right up until you lift it out. This will give you the crisp skin and juicy meat that makes fried chicken so tasty. You can also adapt this method to other birds. I've made a great, crunchy and delicious quail.

1 quart buttermilk

¼ cup Tabasco sauce

2 3½- to 4-pound frying chickens, cut into serving pieces, thoroughly rinsed and patted dry

4 cups all-purpose flour

3 tablespoons coarse salt

1 tablespoon cayenne pepper

4 cups vegetable oil

Coleslaw (recipe follows)

Home-Style Green Beans (recipe follows)

Mashed Potatoes (recipe follows)

Cornbread Biscuits (recipe follows)

Combine the buttermilk and Tabasco in a large nonreactive bowl. Add the chicken pieces and toss to coat them well. Cover the chicken with plastic wrap and allow to marinate for 3 hours.

Line two baking sheets with parchment paper. Set aside.

Place the flour in a large plastic bag. Combine the salt and cayenne. When well blended, add to the flour and shake to blend. Add the marinated chicken to the flour mixture, one or two pieces at a time, and toss to coat well. When nicely coated, transfer to the parchment-lined baking sheets. Continue coating the chicken until all of the pieces are done.

Heat 2 cups of oil in each of two large, heavy-duty, frying pans until very hot but not smoking. Add the chicken pieces to the hot oil, taking care not to crowd the pans, and fry the chicken, turning it occasionally, for about 25 minutes, or until the chicken is cooked through and golden brown and crisp. Using tongs, transfer the fried chicken to paper towels to drain. (If you need to make more than two batches, preheat the oven to low. Place the fried chicken on baking sheets and into the preheated oven with the door slightly ajar. This will keep the chicken warm and crisp while you continue frying.) Place the chicken on a large serving platter and serve it, family style, with the coleslaw, green beans, potatoes, and biscuits on the side.

Coleslaw

1 medium head Savoy cabbage
1 large carrot, shredded
1 cup mayonnaise
1 tablespoon Dijon mustard
½ cup fresh lemon juice

1 teaspoon ground cumin
1 teaspoon cayenne pepper
1 tablespoon minced fresh cilantro
Coarse salt and freshly ground black
    pepper

Using a chef's knife, cut the cabbage into fine shreds. Place it in a large mixing bowl along with the carrot.

Place the mayonnaise and mustard in a small mixing bowl. Add the lemon juice and stir to combine. Whisk in the cumin and cayenne. Using a spatula, fold in the minced cilantro. Scrape the dressing over the vegetables, season them with salt and pepper to taste, and toss them to coat well. Cover the coleslaw with plastic wrap and refrigerate for at least 1 hour to allow the flavors to blend. Serve chilled.

Home-Style Green Beans

¾ pound slab bacon, diced
2 tablespoons water
1 medium onion, julienned

1 pound green beans, trimmed
Coarse salt and freshly ground black
    pepper

Preheat a large sauté pan over medium heat. When hot but not smoking, add the diced bacon along with the water. Cook the bacon, stirring frequently, for about 3 minutes, or until the water has evaporated and the bacon begins to render its fat. Continue to fry, stirring occasionally, for about 10 minutes, or until the bacon is golden and beginning to crisp. Add the onions and sauté for 3 minutes. Add the beans and sauté for 5 minutes, or until the beans are just tender. Season to taste with salt and pepper. Remove from the heat and serve.

Mashed Potatoes

2 pounds Idaho potatoes, peeled

¼ cup (½ stick) unsalted butter, softened

½ cup warm heavy cream

Coarse salt and freshly ground white pepper

Place the potatoes in a medium saucepan with cold, salted water to cover. Place over high heat and bring to a boil. Lower the heat to a simmer and cook for about 15 minutes, or until the centers of the potatoes are tender when pierced with the point of a sharp knife. Drain the potatoes well and transfer them to a potato ricer. Push the potatoes through the ricer into a clean saucepan. Add the butter and cream along with salt and pepper to taste. Place over very low heat and, using a wooden spoon, beat the potatoes until smooth. Serve immediately.

Cornbread Biscuits

5 cups all-purpose flour

1 cup plus 2 tablespoons yellow cornmeal

½ cup sugar

3 tablespoons baking powder

2 teaspoons salt

3 cups plus 1½ tablespoons heavy cream

Preheat the oven to 375 degrees.

Lightly grease a nonstick baking sheet. Set aside.

Combine the flour, cornmeal, sugar, baking powder, and salt in a mixing bowl. When the mixture is well blended, make a well in the center of it and pour the heavy cream into it. Using a spatula, slowly blend the cream into the dry ingredients, working from the outside in until the dough forms a soft mass that does not stick to your hands.

Lightly flour a clean, dry surface. Pat the dough out onto the floured surface to a thickness of about ½ inch. Using a biscuit cutter, cut out circles until you have used all of the dough. You can pull the loose pieces together to make additional biscuits. Place the biscuits on the prepared baking sheet and into the preheated oven. Bake for about 15 minutes, or until golden brown. Serve hot with butter and honey, if desired.

Soy-Soaked Tempura Chicken with Vegetable Stir-Fry

SERVES 6

As good as traditional fried chicken is, this Asian version really hits a contemporary note. Everybody seems to love the flavor that the combination of ginger, soy, and cilantro bring to the "fusion" table. All of the elements in this dish work together to make a very inviting meal with more than a hint of Asia. The Tempura Chicken, alone, would make a great hors d'oeuvre or salad topping. If you want to make the Second Day Dish of Chicken and Cabbage Spring Rolls, make sure that you prepare extra chicken and stir-fried vegetables as you will need both for the recipe.

3 cups soy sauce

1 cup honey

1 cup water

½ cup chopped fresh cilantro leaves

3 cloves garlic, smashed

2 star anise

2-inch piece fresh ginger, peeled and smashed

4 8-ounce skinless, boneless chicken breasts, trimmed of any fat, rinsed and dried

1½ cups all-purpose flour

¾ cup cornstarch

2 tablespoons baking powder

2 tablespoons coarse salt plus more

1½ tablespoons sugar

1¾ cups plus, if needed, 2 tablespoons club soda

4 cups vegetable oil

Freshly ground black pepper

Vegetable Stir-Fry (recipe follows)

To make the Soy-Ginger Vinaigrette, whisk the soy sauce, honey, and water together in a nonreactive container. Add the cilantro, garlic, star anise, and ginger and stir to blend. (This can be done up to 2 days in advance. Bring to room temperature before using.) Reserve 1 cup of the marinade for later.

Add the chicken breasts to the marinade. Cover them with plastic wrap and allow to marinate for 90 minutes.

To make the tempura batter, combine the flour, cornstarch, baking powder, 2 tablespoons salt, and the sugar in a medium mixing bowl. Slowly add the 1¾ cups of club soda, whisking vigorously to smooth the batter; the batter should be smooth and thick enough to coat the back of a wooden spoon. Allow the batter to set for 5 minutes and test it again for thickness. If it is too thick, add the remaining 2 tablespoons of club soda.

Remove the chicken from the marinade and, using a chef's knife, cut the chicken into 2-inch strips.

Heat the oil to 350 degrees in a deep-fat fryer.

Using tongs, dip the chicken strips into the tempura batter, shaking off excess batter as you lift. Working with a few coated chicken strips at a time, drop them into the hot oil. The chicken should float to the top within 15 seconds and should take no longer than 2 minutes to cook to a crisp, golden brown. Using a slotted spoon, lift the strips from the oil and place them on paper towels to drain. Season to taste with salt and pepper. Continue coating and frying until you have cooked all of the chicken.

Mound the Vegetable Stir-Fry in the center of a platter and place the chicken over the top. Drizzle the reserved Soy-Ginger Vinaigrette around the edge of the platter and serve.

Vegetable Stir-Fry

2 tablespoons blended oil
1 tablespoon finely minced fresh ginger
1 tablespoon finely minced garlic
1 medium onion, julienned
1 small bunch celery, trimmed and julienned,
   leaves reserved
3 large carrots, julienned
½ pound snow peas, trimmed and julienned
1 cup celery leaves
Coarse salt and freshly ground black pepper

Heat the oil in a wok over high heat until very hot but not smoking. Add the ginger and garlic and cook, stirring constantly, for about 3 minutes, or until the ginger and garlic is lightly toasted. Add the onion and sauté for 1½ minutes. Add the celery and sauté for 1½ minutes. Follow with the carrots and sauté for 1½ minutes. Finally, add the snow peas and sauté for about 30 seconds, or just until they are crisp-tender and still bright green. Add the celery leaves and salt and pepper to taste. Toss to combine and serve immediately.

Chicken and Cabbage Spring Rolls

SERVES 2

These are also perfect for a snack, a light lunch or, if you make very small ones, terrific as hors d'oeuvres. The basic recipe would work just as well for vegetarians, just omit the chicken. You could also use leftover pork or some shrimp or lobster. If you don't have any leftover Vegetable Stir-Fry, start with a new mix and a fresh sauté.

1 tablespoon vegetable oil plus additional
  oil for baking or frying
1 cup julienned green cabbage
2 ounces green beans, trimmed and sliced
  into thin pieces on the bias
Coarse salt and freshly ground black pepper
½ cup Vegetable Stir-Fry (see page 90)

4 spring roll wrappers (see Note)
4 ounces Soy-Soaked Tempura Chicken (see
  page 89)
1 tablespoon cornstarch dissolved in
  1 teaspoon cold water (known as a slurry)
⅔ cup Soy-Ginger Vinaigrette (see page 89)

Heat the oil in a large wok over high heat. Add the cabbage and beans and season with salt and pepper to taste. Sauté them for about 3 minutes, or until crisp-tender. Remove the cabbage and beans from the heat and toss in the leftover Vegetable Stir-Fry. Drain off any excess oil and set aside.

Working with one spring roll wrapper at a time, place about 2 ounces of the vegetable mixture in the center of the wrapper. Place about 1 ounce of the chicken on top of the vegetables. Fold the wrapper over the vegetables and chicken; then fold the ends in and over to cover. Roll the enclosed pouch up and over to make a firm, neat roll. Using a pastry brush, lightly coat the edge with the cornstarch-water slurry and press to seal. Continue making spring rolls until you have completed 4.

To Bake: Preheat the oven to 500 degrees.

Lightly coat a nonstick baking sheet with vegetable oil. Place the spring rolls on the prepared baking sheet and bake them in the preheated oven, occasionally turning and brushing the rolls with vegetable oil, for about 20 minutes, or until golden brown. Remove them from the oven and place them on a double layer of paper towels to absorb any excess oil. Lay each spring roll on its side and, using a serrated knife, cut each in half on the bias. Place two spring rolls, with two halves laying on their side and the others resting against them, cut side up, on each of two small plates. Drizzle some Soy-Ginger Vinaigrette around the edge of the plate. Pass any remaining vinaigrette on the side.

To Fry: Preheat 4 cups of vegetable oil in a large, heavy-duty frying pan. Carefully holding each spring roll by your fingertips, place the sealed edge in the hot fat for 10 seconds to ensure that the seal holds. Then, drop the spring rolls into the hot oil and fry, turning occasionally, for 5 minutes, or until golden brown. Using a slotted spoon, lift the spring rolls from the oil and place them on a triple thickness of paper towels to drain. Lay each spring roll on its side and, using a serrated knife, cut it in half, on the bias. Place two spring rolls, with two halves laying on their side and the others resting against them, cut side up, on each of two small plates. Drizzle some Soy-Ginger Vinaigrette around the edge of the plate. Pass any remaining vinaigrette on the side.

BARBECUED CHICKEN

For as long as man has been eating meat, he has probably been cooking it over an open fire. Although, technically, barbecue means to cook a whole animal or large pieces of tough meat for a very long period of time in an enclosed space on a very low fire, almost all outdoor cooking is now referred to as barbecuing. The important aspects of true barbecue are the type of wood used to flavor the meat, the temperature of the fire (usually around 220 degrees) to produce a constant, mellow smoke, and the space itself. The original barbecue is a direct pit fire in which the fire is allowed to burn down to embers and upon which a raised metal (or other fire-resistant material) grid is placed, with rocks often lining the pit and covering the edges so that heat is retained. The food is slow-cooked on the grid over the hot embers.

From this evolved fireless-pit cooking where the pit is lined with rocks and the fire is built to heat the rocks. Once the rocks are extremely hot, the fire is scraped aside and the pit is lined with seaweed, cornhusks, or fresh leaves and, perhaps, some herbs and spices. The food to be cooked is placed directly on the lined bed and covered with another layer of seaweed, husks, or leaves. Hot rocks are placed on top and the pit is covered with a tarp or other heavy material. Then, all the cook has to do is sit and wait—of course, some cold beer or chilled wine will help the time pass quickly.

Unless you are in Hawaii or down south, most barbecue refers to foods that have been placed on an outdoor grill, either charcoal or gas. This method of cooking is technically called grilling and can be accomplished on an open grill or a covered (or kettle) grill. For fuel, I prefer hardwood lump charcoal with the addition of some aromatic wood chips or vines to create a nice, woody tinge to the finish. It is important to grill over a low, even fire to give the nearest approximation to real barbecue as the low heat will cook the exterior to a crisp, smoky crust and leave the interior mellow and juicy. Since real barbecue is impossible to do in a home kitchen (or even in many urban restaurants where a large smoking pit would be a fire hazard), when I refer to barbecue, I mean open grilling.

When it comes to the sauce that either coats the meat or is used for dipping, the cook can really have fun. And, this is where the real barbecue debates occur. Do you use vinegar and spices? Do you use beer? Tomatoes or not? Every region has its own style. I like to experiment with all kinds of flavors. At the moment, coffee-scented barbecue sauce is my favorite, but who knows what next year will bring? Try your hand with your own favorite flavors. Citrus, wine, Asian sauces, chilies—almost anything can season a great barbecue sauce.

CLASSIC

Barbecued Chicken Parts with Corn on the Cob and Grilled Vegetables

SERVES 6

Rather than put my barbecued chicken on the grill, I give it a quick poach and then a finish in a very hot oven. This guarantees perfectly cooked chicken all year long and brings the taste of summer into a cold winter day. If the weather is not conducive to outdoor grilling, you can also prepare the vegetables on a stove-top grill pan. If you are lucky enough to have a fireplace, you might try to find a Tuscan grill, which is a simple (and usually adjustable), metal, cooking grill that will fit into a fireplace.

2 zucchini, cut into ¼-inch-thick slices on the bias

2 yellow squash, cut into ¼-inch-thick slices on the bias

2 portobello mushrooms, cleaned, stems removed and cut crosswise into ¼-inch-thick slices

2 red onions, cut crosswise into slices

2 Japanese eggplants, trimmed and cut lengthwise into 3 slices

½ cup extra virgin olive oil

Coarse salt and freshly ground black pepper

6 ears fresh corn, in their husks

2 gallons water

2 cups ketchup

2 cups white vinegar

2 cups molasses

¼ cup coffee beans

1 bay leaf

2 4-pound frying chickens, thoroughly rinsed and cut into serving pieces

Barbecue Sauce (recipe follows)

Combine the zucchini, yellow squash, mushrooms, onions, and eggplant in a large bowl. Add the oil and salt and pepper to taste. Toss to combine. Cover the vegetables with plastic wrap and set aside.

Preheat the oven to 375 degrees.

Place the corn in a large pot, add cold water to cover, and soak for 30 minutes. Shake off any excess water and place the corn on a baking sheet. Roast in the preheated oven, turning it occasionally, for 40 minutes, or until it is cooked through, lightly toasted, and very aromatic.

While the corn is roasting, prepare the poaching mixture. Combine the water, ketchup, vinegar, molasses, coffee beans, and bay leaf in a large, deep pot over high heat and bring to a boil. Add the chicken pieces to the poaching liquid, and return the liquid to a boil. Immediately turn off the heat and allow the chicken to sit in the hot liquid for 20 minutes. Transfer the chicken to two nonstick baking sheets. Using a pastry brush, lightly coat each piece of chicken with the Barbecue Sauce and place on the baking sheets. Place the baking sheets in the preheated oven, along with the corn, and bake the chicken for 15 minutes, or until it is cooked through and nicely caramelized. (If the chicken is not caramelizing as it bakes, you may want to lightly brush on additional Barbecue Sauce.)

Preheat and oil the grill.

While the corn and chicken are in the oven, grill the vegetables. (You can also grill them early in the day, as they taste almost as good served at room temperature.)

Without overcrowding, place the reserved seasoned vegetables on the preheated grill. Grill, turning occasionally, for about 3 minutes per side, or just until the vegetables are nicely marked and barely cooked. Transfer to a serving platter and continue grilling until all of the vegetables are cooked.

Remove the chicken and corn from the oven. Place the chicken on a serving platter and, if you are eating outdoors, leave the corn in the husks and let everyone peel them at the table. If you are eating indoors, it is a good idea to remove the messy husks in the kitchen before bringing the corn to the table on a serving platter. Serve the chicken, vegetables, and corn family style.

Barbecue Sauce

3 cups red wine vinegar
½ cup firmly packed light brown sugar
½ cup honey
3½ cups ketchup
3½ cups tomato purée
¼ cup soy sauce
¼ cup coffee beans
¼ fresh lemon

¼ fresh orange
1 teaspoon paprika
½ teaspoon ground cumin
½ teaspoon ground coriander
½ teaspoon celery seed
½ teaspoon chili powder
¼ cup chopped cilantro leaves
Coarse salt and freshly ground black pepper

Combine the vinegar, brown sugar, and honey in a tall, heavy-duty pot over medium heat. Bring the mixture to a boil and then lower the heat to a simmer. Simmer for about 15 minutes, or until the mixture is reduced by one-half. Stir in the ketchup, tomato purée, soy sauce, coffee beans, lemon, orange, paprika, cumin, coriander, celery seed, chili powder, cilantro leaves, and salt and pepper to taste. Raise the heat and bring the mixture to a boil. Immediately reduce the heat to a simmer and cook, stirring occasionally, for about 40 minutes, or until the mixture is reduced by one-half. Strain the mixture through a fine sieve into a nonreactive container and allow it to cool. If not using immediately, cover and refrigerate for up to 1 month.

CONTEMPORARY

Pretzel-Onion Crusted Barbecued Chicken with Pretzel Latkes, Corn, and Mustard

SERVES 6 TO 8

You need a really big grill to prepare this recipe. When I created it, I even cooked the potato latkes (pancakes to the non-Yiddish speaking crowd) on the grill. I've given you the option of cooking them on top of the stove. If you don't have three 6-inch-round, cast-iron skillets, you could make one large pancake and cut it into wedges. You could also roast the corn in the oven. However, try to keep the carrots (use real baby carrots with tops, not those little stubby ones in the plastic bag) on the grill, as I think that the grill flavor heightens their sweetness and makes them especially delicious.

6 ears fresh corn, in their husks

1½ cups chopped pretzels

½ cup crisply fried onions

2½ tablespoons clarified butter
(see page 7)

1 tablespoon mustard oil (see page 49)

4½ cups Barbecue Sauce (see page 96)

½ cup chicken stock

2 tablespoons Dijon mustard

18 baby carrots, with tops

¼ cup canola oil

Coarse salt and freshly ground black pepper

6 10-ounce chicken breasts with wing bone
on (see Illustration)

6 boneless, skinless chicken thighs, rinsed
and patted dry

2½ tablespoons chopped fresh chives

1 tablespoon extra virgin olive oil

2 tablespoons fines herbes (see page 65)

Pretzel Latkes (recipe follows)

Wrap the corn in aluminum foil, sealing tightly. Set aside.

Combine the chopped pretzels and crispy onions in a mixing bowl. Drizzle on the clarified butter and toss to combine. Continue tossing as you add the mustard oil. Set aside.

Combine 2¼ cups of the Barbecue Sauce with the chicken stock in a small saucepan over medium heat. Bring the mixture to a boil; then remove it from the heat and whisk in the mustard. Do not cook the mustard, or it will turn grainy. Cover lightly with aluminum foil and keep warm.

Remove the tops from the carrots, leaving about an inch of green. Peel the carrots and, using about 1 tablespoon of the oil lightly coat the carrots. Season with salt and pepper to taste. Set aside.

Preheat and oil the grill.

Place the aluminum-wrapped corn on the slowest part of the grill, usually around the outside perimeter. Grill, turning occasionally, for about 35 minutes. Remove the corn from the grill and keep it wrapped until ready to serve.

Wash the chicken thoroughly under cold running water and pat dry with paper towels. Season the chicken with salt and pepper and lightly rub it with the remaining oil. Place the pieces on the hot grill, with the breast pieces toward the slowest part of the grill. Grill the breast pieces for about 25 minutes and the thigh pieces for about 20 minutes. During the final 10 minutes of grilling, using a pastry brush, lightly coat the chicken with the remaining Barbecue Sauce two or three times, allowing the sauce to caramelize slightly between brushings. Take care that you do not burn the chicken, you want it to be nicely glazed and slightly crisp. Remove the chicken from the grill and place it on a baking sheet. Toss the chives into the reserved pretzel mixture and then sprinkle it over each piece, lightly pressing it into the skin to make a crunchy crust.

About 10 minutes before the chicken is ready, place the carrots on the grill. Grill, turning them occasionally, for 7 to 10 minutes, or until crisp-tender and nicely marked. Remove the carrots from the grill and place them in a medium bowl. Toss the carrots with the extra virgin olive oil and fines herbes to coat. If necessary, season with additional salt and pepper. (If your grill is not large enough to handle the corn, chicken, and carrots, grill the carrots after you have removed the chicken from the grill, as the chicken will be just fine even if it cools down a bit.)

Line a large serving platter with the latkes. Transfer the chicken to the platter. Unwrap the corn and garnish the platter with the corn and seasoned carrots. Pass the sauce on the side. Serve family style with lots of napkins.

Pretzel Latkes

2 to 3 cups pretzels	1 cup chopped scallions
2 large Idaho potatoes, peeled and shredded	½ cup fresh corn kernels
2 large red onions, peeled and shredded	Coarse salt and freshly ground black pepper
3 large eggs, beaten	Approximately 3 cups clarified butter (see
1½ cups milk	page 7)

Place the pretzels in the bowl of a food processor fitted with the metal blade and process to a fine powder. Remove the powder from the bowl and set aside.

Combine the potatoes and onions in a large mixing bowl. Add the eggs and milk and stir to combine. Stir in the scallions and corn and blend well. Fold in the reserved pretzel flour, about ¼ cup at a time, blending until the mixture is slightly thick. If necessary, season it with salt and pepper.

Place about ¼ cup of the clarified butter in each of three 6-inch-round, cast-iron skillets over medium heat. Place one-sixth of the potato mixture into each pan and pat the potatoes down into the pans. Fry for about 12 minutes, or until the bottom of the pancakes are golden-brown and the tops have begun to cook. Flip the latkes over, add another ¼ cup of clarified butter and continue to fry, adding additional butter if needed, for about 10 minutes or until golden brown. Remove the pancakes from the skillets and place them on a triple layer of paper towels to drain. Place the latkes on a baking sheet in the preheated oven to keep them warm while you prepare the remaining three latkes. Serve hot.

Barbecued Chicken Sticky Buns

MAKES APPROXIMATELY 16

This recipe combines two classics of the American kitchen, leftovers and Parker House Rolls. Made from a soft, milk dough, Parker House Rolls get their name from the Boston hotel where they made their debut in the 1850s. The standard shape begins by forming the dough into 1-ounce balls that are allowed to rise slightly. After the dough has risen, each piece is rolled down the center, outward, with a rolling pin to form an oval, leaving the sides elevated a bit. The top is brushed with melted butter and then folded over. The rolls are allowed to rise and then given an egg wash and baked to a golden brown. The fold creates a roll that is easily pulled apart. If you don't have the time or inclination to make the dough, do what I often do, just purchase refrigerated biscuits and form them as directed in the recipe.

Parker House Roll Dough (recipe follows) or refrigerated biscuit dough
1½ cups chopped Barbecued Chicken meat (see page 94)
½ cup chopped grilled onions
½ cup chopped Jalapeño Jack cheese

½ cup Barbecue Sauce (see page 96)
Coarse salt and freshly ground black pepper
1 large egg
2 tablespoons water
½ cup finely chopped onion
1 tablespoon cumin seeds

Prepare the dough.

Preheat the oven to 350 degrees.

Line a baking sheet with parchment paper. Set aside.

Lightly flour a clean work surface and, using a rolling pin, roll the dough out into a circle about a ½ inch thick. Then, using a cookie or biscuit cutter, cut the dough out into 3-inch circles. You should yield between 14 and 16 circles.

Combine the chicken, grilled onions, Jack cheese, and Barbecue Sauce in a mixing bowl. Taste it and, if necessary, season it with salt and pepper. Set aside.

Whisk the egg and water together in a small mixing bowl.

Place about 2 tablespoons of the chicken mixture in the center of each dough circle. Using a pastry brush, lightly coat the edges of the dough circles with the egg wash. Working with one piece at a time, pull up the edges of the circle to form a pouch, twisting to enclose the filling. Transfer the finished pouch to the prepared baking sheet, twisted side down. Continue making buns until all of the filling is used.

Once all of the buns have been transferred to the baking sheet, using the pastry brush, lightly coat the tops with the remaining egg wash. Sprinkle the buns with the chopped raw onion and cumin seed and place in the preheated oven. Bake for about 18 minutes, or until golden brown.

Remove from the oven and serve hot with a soup or salad.

Parker House Roll Dough

3 pounds (about 10 cups) bread flour	1½ ounces yeast
2 tablespoons coarse salt	2 tablespoons sugar
3½ cups milk	6 tablespoons plus ¾ teaspoon warm
¼ cup (½ stick) unsalted butter	(120 degrees) water

Sift the flour and salt together. Set aside.

Combine the milk and butter in a small saucepan over low heat. Heat to 120 degrees on a candy thermometer. Remove the mixture from the heat and set it aside.

Combine the yeast and sugar with the warm water in the large bowl of an electric mixer fitted with a dough hook. Turn the machine on to medium speed and mix for 3 minutes. Add the reserved, warm, milk mixture. Slowly begin adding the flour mixture, stirring for about 10 minutes, or until all of the flour is incorporated and the dough is quite smooth and has pulled into a ball. Scrape the dough from the bowl and transfer it to a large, clean bowl. Place the bowl in a warm, draft-free spot, cover it with a clean kitchen towel, and allow it to rest for about 1 hour, or until the dough has doubled in size.

Form the dough into circles for the Barbecue Chicken Sticky Buns recipe or into the regular Parker-House-Roll shape or into any style roll you like. You can also form the dough balls into a circle around the edge of ovenproof dinner plates, bake them in a preheated 350-degree oven for about 15 minutes, and then fill the center of the plate with warm stews or cold salads.

ROAST LONG ISLAND DUCKLING

Duck farming on Long Island goes back well over a hundred years, but there was a real surge in the demand for duck when Eastern European immigrants arrived in the early part of the 1900s. Duck was so much a part of the cuisines of countries such as Poland, Hungary, and Czechoslovakia that these new Americans were delighted to find a cheap and ready supply in their new homeland. Americans took some time to embrace farmed duck. In fact, it was not until recent years that duck made its way to moderately priced restaurant menus and became readily available in supermarkets.

The original Long Island ducks supposedly evolved from four, heavy-breasted Peking ducks brought in on clipper ships in the 1870s. Most of their descendants made their way to the tidewater streams of eastern Long Island, about one-hundred miles east of New York City. From this small beginning has risen a major industry.

Only French restaurants or high-end, hotel dining rooms first featured classic dishes such as *Canard à l'orange*. At the beginning of my career, duck was almost never cooked in restaurants and young chefs were taught only the classic preparations such as *pâté de foie gras* and duck confit. In Périgord and Normandy, duck is widely prepared by home cooks and starred on restaurant menus. It is always paired with an acidic sauce, most often a citrus-based one. It is the complexity of this traditional combination of the rich sweetness of the duck and the sour acidity of the sauce that makes a duck dish so appealing. In fact, it was not until I spent time in France that I began to learn the full range of duck preparations.

With the revolution in American cooking in the 1980s, duck, at long last, made its way onto the restaurant menu. I believe that one of the reasons it took so long was the perception that it was exceedingly fatty and difficult to cook successfully. There is no question that duck is fatty but, with a little care, the fat can be rendered out leaving deliciously tender, rich meat. Duck breasts are now available, sealed in Cryovac, for convenience. They are very easy to cook and take to almost any type of sauce or condiment; even a store-bought chutney will make a four-star meal.

I love the versatility of duck. Roasted, it is as satisfying as a slab of beef; grilled, it can easily taste as good as a steak; and prepared on top of the stove, it becomes almost anything you want it to be. Following in the French tradition, I always use some kind of acid to mellow the richness and finish the preparation with a slightly sweet-tart sauce.

Classic Roast Duck with Oranges

SERVES 6

Canard à l'orange is one of the basics in classic French cooking. However, it made its debut on the fancy restaurant menus of New York in the latter part of the nineteenth century, so very early on it became associated with fine, American dining. Yet you would be hard-pressed to find it on a menu today except at an old-fashioned country club or a large hotel dining room. I still think it is a delicious preparation. There is nothing to compare to the marriage of the rich, fatty duck meat and the slightly tart, yet sweet, orange sauce. To me, it's a classic.

1½ cups orange marmalade
1 cup fresh orange juice
½ cup plus 2 tablespoons white vinegar
5 tablespoons ketchup
1 tablespoon chopped green peppercorns
½ teaspoon cracked black pepper
2 teaspoons chopped fresh thyme leaves
1 pound wild rice, well-washed and drained

4 cups water
Pinch coarse salt plus more to taste
2 4-pound Long Island duck, thoroughly
    rinsed and patted dry
Freshly ground pepper
¼ cup (½ stick) unsalted butter
½ cup minced shallots

Combine the marmalade, orange juice, vinegar, ketchup, peppercorns, and cracked pepper in a medium heavy-duty saucepan over medium heat. Bring the mixture to a boil; then lower the heat and simmer for about 5 minutes, or until the flavors are well blended and the sauce is slightly thick. Remove it from the heat and stir in the thyme. Set aside.

Combine the wild rice and water in a heavy-duty saucepan over high heat. Add a pinch of salt and bring the rice to a boil. Lower the heat to a simmer; cover, and simmer the rice for about 20 minutes, or just until it has cracked open. Remove the rice from the heat and drain through a colander. Set aside to cool.

Preheat the oven to 450 degrees.

Season the ducks, inside and out, with salt and pepper. Place them on a rack in a roasting pan. Roast in the preheated oven for 20 minutes, or just until the skin has begun to color. Reduce the heat to 350 degrees and continue roasting for an additional 40 minutes, or until all of the fat has rendered out, the duck skin is dark brown and crisp, and an instant-read thermometer reads 165 degrees when inserted into the thickest part of the duck.

Just before the duck is ready, finish the rice. Heat the butter in a large sauté pan over medium heat. Add the shallots and sauté for about 5 minutes, or just until the shallots begin to take on some color. Add the rice and sauté it for about 5 minutes, or until heated through. Season to taste with salt and pepper. Remove the rice from the heat and keep it warm. (It is this shallot-flavored wild rice that you will use in the Second Day Dish of Duck Pithiviers {see page 105}).

Cut the duck into eight pieces; 2 thighs, 2 legs, and the 2 breasts cut in half crosswise. Place a large spoonful of the rice in the center of each of six dinner plates. Place a duck piece on top of the rice and spoon some of the orange sauce over the top of the duck. Serve immediately with any green vegetable.

Soy-Honey Roast Duck

SERVES 6

Marinating the duck helps keep the meat juicy and infuses the skin with wonderful flavor. I've found that it also helps render out the fat. The Asian-flavored soak really makes the roasted skin glisten and crack with crispness and tang. The complete dish is a very contemporary take on the classic Peking duck served in many Chinese restaurants.

3 cups soy sauce

1 cup honey

½ cup water

½ cup chopped cilantro

3 cloves garlic, crushed

2 star anise

½ inch piece ginger, peeled and crushed

2 4-pound Long Island ducks, thoroughly
   rinsed and patted dry

1 tablespoon peanut oil

½ cup minced shallots

2 teaspoons minced garlic

1 teaspoon minced fresh ginger

1 small onion, julienned

1 cup julienned celery

1 cup julienned carrots

½ cup sliced shiitake mushroom caps

2 tablespoons chicken stock

½ cup julienned snow peas

2 tablespoons chopped scallions,
   including some of the green part

Coarse salt and freshly ground black
   pepper

Cracked Pepper Pineapple Rings
   (recipe follows)

Combine the soy sauce, honey, water, cilantro, garlic, star anise, and ginger in a deep, non-reactive container large enough to hold the 2 ducks. Add the ducks, making sure that they are covered with the marinade. Cover and refrigerate for 12 hours.

Preheat the oven to 325 degrees.

Remove the ducks from the marinade and place them on a wire rack in a roasting pan. Cover with aluminum foil and place in the preheated oven. Roast the ducks for 1 hour, or until the skin is crisp and an instant-read thermometer inserted into the thickest part reads 165 degrees. If the skin is not crisping, lift off the aluminum foil for the last 15 minutes of roasting.

Place the marinade in a small saucepan over medium heat and bring it to a boil. Immediately remove it from the heat and set aside.

About 15 minutes before the ducks are ready, prepare the stir-fry. Heat the oil in a in a large wok over medium-high heat. Add the shallots and minced garlic and allow them to sweat for about 4 minutes, or until the vegetables are translucent. Add the minced ginger and sauté it for about 2 minutes, or just until the ginger has softened slightly. Add the onion, celery, and carrots and stir-fry them for 2 minutes. Raise the heat to high and add the mushrooms and chicken stock. Stir-fry vigorously to help the liquid evaporate. Add about ¼ cup of the reserved marinade and again stir-fry vigorously to deglaze the pan. Stir in the snow peas and remove the mixture from the heat. Stir in the chopped scallions along with salt and pepper to taste.

Using a chef's knife, cut the duck into eight pieces; 2 thighs, 2 legs, and the 2 breasts cut in half. Place a mound of the stir-fried vegetables into the center of each of six dinner plates.

Place a piece of duck on top of the vegetables and then a pineapple ring on top. Drizzle some of the reserved marinade around the edge of the plate and serve immediately.

Cracked Pepper Pineapple Rings

1 medium pineapple
½ cup cracked black pepper

Coarse salt
3 tablespoons olive oil

Using a chef's knife, slice off the top and bottom of the pineapple to make a smooth, even cut on each end. Peel the pineapple and, using the end of a vegetable peeler or the point of a small knife, carefully remove all of the eyes. Cut the pineapple crosswise into 6 ¼-inch-thick slices of equal diameter, reserving the remaining pineapple for another use. Using a 1-inch-round cookie cutter, remove the center core from each slice.

Place the pepper in a small plate and, working with one slice at a time, dredge both sides of each piece of pineapple in the pepper and season with salt to taste.

Place the oil in a large sauté pan over medium-high heat. When it is very hot but not smoking, add the seasoned pineapple rings. Sear them for 3 minutes, or until golden, without shaking the pan or moving the slices, which can dislodge the pepper. Turn and sear the other side for about 3 minutes, or until well caramelized.

Using a slotted spatula, transfer the caramelized pineapple rings to a double layer of paper towels to drain. Serve warm.

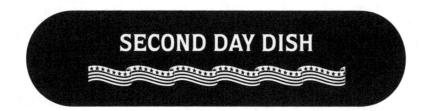

Duck Pithiviers

SERVES 2

In classic French cooking a Pithiviers is, in its first incarnation, a flaky pastry filled with any type of savory filling. In the town of Pithiviers, north of Orléans, a delicious lark pâté is also called by this name. Here, I combined very American white bread and a savory bird filling. If company is coming for lunch, you could put the "sandwiches" together early in the day and bake them just before serving. This method will work for almost any type of savory filling. You could also use any fruit filling, even jam, and then glaze it with a brush of clarified butter and a sprinkle of confectioners' sugar for a really delicious and easy dessert.

4 slices sandwich-style white bread, crusts removed

1 large egg whisked into 2 tablespoons water

1 cup shredded, leftover, roast duck (either Classic Roast Duck with Oranges or Soy-Honey Roast Duck, see pages 102 and 103)

1 cup leftover wild rice (see page 102) or stir-fried vegetables (see page 90)

Approximately 2 tablespoons sesame oil

1 tablespoon toasted sesame seeds

2 cups mesclun greens

2 tablespoons cilantro leaves

1 tablespoon chopped scallions

1 tablespoon David Burke's Vinaigrette (recipe follows) or other flavorful vinaigrette

Approximately 2 tablespoons hoisin sauce (see Note)

NOTE: Hoisin sauce, a spicy-sweet, soybean-based Chinese condiment, is available at Asian markets, specialty food stores, and some supermarkets.

The recipe for David Burke's Vinaigrette makes much more vinaigrette than needed, but it keeps well and is a delicious dressing for almost any type of salad.

Preheat the oven to 375 degrees.

Using a rolling pin, flatten each slice of bread. Lay two slices out on a clean, flat surface. Using a pastry brush, lightly coat the edges of each slice with the egg wash. Set the bread aside, separately reserving the remaining two slices.

Combine the duck and wild rice (or stir-fried vegetables) and toss them to blend well. Place an equal portion of the duck mixture on top of each of the two slices of bread, leaving room around the edge. Top each piece with one of the reserved slices, pushing down against the egg-washed edge to enclose the filling.

Using a clean pastry brush, lightly coat each side of bread with sesame oil. Place the pithivers on a nonstick baking sheet. Sprinkle the tops with sesame seeds and place into the preheated oven. Bake for about 10 minutes, or until golden brown. Remove the pithivers from the oven and set aside.

Combine the mesclun greens with the cilantro and scallions in a small mixing bowl. Drizzle the vinaigrette over the top and toss to combine.

Place a pithivier in the center of each of two luncheon plates. Mound some salad over each one. Make a small half-moon of hoisin sauce at the edge of the plate to dip the pithivier in and serve immediately.

David Burke's Vinaigrette

½ cup sherry wine vinegar
2 tablespoons Dijon mustard
1 cup olive oil

¾ cup extra virgin olive oil
Coarse salt and freshly ground black pepper

Combine the vinegar and mustard in a small mixing bowl. Slowly add the oils, whisking constantly to emulsify. Season with salt and pepper to taste. Hold at room temperature until ready to serve.

ROAST TURKEY

It doesn't matter that you can find turkey in the market all year round, for most people turkey means Thanksgiving with its Norman Rockwell table centered with a gigantic, burnished-gold roast turkey and overflowing with a cornucopia of harvest foods. No one really knows exactly how turkeys came to be associated with Thanksgiving, but, by the middle of the nineteenth century, Thanksgiving and the bird became synonymous. Perhaps it all started with Alexander Hamilton, who was once quoted as saying that "No citizen of the United States should refrain from turkey on Thanksgiving Day." And, this was almost one hundred years before Abraham Lincoln declared that Thanksgiving was to be celebrated, annually, on the fourth Thursday of November.

Other countries also eat turkey but none so much as we do. This might be because turkey is not mentioned in old world cuisine until after the discovery of America so it is presumed that it was one of America's gifts. In France, turkey, or *dinde*, is most often served stuffed with foie gras and truffles or a mousselike *farce* with more truffles inserted under the skin. It is a special occasion dish that is either roasted or poached. Turkey is also used to make a classic *galantine*.

For a great many years, Thanksgiving has found me roasting turkeys in a restaurant kitchen. I usually opt for a smaller turkey, about twelve to fifteen pounds. Birds twenty-five pounds and over look great on the platter, but they are very hard to roast evenly. The smaller birds are most often hens with a somewhat larger breast. You will need about 1 pound of raw turkey per person with, of course, some extra pounds for those sandwiches and Second Day Dishes. I prefer a free-range turkey only because these are generally free of antibiotics and growth enhancers. There remains much argument about whether or not the free-range or organic turkeys actually taste better than those raised in other ways.

The timetable for roasting a turkey is pretty simple: 10 to 12 minutes per pound for an unstuffed bird, and 12 to 15 minutes per pound for a stuffed bird. You will want to roast the bird until the skin is golden brown, the juices run clear, and an instant-read thermometer reads 165 degrees when inserted into the stuffing (or for an unstuffed turkey, 175 degrees when inserted into the thickest part of the leg and thigh).

Let the turkey rest for about 20 minutes before attempting to carve it. Sharpen whatever knife you are going to use. I use my trusty chef's knife but some people recommend a meat-slicing knife. Those without confidence opt for an electric carving knife. First, slice through and remove the drumsticks at the joint. Pull the wings off at the joint. You might have to give a couple of tugs at the drumstick joint to speed up the process. Next, remove the filet section of the breast. Make a horizontal cut about half-way down the breast. Then, from the top of the breast make a vertical cut until you reach the other cut and the wedge of meat falls free. Place the filet on a cutting board and peel off the skin. Cut the filet, on the diagonal against the grain, into ¼-inch-thick slices. If you like the skin, cut it into pieces with kitchen shears and arrange it on the platter with the sliced meat. If you prefer the skin very crispy, throw it in a microwave for a minute or two before serving.

The thigh comes next. Using a boning knife, cut the thigh at the joint and pull it off. Cut the meat into sections and place it on the platter with the breast meat.

Go back to the breast and, using the slicing knife, make a 1½-inch-horizontal cut all the way to the bone and loosen the meat. I call this the turkey sirloin.

The breast meat attached to the wing bone is my favorite. I refer to it as the king piece because it is the most moist and flavorful since it is near the bone and also has the most skin. Run the boning knife right by the joint and make a vertical cut, and pull the meat from the turkey.

The drumsticks can be served whole or cut into sections. Cutting is rather difficult to do, but if you stand the drumstick, ankle side up, and cut downward, the meat should come off neatly.

While the turkey is being carved, the gravy can be made and all of the side dishes can be served up. Can't you just smell the heavenly aromas?

Traditional Roast Turkey with Condiments

SERVES 6 TO 8

Here it is, a complete Thanksgiving dinner. All you have to do is remember to thaw the turkey (if frozen), take the plastic bag of giblets out of the cavity, and get your timing straight. If you undercook the turkey, cut it into pieces and microwave the pieces. If you overcook it, pre-slice it in the kitchen, place the slices on a platter, and cover them with the gravy. If it just happens to be burned, call it Cajun, or remove the skin and tell your guests that you have health concerns. If you want to make the Second Day chowder, make sure that you double the recipe for Sweet Potato and Vanilla Purée as well as reserve one cup of chopped turkey meat.

1 15-pound free-range turkey, thoroughly rinsed and dried

Coarse salt and freshly ground black pepper

5 tablespoons olive oil

Cornbread and Sausage Stuffing (recipe follows)

¼ cup (½ stick) unsalted butter

¼ cup Wondra flour (see page 70)

4 cups turkey or chicken stock (see Note)

3 carrots, cut into sticks, blanched

3 stalks celery, cut into sticks, blanched

2 cups peeled pearl onions, blanched

1 pint Brussels sprouts, trimmed, and blanched

Sweet Potato and Vanilla Purée (recipe follows)

Cranberry-Pineapple Compote (recipe follows)

NOTE: You can make a light turkey stock that is great for gravy making, if your turkey came with giblets. Place the giblets in a large saucepan with cold, salted water to cover. Add a chopped onion and carrot along with salt to taste and bring to a boil. Lower the heat and simmer for about 45 minutes. Strain, discarding the solids. For a richer stock, you can also cook the giblets in canned chicken broth.

Preheat the oven to 350 degrees.

Season the turkey, inside and out, with salt and pepper. Using about 3 tablespoons of the oil, generously coat the skin. Stuff the turkey with the Cornbread and Sausage Stuffing and truss it together. Place the stuffed turkey on a wire rack in a roasting pan and roast in the preheated oven for 15 minutes. Lower the heat to 325 degrees and continue to roast for about 2½ hours, or until an instant-read thermometer inserted into the stuffing reads 160 degrees. Remove the turkey from the oven and transfer it to a serving platter. Allow it to rest for 15 minutes before carving. Do not turn off the oven.

While the turkey is resting, prepare the gravy and blanch the vegetables.

Melt the butter in a medium saucepan over medium heat. Whisking constantly, add the flour, making sure that no lumps form. Whisking constantly, add the stock in a slow, steady stream. Bring to a simmer and simmer for 5 minutes. Taste and adjust the seasoning with salt and pepper. Pour the liquid into a gravy boat and lightly tent it with aluminum foil to keep it warm.

Place the carrots, celery, onions, and Brussels sprouts on a baking sheet and toss them with the remaining oil and salt and pepper to taste. Place the vegetables in the preheated oven and roast them for about 10 minutes, or just until they begin to take on some color.

Place the vegetables, purée, and compote in serving bowls on the table. Place the turkey on the table (and take any offers for the carving). Serve family style with the stuffing taken directly from the turkey and with the gravy on the side.

Cornbread and Sausage Stuffing

2 pounds sweet or hot (or mixed) Italian
    sausage
½ cup diced onion
½ cup diced celery
1 clove garlic, minced
¾ teaspoon minced fresh rosemary

¾ teaspoon minced fresh sage
¾ teaspoon minced fresh thyme
2 cups ½-inch fresh white bread cubes
2 cups fresh cornbread crumbs
Coarse salt and freshly ground black
    pepper

Line a platter with a triple layer of paper towels. Set aside.

Release the sausage from its casing and break apart in a large sauté pan. Place the meat over medium heat and cook it, stirring frequently, for about 12 minutes, or until the sausage is almost cooked. Using a slotted spoon, transfer it to the paper towel–lined platter and allow the excess fat to drain off.

Place the onion, celery, and garlic in the same sauté pan over medium heat and sauté for about 4 minutes, or just until the vegetables are translucent but have not taken on any color. Stir in the rosemary, sage, and thyme and remove the mixture from the heat.

Combine the bread cubes and crumbs in a large mixing bowl. Scrape the onion mixture into the bowl, add the reserved sausage, and stir well to combine. Taste and, if necessary, adjust the seasoning with additional salt and pepper.

Sweet Potato and Vanilla Purée

2 pounds sweet potatoes, peeled and cubed
1 vanilla bean
½ cup (1 stick) unsalted butter, softened

½ cup hot milk
Coarse salt and freshly ground white
   pepper

Preheat the oven to 350 degrees.

Place the sweet potatoes in a medium saucepan. Add cold, salted water to cover the potatoes by 1 inch. Bring to a boil over medium-high heat. Lower the heat and simmer the potatoes for about 15 minutes, or until they are tender when pierced with the point of a sharp knife. Drain well. Transfer the potatoes in a single layer to a nonstick baking sheet.

Place the sweet potatoes in the preheated oven for 5 minutes, or just until their exterior is quite dry. Transfer them to the bowl of a food processor fitted with the metal blade.

Split the vanilla bean lengthwise and, using the edge of a paring knife, scrape the seeds into the sweet potatoes. (Do not discard the bean. Save it to flavor sugars, teas, or beverages.) Add the butter and milk and process to a smooth purée. Season to taste with salt and pepper. Transfer the purée to the top half of a double boiler over very hot water. Cover and keep it warm. (The purée may be made up to 3 days in advance; and stored, covered and refrigerated. Reheat it as above or in a microwave oven.)

Cranberry-Pineapple Compote

4 cups fresh orange juice
¾ cup fresh lime juice
2 cups honey
½ cup sugar
1 teaspoon freshly grated orange zest

1 teaspoon freshly grated lemon zest
1 sprig fresh rosemary
12 ounces fresh cranberries thoroughly
   washed
4 cups finely diced fresh pineapple

Combine the orange and lime juices in a large, heavy-duty saucepan over medium-high heat. Add the honey and sugar and stir until dissolved. Add the orange and lemon zest and the rosemary sprig and bring the mixture to a boil. Lower the heat and simmer, stirring occasionally, for about 30 minutes, or until the mixture is thick and syruplike. Add the cranberries and pineapple and raise the heat. Again, bring it to a boil; then lower the heat and simmer for about 20 minutes, or until the mixture has returned to a syruplike consistency.

Remove the syrup from the heat, transfer it to a nonreactive container, and allow to cool to room temperature. The compote can be stored, covered and refrigerated, for up to 1 week.

CONTEMPORARY

Roast Half Turkey with Bread Pudding, Chestnut-Turkey Cappuccino, and Candied Lemon Peel

SERVES 6

This recipe takes a little skill in getting the turkey breasts deboned and placed into their roasting pans. It also requires two 9-inch cake pans, six ramekins, a cappuccino machine, and six cappuccino cups. But it's a great recipe and worth the work. It would be a sensational change from the traditional bird and fixings, or a winter dinner-party special. The pudding, the cappuccino, and the lemon peel can all be made in advance.

1 cup (2 sticks) unsalted butter, at room temperature
3 tablespoons fresh lemon juice
2 tablespoons minced fresh thyme leaves
Coarse salt
Freshly ground white pepper
1 12- to 15-pound free-range turkey, halved and deboned, with leg bone attached, well rinsed and dried

Freshly ground black pepper
3 cloves garlic, cut into slivers
Bread Pudding (recipe follows)
Chestnut-Turkey Cappuccino (recipe follows)
Candied Lemon Peel (recipe follows)

Preheat the oven to 350 degrees.

Combine the softened butter with the lemon juice and thyme. Add salt and white pepper to taste and, using a wooden spoon, mash it all together to combine well. Form the flavored butter into two equal pieces and place them into the refrigerator to firm up slightly.

Season the turkey with salt and black pepper. Place a piece of flavored butter and some garlic slivers under the skin of each turkey half. Holding the leg bone up in the air, swing the breast around the leg and fit the turkey half into a 9-inch-round, cake pan. Do the same with the remaining turkey half.

Place the turkey halves into the preheated oven and roast them for about 1 hour, or until an instant-read thermometer inserted into the thickest part of the bird reads 160 degrees.

Place the turkey halves on a large serving platter with the Bread Pudding and Chestnut-Turkey Cappuccino set around the edge. Sprinkle the Candied Lemon Peel over the turkey halves and serve.

Bread Pudding

2 tablespoons unsalted butter, softened	2 tablespoons thinly sliced scallions
3 large eggs, beaten	1 tablespoon Roasted Garlic Purée (see
2 cups milk or heavy cream	page 12)
¼ pound cooked, lean bacon, crumbled	Coarse salt and freshly ground black pepper
2 tablespoons minced flat-leaf parsley	6 cups ½-inch fresh white bread cubes

Preheat the oven to 350 degrees.

Lightly coat the interior of each of six 4-ounce ramekins with the softened butter. Set aside.

Whisk the eggs and milk together in a large mixing bowl. Stir in the bacon, parsley, scallions, and garlic purée. Season the mixture with salt and pepper. Add the bread cubes and fold them into the liquid. Allow the bread to soak up the egg mixture.

When the bread mixture is very moist, spoon an equal portion of it into each of the prepared ramekins. Place the filled ramekins into a roasting pan and pour in warm water to come halfway up the sides of the ramekins. Place the entire pan in the preheated oven and bake for 45 minutes, or until the edges of the filled ramekins are beginning to brown and the center is almost set. Raise the oven temperature to 400 degrees, and bake the puddings for an additional 10 minutes. (These can be baked early in the day and reheated in a microwave oven, or for 15 minutes in a 325-degree oven just before using.) Remove from the oven and serve immediately.

Chestnut-Turkey Cappuccino

10 ounces dried chestnuts	1 cup skim milk
9 cups turkey stock (see page 110)	1 tablespoon dried porcini powder
Coarse salt and freshly ground black pepper	(see Note)

NOTE: Porcini powder can be purchased in some specialty food markets, or you can make your own by placing a small amount of dried porcini mushrooms in a clean spice grinder and processing to a fine powder. Porcini powder will keep indefinitely in an airtight container placed in a cool, dark place.

Place the chestnuts in a medium saucepan, add boiling salted water to cover, and place over medium heat. Blanch them for 2 minutes. Drain them well and push off any bits of skin.

Combine the chestnuts with the stock in a medium saucepan over medium-high heat and bring them to a boil. Lower the heat and simmer the stock for about 30 minutes, or until it has reduced by one-half and the chestnuts are falling apart. Transfer the mixture to a blender and process it to a smooth purée. (This can be done up to 3 days in advance. Cover and refrigerate the purée until ready to use. Reheat it before using.)

If the purée has cooled down too much, reheat it in a clean, small saucepan. Place the milk in a heat-proof container and, using the steamer on a cappuccino machine, foam the milk.

Pour the hot purée into each of six cappuccino cups. Spoon the foamed milk on top of each cup. Sprinkle the tops with porcini powder and serve immediately.

Candied Lemon Peel

2 large organic lemons
¼ cup sugar
¼ cup water

Using a vegetable peeler, remove the rind from the lemons in strips as large as possible, taking care that it is free of any white pith. Cut the rind lengthwise into fine strips. Set aside.

Combine the sugar and water in a small, heavy saucepan over high heat and bring it to a boil. Lower the heat and simmer the mixture for about 10 minutes, or until the liquid reaches 220 degrees on a candy thermometer. Add the lemon rind and remove the pan from the heat. Allow the rind to sit in the liquid until it is cool. Using a slotted spoon, transfer the rind to wire racks to drain. Store the candied peel, uncovered, until ready to use.

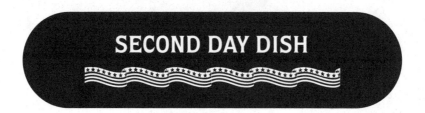
Sweet Potato-Turkey Chowder

SERVES 2

This soup is so delicious that no one will ever take it to be a Second Day Dish. The purée replaces the rich cream usually found in a traditional chowder but still creates the smooth creaminess necessary. The sausage adds a slightly spicy zest to the other mild and simple ingredients. A nicely chilled glass of white wine or rosé, some sweet potato biscuits, and a tossed salad would make a perfect late fall–early winter meal.

2 ounces breakfast sausage meat
½ cup finely diced sweet potatoes
⅓ cup finely diced onions
¼ cup finely diced carrots
¼ cup finely diced celery
1½ cups Sweet Potato and Vanilla
　Purée (see page 112)

⅓ cup chopped cooked turkey meat
3 cups turkey stock (see page 110)
　or chicken stock
Coarse salt and freshly ground black
　pepper

NOTE: If you don't have leftover Sweet Potato and Vanilla Purée, substitute the same amount of mashed sweet potatoes (you will probably need 2 baked sweet potatoes) and 1 cup of heavy cream.

Place the sausage meat in a large, heavy-duty saucepan over medium heat. Cook it, stirring frequently, for about 5 minutes, or until the fat has rendered out of the meat. Drain off the excess fat. Add the diced sweet potatoes, onions, carrots, and celery and sauté them for 4 minutes, or just until the onions are translucent. Stir in the purée and turkey. When the mixture is well blended, add the stock and bring it to a simmer. Simmer, stirring occasionally, for about 15 minutes, or until the mixture is chowderlike in consistency. Taste it and, if necessary, adjust the seasoning with more salt and pepper. Serve hot.

BEEF

I think I started haunting meat markets as soon as I decided to be a cook. First it was the local butcher and then I went to the Fourteenth Street meat markets in Manhattan. Finally, I made my way to the stalls of Les Halles in Paris. I still seek out butchers and markets wherever I travel. I can still remember my first taste of Kobe beef, Japan's incredibly tender and flavorful national treasure. I grew up on corn-fed beef and I'm always on the lookout for a great steak, hamburger, or roast.

I'm not alone in my love for beef. It has been, for years, the most popular meat in America. In fact, beef is consumed with abandon all across the world, but we consume more per capita even though we eat far less red meat than we did ten years ago.

Most of the beef that we eat comes from just a few breeds, mainly Angus, Hereford, and Shorthorn, bred in Texas and the Plains states. The legendary stockyards of Chicago, Kansas City, and Omaha still process and send most of our beef to cities across the country (and the world). In America, superb breeding and excellent feed have combined to produce some of the world's best beef cattle.

Cattle are now raised to be much leaner, but beef remains an excellent source of protein, B-complex vitamins, iron, and other minerals. There are eight USDA grades of beef, but the average consumer has to be concerned with only three of them: prime, choice, and select. Prime, the costliest and most reliably well textured and flavorful, comprises only about 5 percent of the market and is usually sold to steak houses, fine restaurants, and a few select butchers. Choice is, by far, the most available grade and is found in almost all supermarkets and most moderate-priced restaurants. The best of choice is labeled "top choice" and should be your selection when offered. Select is infrequently offered to the average consumer.

Beef has five basic cuts from the sides and one basic cut from the underbelly. Starting from the neck and moving backward, you have the chuck, rib, loin, sirloin, and round. On the underside, you have the brisket, plate, and flank. The leg is known as the foreshank. As is true with almost all animals, the tastiest, most expensive meat comes from the back half with the very best coming from the meaty hindquarters. Chuck is used for hamburger, pot roasts, and stews; rib provides roasts and, obviously, rib cuts; loin gives the tenderest meat as in the tenderloin (for the classic Beef Wellington, a dish rarely done anymore), filet mignon (cut from the thinnest part), and Châteaubriand (the thick steak cut from the wide end) as well as T-bone and porterhouse steaks; sirloin produces steaks and top and bottom roasts; round is used for rump roasts, stews, and other dishes requiring moist heat. The underbelly gives us specialty cuts such as brisket, flank, and skirt or hanger steaks and London broil. The fore-shank is used for stews and braises. The greatest delicacy of all is the marrow found inside the large bones, particularly the leg bones.

It is fairly easy to judge a prime piece of beef. It will be bright red, with the exception of long-aged beef whose exterior will be covered with an almost black-red dry crust. The best beef is always aged, usually for about three weeks, sometimes longer to ensure tenderness and flavor. The aging process does result in a loss of moisture that, in turn, increases the cost of the final product. The meat should have an excellent marbling of fat, that is, streaks and specks of fat running through it and the external fat should be clean, firm, and white. Some-times the fat will have a slightly yellow cast brought about by the type of feed. When buying a piece of choice or top-choice meat in your local supermarket, you can improve its flavor by aging it for a few days, uncovered, in the refrigerator.

I can't talk about beef without a quick discussion of hamburger. Usually ground from bits and pieces of meat trimmed from a primal cut, hamburger can range from 60- to 90-percent lean. I think that meat that is about 80-percent lean makes the juiciest burger. By law, wrapped packages have to be labeled with lean percentages.

STEAK AND POTATOES

Can you believe that steak has been America's most popular meal for over 150 years? As early as the 1850s, discerning diners were ordering steak and potatoes and the demand has continued into the twenty-first century. Steak houses are the fastest growing dining establishments in the United States. It seems that American diners never tire of a great steak no matter the current health trend.

A steak and potatoes dinner was so popular in New York in the 1800s that it was referred to as a "New York beefsteak dinner" and was compared, in importance, to regional meals like New England clambakes and Texas barbecues. The ready availability of good beefsteak came from the proximity of slaughterhouses along the East River so that the cattle were slaughtered and the meat aged and then cooked and eaten in locations within blocks of one another.

Due to genetic breeding improvements, steaks are much leaner than they once were. But, it is the fat that helps ensure a juicy, tender, and tasty steak. The melting fat is also greatly responsible for the wonderful aroma that rises from a grilling steak.

The type of steak will very definitely define the taste. Rib steaks are generally well marbled and consequently have better flavor than those cut from the leaner loin. A filet mignon (or tenderloin steak) has the least amount of fat. Strip steaks are the most confusing because they come with so many other names. In New York, they are often called Kansas City strips while in Kansas City they are called Texas strips. In Texas, they are called, what else, New York strips. They are also known as shell steak, strip loin, and top loin. Whatever cut you prefer, just know that a really great steak is also going to be an expensive steak.

I look for great texture in a steak, which is measured by the density of the surface meat, and perfect marbling, which is the integration of fat throughout the meat and is most responsible for the juiciness of a well-cooked steak.

Aging, particularly for those steaks cut from prime meat, is extremely important because the age requirements for an animal to be labeled "Prime" (no more than 30 months but usually about 14 months) leave the meat with less flavor than that of an older, fatter animal. Aging, which entails hanging the meat in a cooler for anywhere from one to three weeks, improves the flavor of the meat immeasurably. A well-aged, well-marbled steak needs little help to become great eating. Just cook it at the perfect temperature and season it with salt and pepper to taste.

How and for how long a steak is cooked helps create great flavor. I once did a taste test based on the degree of doneness and found, surprisingly, that well-done steaks often had much more flavor than the rare I always order. (It didn't change my preference however.) Since it is the caramelization of the proteins in the meat that gives enormous flavor, it is important that the exterior of the steak be well-cooked. Generally this is best done on a very hot grill that instantly gets the caramelization process in motion and sets the crust. Steaks can also be seared on top of the stove, a ridged grill pan works well for this method, or placed under a very hot broiler. Small steaks can also be sautéed with their pan juices creating a nice sauce.

If you are grilling steaks outdoors, be sure that you get the fire going a good 40 minutes before you put the steaks on. The fire is perfect when the coals are ashy and you can hold the palm of your hand, without burning, about 4 inches from the coals for 4 seconds. A 1 inch-thick steak will take about 12 minutes to grill to medium-rare. You can always do the touch test, very soft to the touch and the meat is still quite rare; when the meat is soft it is rare; when the meat gives only slightly, it is medium, and when the meat is firm to the touch, the meat has stayed on the grill much too long. If you are grilling steaks that are thicker, use an instant-read thermometer to test the doneness, 145 degrees for medium-rare and 160 degrees for medium. (You should give the meat about 5 to 10 minutes resting time for the juices to set; the meat will continue to cook as it sets.)

A word about the potatoes that accompany the steak. Every steak house serves at least a couple of potato side dishes. They can be home fries, cottage fries, French fries, Delmonico, baked with sour cream and chives, stuffed, au gratin, mashed, or even spicy potato skins. Whatever you choose will be just fine because all will sop up the steak's rich juices.

Grilled Sirloin Steak with Garlicky Spinach

SERVES 6

So many people love nothing better than a good steak. I can almost smell this steak along with the garlicky spinach.

4 cups blended oil

1 tablespoon Roasted Garlic Purée
  (see page 12)

1 tablespoon dry mustard

1 tablespoon coarsely ground black pepper

1 teaspoon cayenne pepper

1 teaspoon coarse salt plus more to taste

6 8-ounce sirloin steaks

David Burke's Table Sauce (see Sources)

Freshly ground pepper

2 tablespoons clarified butter (see page 7)

2 pounds spinach, tough stems removed,
  thoroughly washed and dried

1 tablespoon minced garlic

Mashed Potatoes (see page 88),
  optional

Combine the blended oil with the garlic purée, dry mustard, coarse pepper, cayenne, and 1 teaspoon salt in a shallow nonreactive pan large enough to hold the steaks. Add the steaks, turning them once to coat each side with the marinade. Cover the meat with plastic wrap and allow it to marinate, turning occasionally, for 3 hours.

Preheat and oil the grill.

Place the table sauce in a small saucepan over medium heat. Bring it to a simmer. Remove the sauce from the heat and keep it warm.

Remove the steaks from the marinade, season them with salt and pepper, and place them on the preheated grill. Grill them for 4 to 5 minutes per side for medium-rare.

While the steaks are grilling, prepare the spinach.

Preheat the oven to 350 degrees.

Heat the clarified butter in a large sauté pan over medium heat. Add the spinach and garlic and sauté for about 4 minutes, or just until the spinach has wilted slightly and the garlic has taken on some very light color. Season it to taste with salt and pepper.

Place a steak on each of six dinner plates. Place a mound of spinach beside each steak and spoon some mashed potatoes next to the spinach, if you'd like. Ladle the warm table sauce over the top of the steak and serve immediately.

Cracked Pepper Sirloin with Shrimp-Potato Pancake and Roasted Asparagus

SERVES 6

I guess you could call this my take on both surf and turf and the All-American steak-and-potatoes meal. The Worcestershire Compound Butter can be made well in advance, and the pancakes can be made early in the day and reheated in a 300-degree oven for about 10 minutes before serving. Put the asparagus in to roast while you prepare the steaks, call your guests into the kitchen, pour a great glass of red wine, and get the talk going as you pull it all together.

6 8-ounce sirloin steaks
Cracked black pepper and coarse salt
¼ cup clarified butter (see page 7)
Shrimp-Potatoes Pancakes (recipe follows)

6 ½-inch-thick slices Worcestershire Compound Butter (recipe follows)
Roasted Asparagus (recipe follows)

Generously coat each steak in cracked pepper and salt.

Heat the butter in a large, heavy-duty frying pan over medium-high heat. (You will probably need two pans to fry the steaks without crowding.) When the pan is very hot, add the steaks and fry, turning once, for about 10 minutes, or until the outside is nicely browned and crisp and the inside is medium-rare. Remove from the heat.

Place two Shrimp-Potato Pancakes in the center of each of six dinner plates. Place a steak on top of the pancakes on each plate. Top each steak with a slice of compound butter, place an equal portion of the asparagus at the side, and serve.

Shrimp-Potato Pancakes

2 large Idaho potatoes, peeled and grated
3 shallots, minced
1 large egg
3 ounces shrimp, peeled, deveined, and chopped

Coarse salt and freshly ground black pepper
Approximately ¼ cup clarified butter (see page 7) or vegetable oil

Combine the grated potatoes with the shallots and egg in a medium bowl, stirring to blend well. Add the shrimp and season the mixture with salt and pepper.

Heat the butter (or oil) in a large, nonstick sauté pan over medium-high heat. Spoon about 2 to 3 tablespoons of the potato mixture into the pan, pushing down slightly to form neat, pancake shapes. Continue forming pancakes without crowding the pan. You will need 12 pancakes to complete the dish.

Fry the pancakes, turning them frequently, for about 10 minutes, or until golden brown on both sides and cooked through. If necessary, lower the heat to keep the pancakes from burning before the potatoes are cooked.

Using a slotted spatula, transfer the pancakes to a double layer of paper towels to drain. Serve warm.

Worcestershire Compound Butter

½ cup Worcestershire sauce
1 tablespoon sugar

1 cup (2 sticks) unsalted butter, at room temperature

Combine the Worcestershire sauce and sugar in a small nonstick saucepan over medium-high heat. Bring the sauce to a boil; then lower the heat and cook it at a bare simmer for about 10 minutes, or until the mixture is syrupy. Remove it from the heat and set it aside to cool.

Place the butter in the bowl of a food processor fitted with the metal blade. Add 2 tablespoons of the cooled Worcestershire syrup and process it until well blended.

Place a large piece of plastic wrap on the countertop. Using a rubber spatula, scrape the butter mixture into the center of the plastic wrap. Wrap the plastic up and over the butter to enclose it completely. Roll the butter into a cylinder, twisting the ends together to seal. Place it in the refrigerator for at least 1 hour to firm it up before cutting it into slices. (The butter may also be wrapped in freezer wrap, labeled, and frozen for up to 3 months.)

Roasted Asparagus

2 pounds asparagus, trimmed
2 tablespoons extra virgin olive oil
Coarse salt and freshly ground black pepper

Preheat the oven to 400 degrees.

Break off the woody stem ends of the asparagus. Use a paring knife to neaten the ends. If the stalks are very large and tough, peel off the outer layer.

Place the asparagus on a nonstick baking pan. Add the olive oil and salt and pepper to taste and toss the asparagus to coat well. Place them in the preheated oven and roast them for about 20 minutes, or until they are nicely colored and cooked through. Remove the asparagus from the oven and serve them either warm or at room temperature.

Sirloin and Horseradish Knish with Mustard-Russian Sauce

SERVES 2

A knish is the quintessential New York street food. There is nothing like a piping hot, potato knish with a big scoop of deli mustard straight off the vendor's cart. But beyond being great street food, a knish is a wonderfully savory handheld, filled, square pastry made by wrapping a thin dough around either mashed potato, kasha (buckwheat groats), ground meat, or a combination of all three. Knishes come from Eastern Europe and made their way to America with the Jewish migration of the early 1900s. In New York, the most famous knishery is Yonah Schimmel's, which was founded by a Romanian rabbi of the same name via a Lower-East-Side pushcart in the late 1800s. It developed into a store in 1910. Rabbi Schimmel's descendants operate in the same location, selling hundreds of knishes daily. I have never encountered a knish outside of New York except in a couple of delicatessens in Florida and California. So if you want to be the first on your block to introduce knishes to the neighborhood, try my take on the original.

1½ cups Mashed Potatoes (see page 88)

¾ cup finely diced sirloin steak

⅓ cup grated white Cheddar or Monterey
Jack cheese

2 tablespoons bottled horseradish, well
drained

1 tablespoon finely chopped fresh chives

2 large eggs

¾ cup all-purpose flour

Salt and freshly ground black pepper

Approximately 1½ cups fresh white bread
crumbs

2 tablespoons water

Approximately ½ cup peanut oil

Mustard-Russian Sauce (recipe follows)

> NOTE: Alternately, you can fry the knishes in approximately ¼ cup of clarified butter
> for about 4 minutes, turning once, and then place them in a preheated 350 degree
> oven for about 7 to 10 minutes to finish cooking. Serve as below.

Line a baking sheet with parchment paper and set aside.

Place the potatoes, sirloin, and cheese in a medium mixing bowl. Add the horseradish and chives and, using a wooden spoon, stir to combine. Beat in 1 egg. Add ½ cup of the all-purpose flour and beat to blend well. Season with salt and pepper. If the mixture seems very damp, add bread crumbs to firm it up. It should be quite dense.

Form the mixture into balls weighing approximately 6 to 8 ounces. Shape each ball into a hockey puck–like form and place it onto the prepared baking sheet. When finished, cover the baking sheet with plastic wrap and refrigerate the knishes for 45 minutes to allow them to firm up.

Place the remaining egg in a shallow soup bowl, and whisk in the water until well blended.

Place the remaining flour on one plate and the bread crumbs on another larger plate.

Remove the knishes from the refrigerator. Dredge each one in the flour; then dip them into the egg wash to coat well, shaking off any excess. Finally, roll each one in the bread crumbs until well coated. Return the knishes to the baking sheet.

Place the oil in a large frying pan over medium heat. When very hot but not smoking, add the knishes and fry, turning occasionally, for about 10 minutes, or until they are golden brown and crisp and the center is hot. Using a slotted spatula, remove the knishes from the hot oil and place them on a double layer of paper towels to drain. Serve hot with the Mustard-Russian Sauce.

Mustard-Russian Sauce

2 cups mayonnaise

½ cup ketchup

1 tablespoon whole-grain mustard

Coarse salt and freshly ground black pepper

Combine the mayonnaise, ketchup, and whole-grain mustard in a small bowl. Whisk the mixture together to combine. Taste and, if necessary, adjust the seasoning with additional salt and pepper. Cover and refrigerate the sauce until you are ready to use it.

ROAST PRIME RIB OF BEEF

Not many cooks put a standing rib roast on the table anymore, but it remains a simple and spectacular meal. All you need to do is to season the roast with salt and pepper and throw a goodly amount of vegetables into the pan to roast along with the meat. A rib roast is, without doubt, well worth its notable expense, and it is expensive. You will need a three-rib roast to feed six people.

In old butcher's lore, the first three ribs are supposed to be the best and consequently gave the name "prime rib" to a three-rib roast. Often, when ordering "prime rib" in a restaurant you will be asked if you want it "American-cut or English." You can almost guess that the American would be one thick slice and the English a couple of thin slices. With either cut, the meat is usually cut away from the bone before being sliced into serving pieces.

I like to think that a standing rib can be made economical since I always use the bones to make Deviled Beef Bones. This is nothing more than the leftover rib bones covered in a mustard–bread crumb coating and roasted to a crisp finish. There is just enough meat left on the bones to make for great gnawing. If you think ahead, cut the ends from the ribs to make short ribs (not quite as meaty as those cut from the chuck) that can be cooked up to a deliciously rich stewlike concoction. The French, ever mindful of economy in the kitchen, always serve a rib roast boned and rolled, leaving the ribs for other meals.

CLASSIC

Roast Prime Rib with Gratin Potato

SERVES 6

This is a true classic. A standing rib roast used to be *the* Sunday dinner, often with roasted vegetables and Yorkshire pudding, but it is rarely served anymore. This is partly because families don't gather for a big weekend meal the way that they did when I was a child, partly because we don't eat red meat the way we once did and partly because there are no corner butchers showcasing prime meats in their windows. If you have never cooked this traditional meal, this is the time to give it a try.

5 stalks celery

3 large onions, cut crosswise into 1-inch-thick rings

3 large carrots, cut into ¼-inch-thick sticks

6 cloves peeled garlic

1 bay leaf

¼ cup olive oil

5-pound prime beef rib roast, trimmed of excess fat

Coarse salt and coarse black pepper

Gratin Potato (recipe follows)

Preheat the oven to 500 degrees.

Place the celery, onions, and carrots in the bottom of a roasting pan. Stir in the garlic, bay leaf, and olive oil, stirring until the vegetables are nicely coated. Generously season the roast with salt and pepper and place it on top of the seasoned vegetables. Place in the preheated oven and roast for 15 minutes, or just until the meat is beginning to brown. Lower the heat to 425 degrees and continue roasting for 30 minutes (or perhaps a bit longer), or until an instant-read thermometer inserted into the center reads 120 degrees for rare. Remove from the oven and allow the meat to rest for 15 minutes. Remove and discard the bay leaf. Carve the meat at the table and serve with a wedge of Gratin Potato and the roasted vegetables.

Gratin Potato

2 tablespoons softened butter

2 tablespoons minced fresh chervil

1 tablespoon minced fresh thyme

1 tablespoon minced fresh tarragon

1 tablespoon minced fresh chives	Coarse salt and freshly ground black pepper
4 cups heavy cream	6 large Idaho potatoes
2 tablespoons Roasted Garlic Purée	4 cups grated Gruyère cheese
(see page 12)	½ cup freshly grated Parmesan cheese

Preheat the oven to 375 degrees.

Lightly coat a 10-inch-oval casserole dish with the softened butter. Set aside.

Combine the chervil, thyme, tarragon, and chives in a small bowl. Set aside.

Combine the cream and garlic purée with salt and pepper to taste in a medium saucepan over medium heat. Bring the mixture to a boil and immediately remove from the heat. Keep warm.

Peel the potatoes and cut them lengthwise into ¼-inch-thick slices on a mandoline or Japanese vegetable slicer. Ladle ½ cup of the warm cream mixture into the bottom of the prepared casserole. Working quickly, make a ring of slightly overlapping potato slices around the perimeter of the prepared casserole. Continue making slightly overlapping potato rings until the bottom of the dish is entirely covered with potatoes. Lightly season the top with salt and pepper. Sprinkle 1 tablespoon of the reserved herb mixture over the seasoning. Using 1 cup of the grated Gruyère, make a thin layer of cheese over the potatoes. Ladle 1 cup of cream over all of it. Continue making layers of potatoes, seasoning, herbs, cheese, and the cream mixture until you have made 3 additional layers. Finish with a layer of Parmesan. Cover the entire casserole with aluminum foil and place in the preheated oven. Bake, covered, for 1 hour, or until a toothpick is easily inserted into the center. Remove the foil and bake for an additional 10 minutes, or until the top is golden brown. Remove the gratin from the oven and allow to rest for 15 minutes to firm up before cutting into serving pieces.

CONTEMPORARY

Roasted Spice-Crusted Rib with Wild Mushroom-Vegetable Stew, Horseradish-Mustard Mousse, and Popovers

SERVES 6

This is a traditional dish with a real kick. The cumin, pepper, and cayenne really make a strong statement against the rich red meat. The Popovers and mushroom stew add a bit of sweet earthiness and the mousse brings it all together. The stew, the Popovers, and the mousse can be made early in the day. Reheat the Popovers before serving. This is a great dish for entertaining.

½ cup plus 2 tablespoons ground cumin

6 tablespoons coarse ground black pepper

6 tablespoons plus 1 teaspoon cayenne pepper

5-pound prime beef rib roast, trimmed of excess fat

Coarse salt

2 tablespoons unsalted butter

1 onion, finely diced

1 carrot, finely diced

1 stalk celery, finely diced

2 pounds button, shiitake, or portobello mushrooms, wiped clean, stems removed, and sliced

¼ cup Madeira

2 tablespoons all-purpose flour

2 cups boiling chicken stock

Freshly ground black pepper

Popovers (recipe follows)

Horseradish-Mustard Mousse (recipe follows)

Preheat the oven to 425 degrees.

Combine the cumin and black pepper with the 6 tablespoons of the cayenne pepper in a small bowl. Generously coat the entire outside of the roast with the spice mixture and salt. Place the seasoned roast on a wire rack in a roasting pan and roast in the preheated oven for 40 minutes, or until an instant-read thermometer inserted into the center reads 120 degrees. (Check the roast from time to time. If the spice crust starts to burn, cover the roast with aluminum foil and continue roasting it for the desired time.) Remove the roast from the oven and allow it to rest for 15 minutes before carving. Raise the oven temperature to 500 degrees.

While the meat is roasting, prepare the stew. Melt the butter in a large, shallow saucepan (a rondeau is perfect) over medium heat. Add the onion, carrot, and celery and sauté for about 6 minutes, or just until the onion is translucent. Stir in the mushrooms and sauté for an additional 5 minutes. Add the Madeira and stir to deglaze the pan. Raise the heat and cook for about 5 minutes, or until there is about 1 tablespoon of liquid left in the pan. Using a wooden spoon, vigorously stir in the flour, making sure that no lumps form. Cook the mixture, stirring constantly, for 5 minutes. Stir in the boiling chicken stock and bring to a simmer. Season to taste with salt and pepper. Lower the heat and simmer for about 10 minutes, or until the flavors are nicely blended and the sauce is thick. Remove from the heat and tent lightly with aluminum foil to keep warm until ready to serve.

Slice the roast into serving pieces. Place a portion of the roast at the bottom of each of six dinner plates. Cut a hole in the top of each Popover and place one at the top of each plate. Fill each Popover with some of the mushroom stew. Spoon a quenelle (a small oval easily formed between 2 teaspoons) of the Horseradish-Mustard Mousse on top of the meat and serve immediately.

Popovers

1 tablespoon unsalted butter, softened
3 large eggs
1¼ cups milk
1 tablespoon melted unsalted butter
1 tablespoon mixed, minced, fresh herbs

such as parsley, chervil, tarragon
and chives
1 cup all-purpose flour
½ teaspoon salt

Preheat the oven to 450 degrees.

Using the softened butter, generously coat six 6-ounce ramekins or large muffin cups. Set aside.

Combine the eggs, milk, melted butter, and herbs in a medium mixing bowl. Whisk together to blend.

Combine the flour and salt in a separate bowl. Pour the egg mixture over the flour and, using a wooden spoon, mix together until well blended. Fill the prepared ramekins or muffin cups three-quarters full. Place the filled ramekins on a baking sheet in the preheated oven and bake for 15 minutes. Lower the oven temperature to 350 degrees and continue to bake the Popovers for an additional 20 minutes, or until they are golden brown and beautifully puffed. Remove them from the oven and serve warm.

Horseradish-Mustard Mousse

2 cups crème fraîche
2 tablespoons bottled horseradish,
   well-drained

1 tablespoon Dijon mustard
1½ teaspoons coarse salt
¼ teaspoon freshly ground black pepper

Place the crème fraîche in a chilled, stainless steel mixing bowl and whisk vigorously until soft peaks form. Whisk in the horseradish, mustard, salt, and pepper to taste and continue whisking until the mousse is slightly firm. Taste and, if necessary, adjust the seasoning with additional salt and pepper. Cover the mousse with plastic wrap and refrigerate until you are ready to use it.

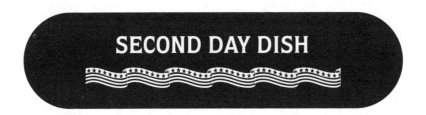

SECOND DAY DISH

Red Chili in a Potato Boat with Minced Crisp Onion

SERVES 2

This is a very easy way to put together a satisfying chili meal. If you don't have time to make the Tomato Sauce you could use tomato purée and some fresh basil or a commercial sauce, but I must warn you, the taste will not be as mellow. Since this is such an easy sauce to make and is so useful, it's a good idea to make a double amount and freeze it. Although this is one of my favorite Second Day Dishes, you could also make it with a freshly purchased ground beef or turkey, which you should fry before adding to the pot.

1 medium sweet onion, sliced crosswise, paper-thin
1 large Idaho potato, scrubbed
Approximately 1 tablespoon vegetable oil
1 cup Wondra flour (see page 70)
2 tablespoons chili powder
2 teaspoons cayenne pepper
Coarse salt

¼ pound slab bacon, diced
¼ cup water
1½ cups Tomato Sauce (recipe follows)
½ pound diced Roast Prime Rib, finely chopped (see page 130)
¼ cup finely sliced scallions, with some green parts
Freshly ground black pepper to taste

Preheat the oven to 350 degrees.

Pull the onion rings apart and place them on a nonstick baking sheet and into the preheated oven. Bake them for 20 minutes, or until they are dry and crisp. Remove the onions from the oven and set aside.

Place the potato in the preheated oven and bake it for 40 minutes, or just until it can be pierced with a toothpick. Remove the potato from the oven and split it in half lengthwise. Using a tablespoon, carefully scoop out the flesh leaving a ⅛-inch-thick shell. Set the shells aside and reserve the flesh for another use. Do not turn off the oven.

Using a pastry brush, lightly coat the potato boats with vegetable oil.

Combine the Wondra flour with 1 tablespoon chili powder, 1 teaspoon cayenne, and salt to taste. Roll the oiled potato boats in the flour mixture, coating all sides well. Place the seasoned potato boats on a nonstick baking pan and bake them in the preheated oven for about 15 minutes, or until they are nicely colored and slightly crisp. Remove them from the oven and set aside.

Place the bacon in a large saucepan over medium heat. Add the water and fry, stirring occasionally, for about 7 minutes, or until the bacon is slightly crisp and brown. Stir in the Tomato Sauce and beef along with the remaining 1 tablespoon chili powder and 1 teaspoon cayenne and bring the mixture to a simmer. Simmer for 10 minutes. Stir in the scallions. Taste and, if necessary, adjust the seasoning with more salt and pepper. Ladle a generous portion of the chili into each potato boat. Garnish with the reserved onions and serve.

Tomato Sauce

1 tablespoon olive oil
1 large onion, finely diced
1 clove garlic, thinly sliced
4 cups canned tomato purée

1 tightly packed cup fresh basil leaves, chopped
Coarse salt and freshly ground black pepper

Heat the oil in a medium saucepan over medium heat. Add the onion and garlic and allow them to sweat, stirring frequently, for about 10 minutes, or until the onion is translucent but has not taken on any color. Add the tomato purée and one-half of the basil and bring the mixture to a simmer. Immediately lower the heat and cook slowly, stirring frequently, for about 40 minutes, or until about 90 percent of the liquid has evaporated. Stir in the remaining basil and season the sauce to taste with salt and pepper. Remove the sauce from the heat and allow it to cool. You can store the sauce, covered and refrigerated, for up to 5 days, or covered, labeled, and frozen for up to 3 months.

POT ROAST

What a great deal for the cook (and the dishwasher)—everything in one pot. Since the meat is usually a fairly large piece of one of the less expensive cuts, it is economical, too. A perfect family meal.

Pot roasts can be made with almost any braising liquid and with the addition of almost any flavor. The addition of vegetables to the pot makes a Yankee Pot Roast (see page 137) while the type of seasoning determines the regional flavor. Add some red wine and leeks and it's French; tomatoes and basil and serve with Chianti; soy and ginger, bring out the chopsticks; chilies and beer, top with taco chips.

Unlike most cooks, I always choose a brisket because I think it is one of the most flavorful cuts of beef and keeps its shape and texture over a long, slow braise. Brisket is the flesh that runs along the breast, quite fatty when left untrimmed. It is the cut used for the traditional New England boiled dinner as well as for corned beef. When well trimmed, it is quite lean and that is what I use for pot roast. You can, of course, use other cuts in my recipes. You just might need to adjust the cooking times as the brisket is somewhat thinner than most other roasts that are cooked with moist heat.

The most important things to remember when making a pot roast are: Always sear all sides to create a nice brown crust; keep the braising liquid to a minimum (you don't want to drown the meat); cover the pot and cook the meat slowly, on top of the stove on a low flame that produces a bare simmer. Or cook it in the oven at a low temperature that will just keep the liquid at the edges of the pot bubbling slightly. When the cooking is done, the meat should be extremely tender but should not fall apart when poked with a fork.

Yankee Pot Roast with Brown Bread Dumplings and Melted Vegetables

SERVES 6

This traditional pot roast is really enhanced by the dumplings. Technically, a pot roast can only be called "Yankee" when vegetables are added to the pot at some point during the cooking process, which I do here. I give the vegetables a final roast to put a beautiful glaze on them.

1 sprig fresh thyme

1 sprig fresh parsley

6 black peppercorns

2 tablespoons peanut oil

1 5-pound beef brisket

Coarse salt and freshly ground black pepper to taste

1 cup red wine

6 stalks celery, trimmed and cut in half lengthwise and then crosswise

3 carrots, peeled, cut into ¼-inch-thick sticks

3 heads garlic, broken into cloves and peeled

2 onions, julienned

16 to 24 cups beef stock (or water)

1 large ripe tomato, peeled, cored, and quartered

Brown Bread Dumplings (recipe follows)

Preheat the oven to 350 degrees.

Make a bouquet garni by placing the thyme, parsley, and peppercorns in a small piece of cheesecloth. Bring the corners of the cheesecloth together and, using kitchen twine, tie the cheesecloth into a small bag or sachet. Set aside.

Heat the oil in a Dutch oven over medium heat. Season the beef with salt and pepper and place it in the Dutch oven. Sear the meat, turning it occasionally, for about 12 minutes, or until all sides have browned. Pour off any excess oil. Add the wine and, using a wooden spoon, stir to deglaze the pot and lift up any browned bits clinging to the bottom of it. Add the celery, carrots, garlic, and onions and stir to distribute the vegetables evenly in the Dutch oven. Add the stock (or water) and tomato along with reserved bouquet garni and salt and pepper. Bring the mixture to a boil; then immediately cover and place it in the preheated oven. Braise the meat for about 90 minutes, or until it is extremely tender and almost ready to fall apart when pierced with a fork. Remove the pot from the oven. Do not turn off the oven.

Uncover and carefully transfer the meat to a serving platter. Tent the meat lightly with aluminum foil to keep it warm.

Using a slotted spoon, carefully transfer the vegetables to a nonstick baking sheet. Place the baking sheet in the preheated oven and roast the vegetables for 15 minutes, or until they are nicely glazed.

Place the Dutch oven over medium heat. Remove and discard the bouquet garni. Bring the gravy to a boil and boil it for about 10 minutes, or until it has thickened slightly and formed a nice glaze. Remove the pot from the heat and return the meat to the gravy. Spoon the gravy over the top of the meat and then return the meat to the serving platter. Carefully transfer the vegetables to the serving platter. Serve, family style, carving the meat at the table and passing the gravy and Brown Bread Dumplings on the side.

Brown Bread Dumplings

¼ cup (½ stick) unsalted butter, softened

1 cup diced onions

1 pound pumpernickel bread, crusts removed, and cubed

1½ cups heavy cream

3 small eggs

1 teaspoon coarse salt to taste

Freshly ground pepper to taste

Using 2 tablespoons of the butter, lightly coat the insides of twelve 2-ounce ramekins. Set aside.

Preheat the oven to 350 degrees.

Heat the remaining butter in a small sauté pan over medium heat. Add the onions and sauté them for about 5 minutes, or until the onions are soft and have sweat off most of their liquid. Remove them from the heat and set aside.

Place the bread in a large mixing bowl. Whisk together the cream and eggs and pour the mixture over the cubed bread. Add the onions and salt along with pepper and toss to combine. Generously pack the mixture into the prepared ramekins. Place the ramekins into a baking pan large enough to hold them, leaving at least an inch between each ramekin. Fill the pan with hot water to halfway up the sides of the ramekins. Place the entire pan in the preheated oven and bake for 20 minutes, or until the dumplings are set and their tops are slightly dry. Remove them from the oven and carefully tip each dumpling from the ramekin. Serve hot.

Asian-Style Pot Roast

SERVES 6

This is cooked in the traditional pot roast manner, but the flavors are Asian. I think you will find the dish very aromatic with only a hint of heat. If you don't want to bother with the fancy cut-out vegetables, feel free to throw some diced veggies into the pot.

1 1-inch piece fresh ginger, peeled
   and crushed
5 cloves garlic, peeled
3 scallions, white part only, chopped
3 star anise
3 whole cloves
1 stick cinnamon
1 tablespoon fennel seeds
1 tablespoon coriander seeds
1 tablespoon allspice berries
1 tablespoon white peppercorns
½ cup peanut oil
1 5-pound beef brisket

Coarse salt and freshly ground black
   pepper
1 cup Chinese rice wine (or red wine)
16 cups beef stock (or a combination
   of stock and water)
1 cup soy sauce
2 large daikon, peeled and cut into
   a medium dice
2 large carrots, cut into a medium dice
1 large turnip, peeled and cut into
   a medium dice
2 large Yukon Gold potatoes, peeled and
   cut into medium dice (optional)

Tie the crushed ginger, garlic, scallions, star anise, cloves, cinnamon stick, fennel seeds, coriander seeds, allspice berries, and peppercorns in a cheesecloth bag. Set aside.

Heat the peanut oil in a Dutch oven over medium heat until smoking. Season the beef with salt and pepper and place it in the Dutch oven. Sear it, turning frequently, for about 12 minutes, or until all sides have browned. Carefully lift the meat from the pot and drain off any excess oil.

Return the pan to medium-high heat, add the rice wine, and stir to deglaze. Add the stock and soy sauce along with the reserved spice bag and bring the mixture to a boil. Return the meat to the pot along with the daikon, carrots, turnip and, if you are using them, the potatoes. Bring to a simmer. Simmer for about 90 minutes, or until the meat is very tender when pierced with the point of a small sharp knife. Remove the meat and vegetables from the pot and place them on a platter. Tent lightly with aluminum foil to keep warm.

Raise the heat to high and bring the cooking liquid to a boil. Boil it for about 10 minutes, or until it is slightly glazed in appearance. Remove the spice bag from the gravy and pour the gravy into a gravy boat or other serving bowl.

Serve the meat and vegetables, family style, with the gravy passed on the side.

Pot Roast Sloppy Joes

SERVES 2

Now here is a great Sloppy Joe. It may make for messy eating, but to me it's a gourmet meal. All you need is plenty of napkins and a beverage of choice.

½ tablespoon olive oil

1 jalapeño, stemmed, seeded, and cut
   crosswise into thin slices

2 tablespoons finely diced red onion

2 tablespoons finely diced red bell pepper

2 tablespoons finely diced green bell pepper

1½ cups cooked shredded pot roast

¾ cup Barbecue Sauce (see page 96)

2 tablespoons water, optional

1 tablespoon sliced scallions

2 hot dog buns, toasted

2 slices Cheddar cheese

Heat the oil in a large saucepan over medium heat. Add the jalapeño and onion and allow them to sweat for about 4 minutes, or just until the onion is translucent. Stir in the bell peppers and sweat for an additional 2 minutes. Stir in the pot roast, Barbecue Sauce, and water and bring the mixture to a simmer. Lower the heat to a bare simmer and cook, stirring constantly, for 15 minutes, or until the mixture is very thick. Stir in the scallions. Scoop the mixture into the hot dog buns and place a slice of cheese on top. Close the buns over the meat and cheese and serve.

MEATLOAF

When working in France with the great restaurateurs Marc Meneau and Pierre Troisgros and later in the kitchens of Fauchon in Paris, I learned much about the evolution of many of the classic French dishes that I was learning to prepare. My French was poor but that didn't stop me from asking questions.

Pâté was one word with which I was quite familiar, but I didn't know much of the history of the dish. It began, I learned, as a royal dish of finely chopped meat or fish (forcemeat) encased in pastry and baked. As pâtés moved from the regal kitchens to everyday life, the recipes were simplified. The forcemeat lost its crust and was baked in an earthenware dish (a terrine). In their beginnings, a pâté and a terrine, although made of similar ingredients, were distinguished from one another by the fact that a pâté could be served hot or cold while a terrine was always served cold. Once a pâté was baked in a terrine, the terms were used almost interchangeably.

From pâtés and terrines evolved *tourtes*. These simple dishes, prepared in a circular shape, were comprised of a mixture of forcemeat baked in crust. Then, new terms evolved: a pâté baked in a rectangular loaf without a crust was called a *pain de viande* (meat bread), since it was baked in the shape of a loaf of bread, and a pâté baked in a circular shape was called a *gâteau de viandes* (meat cake), since it was baked in the traditional round shape of a cake. The language of the French kitchen was, if nothing else, specific in its terminology. From these classic French dishes evolved many of the meat loaves, savory pies, and sausages of other cuisines. And that includes good old-fashioned American meatloaf.

A true American kitchen classic, meatloaf is made of finely ground veal, beef and/or pork and, more recently, ground chicken or turkey, and baked, usually, in a rectangular, loaf shape. Everyone seems to have a favorite recipe, frequently handed down in a family, even if they have not made a loaf in years. People see it as comfort food and not for entertaining. I beg to differ.

Although American meatloaf probably evolved from the traditional English-based savory pie fillings of colonial times, it nonetheless has, in its family tree, the pâtés and terrines that I learned in France. The signs of a good meatloaf are similar to those of a pâté—

chopped meat(s), fine seasoning, just a little filler to cement the whole, and a moist texture. A great meatloaf also features an added hint of intrigue in the form of a special ingredient, unusual garnish, and/or a unique shape and presentation. This kind of meatloaf will move from the family table to a dinner-party menu.

The very simplicity of the ingredients allows you to make a loaf that can take many guises: a potato crust, a juicy bed of croutons, a shiny glaze, a garnish of roasted garlic cloves, some vegetable confetti. You can make one big loaf of any form or individual 4-ounce servings. Meatloaf can be made and frozen, well wrapped, for baking at a later date.

As I began to develop some new versions of the classic meatloaf, I first devised a true loaf: one that derived from the *pain de viande* with a little touch of the classic, cold appetizer, *pâté de campagne.* Since a *pâté de campagne* is often eaten with a crusty piece of bread or toast or as a topping for a simple baguette sandwich, I baked the loaf on a bed of croutons. The croutons lustily soaked up the meat juices, creating a juicy, sandwichlike melange.

To the basic meat and bread combo, I added some aromatic garnish with unpeeled garlic cloves cooked into the top of the meatloaf, lending their fragrance and sweet heat. Bay leaves and thyme, randomly inserted into the loaf, plied their gentle scent and mellow pungency. At serving time, the garlic cloves popped right out of their roasted skin to make a self-contained condiment for the sliced meatloaf.

But then, I thought, what is meat without potatoes? Taking my cue from the roasted garlic, I whipped up a batch of garlic-mashed potatoes. Then, I piped the aromatic potatoes onto the serving platter, making elegant rosettes around the meatloaf. I added a great green salad to properly round out the meal.

Not-So-Basic Meatloaf

SERVES 6

This is my idea of a great meatloaf, perfectly-seasoned, carrying a hint of aromatic intrigue from the Barbecue Sauce (see page 96), horseradish, and bay leaves, and innovatingly garnished. When you transfer the meatloaf to its serving platter, make sure to take all of the croutons too. They will have absorbed the flavorful juices that cooked out of the meatloaf

Roast Half Turkey
with Bread Pudding,
Chestnut-Turkey
Cappuccino, and
Candied Lemon Peel
(Contemporary)

Cracked Pepper Sirloin
with Shrimp-Potato Pancakes
and Roasted Asparagus
(Contemporary)

Roast Prime Rib with
Gratin Potato
(Classic)

Asian-Style Pot Roast
(Contemporary)

Meatloaf Bundt Cake
(Contemporary)

Meatloaf Pancakes
with Goat Cheese Salad
and Fried Eggs
(Second Day Dish)

Rack of Lamb with
Bouquet of Vegetables
(Classic)

Braised Lamb Shank
with Cauliflower-
Rosemary Purée
(Contemporary)

and complete the texture and taste of the dish. Serve with Mashed Potatoes (see page 88) and a lively green salad.

5 strips lean bacon, finely chopped
6 cloves garlic, minced
2 medium onions, finely chopped
1 medium carrot, finely chopped
2 pounds very lean ground beef sirloin
2 large eggs
½ cup milk
1 cup finely ground fresh bread crumbs
¼ cup Dijon mustard
¼ cup Barbecue Sauce (see page 96)
1 tablespoon bottled horseradish, well
    drained

½ cup finely chopped fresh flat-leaf
    parsley
2 tablespoons coarse salt
1 tablespoon freshly ground black
    pepper
1 teaspoon finely minced fresh thyme
    (or ¼ teaspoon dried thyme)
2 to 3 cups croutons
10 whole, unpeeled, garlic cloves
4 bay leaves
1 sprig fresh thyme

NOTE: I prefer to slightly precook any vegetables that I will be adding to a meatloaf so that they can more readily release all of their flavor into the loaf as it bakes. You can also double the amount of vegetables and reserve half of them to spoon around the meatloaf before serving.

If serving with Mashed Potatoes, spoon the potatoes onto the platter before sprinkling with the parsley.

Preheat the oven to 375 degrees.

Place the bacon in a medium sauté pan over medium-low heat. Sauté the bacon for about 5 minutes, or until it has begun to crisp and most of the fat has rendered out. Add the garlic, onion, and carrot and continue to sauté for about 4 minutes, or until the vegetables are soft and the onions are translucent but have not taken on any color. Remove the pan from the heat and allow the vegetables to cool (see Note).

Place the ground sirloin into a large mixing bowl. Add the eggs and milk and, using your hands, work the liquid into the meat. Add the bread crumbs and continue to work the liquid and crumbs into the meat. Add the cooled vegetables, mustard, Barbecue Sauce, and horseradish along with ¼ cup of the parsley, salt, pepper, and thyme. Using your hands, gently work all of the ingredients into the meat until well combined.

Place one-half of the croutons into a shallow baking dish at least 14 inches long.

Transfer the meatloaf mixture onto a clean, flat surface and, again, using your hands, shape it into a loaf about 3½ inches wide × 2½ inches high × 12 inches long (or into a round, breadlike form, a letter of the alphabet, an oval, or into several small loaves). Press the remaining croutons into the loaf, making sure that they are partially pressed down into it. Gently press the unpeeled garlic cloves into the top of the meatloaf. Carefully lay the loaf on top of the croutons in the baking dish (you might need to use a couple of spatulas to facilitate this), reforming the shape with your hands, if necessary. Pierce the meatloaf with the bay leaves and thyme sprig. Place the meatloaf in the preheated oven and bake for 1 hour, or until the internal temperature reads 165 degrees on an instant-read thermometer and the top is nicely browned.

Remove the pan from the oven. Allow the meatloaf to rest for about 5 minutes before transferring it to a serving platter. Remove the bay leaves and thyme sprig and sprinkle the remaining parsley over the top of the loaf and around the platter. Cut crosswise into 1-inch, or thicker, slices and serve.

CONTEMPORARY

Meatloaf Bundt Cake

SERVES 6

In the French kitchen, a *tourte* is a savory pie or tart that it almost always round in shape. Here, working with the classic requirements of a savory dish prepared in a *tourtière* (round pan), I have created an all-American, meat-and-potatoes meal using prepared croissant dough for a Gallic twist. This also makes a great Second Day Dish served at room temperature.

1 tablespoon olive oil	1 cup canned diced tomatoes, well drained
2 cloves garlic, minced	1 cup finely diced Jalapeño Jack cheese
1 large onion, finely diced	4 large eggs
½ cup finely diced celery	2 cups bread crumbs
1 pound lean ground beef	Coarse salt and freshly ground black
1 cup Barbecue Sauce (see page 96)	pepper

<table>
<tr><td>2 tubes commercially prepared, frozen croissant dough, thawed</td><td>4 cups commercially prepared croutons</td></tr>
<tr><td></td><td>1 tablespoon poppy seeds</td></tr>
</table>

Heat the oil in a medium sauté pan over medium heat. Add the garlic, onion, and celery and sauté them for about 4 minutes, or just until the vegetables have softened but not taken on any color. Remove them from the heat and set them aside to cool.

Preheat the oven to 325 degrees.

Place the ground meat in a large mixing bowl. Add the Barbecue Sauce, tomatoes, and cheese along with the reserved aromatics and 3 of the eggs. Using your fingers, begin to lightly mash the mixture together. Add the bread crumbs, season with salt and pepper, and continue to blend the mixture together without breaking up the cheese.

Form the croissant dough into 2-inch round balls. Set aside.

To make an egg wash, whisk the remaining egg with a tablespoon of water in a small mixing bowl. Set aside.

Lightly spray the interior of a nonstick bundt pan with nonstick vegetable spray. Nestle the croutons into the bottom of the pan, making sure they are evenly distributed in a tight, single layer. Press the meat mixture over the croutons in the pan. Cover the meat with a single layer of croissant balls. Using a pastry brush, lightly coat the croissant balls with the egg wash. Sprinkle the poppy seeds over the top.

Place the meatloaf in the preheated oven and bake it for about 45 minutes, or until an instant-read thermometer inserted into the center reads 145 degrees. Remove the loaf from the oven and allow it to rest for about 10 minutes before turning the "cake" out onto a serving platter. Using a serrated knife, cut the meatloaf into slices and serve.

SECOND DAY DISH

Meatloaf Pancakes with Goat Cheese Salad and Fried Eggs

SERVES 2

Meatloaf can be the basis for a Second Day Dish as simple as a baguette sandwich with Dijon mustard and cornichons. But here, my meatloaf sandwich begins with rich pancake batter.

I tried crêpe batter, but it was too delicate to handle the hearty meatloaf. I add a slightly tart goat cheese salad and a fried egg for the perfect meal at any time of the day.

2 large warm Buttermilk (or other plain breakfast) Pancakes (see page 14)

Approximately 1½ tablespoons melted, unsalted butter

2 large eggs

2 1-inch-thick slices Not-So-Basic Meatloaf (see page 142)

2 cups frisée

¼ cup crumbled fresh goat cheese

2 tablespoons Basic Vinaigrette (see page 61)

> NOTE: If you are making fresh pancake batter, you might want to add ½ cup of blanched, fresh corn kernels (or thawed and well-drained, frozen kernels) to it for extra texture and sweet flavor.
>
> If you have any cooked garlic cloves remaining with the meatloaf, peel and mash them into the batter for a savory pancake.
>
> If it is asparagus season, replace the salad with steamed fresh asparagus spears tossed with a little vinaigrette.

Preheat the oven to low.

Place the pancakes on a piece of aluminum foil in the warm oven.

Heat the butter in a medium, nonstick frying pan. When the butter is very hot but not smoking, add the eggs and fry according to your taste. (I prefer sunny-side up.)

Place one warm pancake in the center of each of two luncheon plates. Place a meatloaf slice on top of each pancake.

Place the frisée, goat cheese, and vinaigrette in a mixing bowl and quickly toss together. Place an equal portion on the top of each pancake. Lay a fried egg on top of each salad and serve immediately.

PORK

Did you know that pigs are thought to be the first wild animals to be domesticated by man? I would guess that was because pigs eat almost anything and are relatively docile when well fed, which, I'm sure, helps produce their usual bountiful twice-yearly litters. In Ireland, pigs were considered so important that farmers referred to them as "The Gentleman That Pays the Rent."

When I was a young cook working in France, I fell for one of the classic pork preparations, rillettes. These were and still are made in the fanciest restaurants and in the humblest homes. Rillettes are made from the cheapest cuts of pork (or rabbit, poultry, or game) that are cooked, long and very slowly, in seasoned fat. The meat is pulled apart or shredded and stored, tightly packed into crocks or terrines, preserved in its own fat. In the old days, every house had crocks of rillettes all year long. As long as the fat seal was not broken, the rillettes would keep for weeks and make a ready meal. Once the fat seal was opened, the rillettes required cold to keep them. Rillettes are not meant to be a main course but are served as you would any other cured meat, pâté, or terrine although in some households rillettes, a baguette, and some wine would constitute the meal.

Pork remains the most popular meat in the world. Prior to the Second World War, there were many uses for pig fat all over the world, from cooking to the manufacture of explosives, so the animals were bred to gigantic size with an emphasis on their fattiness. With a decrease in the demand for fat and an increase in health awareness, commercial breeders began to raise hogs that had meat rather than fat as a high percentage of the total weight. Within the past few years, the breeding patterns have continued to change with today's pork, "the new white meat," having less than 250 calories per serving with more protein and a minimal amount of fat and cholesterol. With this leaner meat comes less flavor and far less tenderness; I am sure breeders are working on that.

Prime pork meat is finely textured with a soft pale pink color. The fat should be very firm and almost stark white. Most pork in the market comes from pigs that are between six and nine months old unless it is labeled "suckling pig," which is slaughtered at about three weeks. It is butchered into many, many cuts ranging from holiday ham to everyday chops and breakfast bacon. Graded on a numbered system with No. 1 being the best available, and classified by age (suckling pigs: those up to four months and about 120 pounds, and hogs: those up to nine months and about 210 pounds), pork is not seasonal and is very economical, which is, in part, why it remains so popular.

Some of the cheaper cuts of pork, with a higher-fat content, are best cooked for a long period of time and served with starches or legumes to soak up the fattiness. The leaner cuts are best paired with fruits such as in the classic prune- or apricot-stuffed loin. Lean or fat, pork is often cooked in a rich lager or a dense cider, or on a bed of red cabbage or sweet turnips. In almost every cuisine, you will find an aromatic and substantial classic pork dish.

One of today's most often asked culinary questions is, How long should you cook pork. When I was a beginning cook, all pork was cooked to 185 degrees. Chefs and home cooks alike were terrified of trichinosis, a disease caused by the presence of trichinae (the larvae of parasitic worms) in the intestines and muscle tissues, which was caused by eating under-cooked meat from an infected hog. It was not unusual for chops to be cooked for over an hour, which, of course, left them dry and rubbery. It is now generally agreed that pork can be safely cooked to an internal temperature of 140 degrees. It is then recommended that the meat be allowed to sit for about 15 minutes during which time it continues to cook and will reach an internal temperature of about 155 degrees. This method leaves the meat juicy and tender and yet cooked to a degree of safety. However, the USDA still recommends that pork be cooked to an internal temperature of 160 degrees, so you must make that decision. It is helpful to know that through improvements in raising, butchering, and shipping pork, parasites are no longer the huge problem that they were years ago. Also remember that lean pork cooks much more quickly than the fatty pork of the past, so if you want to cook pork from an old recipe, be sure to adjust the time accordingly.

FRESH HAM

What is more evocative of a special family occasion than a big, beautiful candy-coated ham sitting on the sideboard ready to be carved? It is amazing that something so simple calls out "Celebration!" A ham is nothing more than the rear leg of a hog, cut from the aitchbone (hip bone) through to the meaty shank bone. Once eaten fresh or home-cured straight from a farm, there are now a number of types of ham readily available in supermarkets and through butchers and specialty food shops. The taste differential in ham is very dependent upon the type of hog the meat was cut from as well as the food it was fed. With cured hams, the type of cure will also affect the flavor tremendously; sometimes it is dry and salty, other times moist and sweet. And wild boar, available from specialty markets, has a very unique and intense flavor quite different from that of his corn-fed brethren. Finally, the herbs, spices, fruit, and/or liquid used in precooking, roasting, and basting the hams will add their stamp to the taste. Cured hams such as those that are brine cured, dry cured, or smoke cured are the ones with which we are now most familiar, but fresh (non-cured) hams are making a comeback, particularly in areas with a large Hispanic population.

Brine-cured hams are those that have been injected with a saline solution (usually water, salt, sodium nitrate, and nitrates) along with sugar and/or honey. Those that are dry-cured have a blended cure (usually salt, sodium nitrate, nitrites, and sugar) rubbed directly onto the surface of the ham and hung to allow the moisture to be drawn out and the flavor to intensify. Smoke-cured hams have been cured, but are then given some additional time in a smokehouse to continue the drying and aging. The type of wood used and the length of time smoked will strongly affect the final taste. Smoked-cured hams are usually the most expensive. Cured hams require either no cooking, such as for prosciutto, Westphalian, and Black Forest hams; minimal roasting, as for fully-cooked, spiral-cut, or canned hams; or specialized cooking, as for Smithfield or American country-style hams.

Fresh hams are just that. They have not had any type of cure or processing so that they require a goodly amount of time in the oven to roast through to the bone. A whole fresh ham can weigh up to fifteen pounds as it is comprised of both the butt and the shank sections. However, fresh hams are, like cured hams, sold bone-in or boneless, whole, half (shank or butt), or end (shank or butt) as well as cut into 1- to 3-inch-thick slices. Whether you get the whole or part really depends upon need and taste. Obviously the two separate sections offer a smaller piece of meat with the butt end meatier and the shank end bonier.

With a fresh ham, the herbs, spices, fruit and/or liquid used for precooking, roasting, and basting will impart even more flavor than they do with cured hams. The thick layer of external fat on a fresh ham should be very white and firm and the meat should be a rosy pink. The lean meat should be finely grained, well marbled with fat, and firm, and the bone should be porous and slightly pink. You will want to trim off the excess fat and rind but leave just enough of both to flavor the meat and create a crisp exterior during roasting. After roasting, the meat will be almost beige not the familiar bright pink of a cured ham. The taste, too, will be quite different, twice as moist but no less delicious.

Roast Fresh Ham with Pineapple Tarte Tatin

SERVES 6

This is a classic baked fresh ham recipe updated with the Pineapple Tartes Tatin that replace the pineapple rings, maraschino cherries, and cloves that are usually found garnishing the burnished meat. The *tartes* are beautiful and easy to make. However, you do need six 3-inch-round, nonstick, flat-bottomed molds to successfully make them. If you have an oversized, nonstick muffin tin, it will make a handy substitute for the molds. A great thing about a ham is that it almost always (unless feeding a big crowd) leaves a lot for Second-Day Dishes.

    1 14-pound fresh ham, trimmed of excess fat and rind (see Note)

    Coarse salt and freshly ground black pepper
    Pineapple Tarte Tatin (recipe follows)

> NOTE: Make sure that you leave about a ½-inch-thick layer of fat so that the outside can be nicely scored.

Preheat the oven to 375 degrees.

Generously season the ham with salt and pepper. Place the seasoned ham on a rack in a roasting pan. (It is important to place the ham on a rack so that the fat can drip off.) Roast the ham in the preheated oven, uncovered, for about 5½ hours, or until an instant-read thermometer inserted into the center of the ham near to but not touching the bone reads 160 degrees. Remove the ham from the oven and transfer it to a serving platter. Place the Pineapple Tartes Tatin on the platter and carve the ham, family style, at the table.

Pineapple Tarte Tatin

1 large pineapple	¼ cup plus 1 tablespoon water
3 tablespoons coarse black pepper	2 cups sugar
3 tablespoons green peppercorns	2 tablespoons unsalted butter, chilled
1 tablespoon unsalted butter, softened	6 3-inch-round puff pastry circles
1 large egg yolk	

Cut off each end of the pineapple, peel, and core. Cut the pineapple crosswise into ½-inch-thick rings. Season each pineapple ring with ¼ teaspoon coarse black pepper and 4 green peppercorns. Set aside.

Using the softened butter, lightly coat six 3-inch-round, nonstick molds. Set aside.

Preheat the oven to 350 degrees.

To make an egg wash, place the egg yolk and 1 tablespoon of the water in a small bowl and whisk together to blend. Set aside.

Combine the sugar and the remaining ¼ cup of water in a medium, heavy-duty saucepan over high heat. Bring the mixture to a boil; then lower the heat, and simmer for about 15 minutes, or until the sugar has begun to caramelize and the temperature reads 350 degrees on a candy thermometer. Remove the mixture from the heat and immediately beat in the chilled butter until well incorporated. Spoon ½ cup of the caramel into each of the 6 prepared molds. Place a seasoned pineapple ring on top of the caramel. Place the molds in the preheated oven and roast the pineapple for 10 minutes.

Remove the molds from the oven and place a puff pastry circle on top of the roasted pineapple. Using a pastry brush, lightly coat the pastry with the reserved egg wash. Return the molds to the preheated oven and bake for 25 minutes more, or until the puff pastry has risen and turned golden brown. Remove the pastry from the oven and allow it to rest for a couple of minutes. Invert the molds and tap the tartes free. Serve warm.

Crackling Pork Shank with Firecracker Applesauce

SERVES 6

These pork shanks have to cure for 48 hours before cooking. To cook the shanks, you will need a very deep stockpot that can contain the shanks in a single layer as well as two gallons of oil and still fit in the oven. In the end you will have the most amazing pork you have ever eaten. In principle, the dish is a bit like the French rillettes or duck confit but the final deep fry makes a crackling crisp skin around the meltingly tender meat. When I introduced this recipe in a restaurant all of my colleagues swore it would never sell. Not only did it sell, it won *USA Today*'s Dish of the Year (1996) and went on to become one of the most popular dishes I have ever created.

I serve the applesauce in a Ball canning jar that puts a homespun touch on the meal. However, it can be served in any appropriate serving container. Or, if you get the urge, you can make a big batch and can it and, like me, serve it straight from the jar.

1 bunch fresh flat-leaf parsley, chopped
1 cup minced shallots
¼ cup minced fresh thyme
4 teaspoons minced garlic
1 teaspoon crushed bay leaves
½ cup coarse salt plus more to taste
6 3-pound pork shanks (see Note)
2 gallons melted lard, melted duck fat, or canola oil

2 tablespoons olive oil
1 medium onion, julienned
2 medium green cabbage, cored and julienned
1 teaspoon cracked black pepper
4 cups beef stock
Firecracker Applesauce (recipe follows)

NOTE: Pork shanks can be difficult to find. If unavailable in your area, you can substitute pork shoulder with excellent results.

To make plain applesauce, delete the chilies and the bay leaf and cook as below. The applesauce can be made up to 3 days in advance and stored, covered and refrigerated.

Combine the parsley, shallots, thyme, garlic, and bay leaves. When well blended, stir in the salt. Generously coat each pork shank with the herb mixture. Place the pork shanks in a single layer on a baking sheet with sides. Cover them with plastic wrap and refrigerate for 48 hours.

Preheat the oven to 300 degrees.

Place the cured pork shanks in a deep stockpot large enough to hold them in a single layer. Cover with the melted lard, making sure that you have at least a 2½-inch clearance from the top of the pot to ensure that the fat does not overflow while cooking. Place the pot over medium heat and bring to a simmer. Test the fat with an instant-read thermometer; it should be about 225 degrees to maintain a quiet simmer. Place the pot in the preheated oven and cook for 2 hours, or until the meat is beginning to pull away from the bone. Remove the pot from the oven and, using a slotted spoon, carefully remove the shanks from the oil. Place the pot over high heat and bring the fat to 350 degrees. Wearing an oven mitt and standing as far away from the stove as you comfortably can (the shanks may splatter hot fat when lowered back into the pot), carefully return the shanks to the fat and deep-fry for about 5 minutes, or until the outside is crisp. Using a slotted spoon, carefully lift the shanks to a triple layer of paper towels to drain.

Heat the olive oil in a large saucepan over medium heat. Add the onion and sauté it for about 4 minutes, or just until it has begun to sweat its liquid. Add the cabbage and cracked pepper and, using tongs to lift the cabbage up and around, toss the cabbage for about 5 minutes, or just until it has wilted. Add the stock, cover, and cook for 15 minutes. Season to taste with salt. (If desired, you can replace the cabbage with commercially prepared sauerkraut.)

Serve the pork shanks on a bed of braised cabbage with the applesauce passed on the side.

Firecracker Applesauce

6 cups chopped, unpeeled Granny Smith
    apples
1 cup chopped seedless serrano chilies
¼ cup cider vinegar
½ teaspoon coarse salt

1 whole clove
1 bay leaf
1 2-inch cinnamon stick
2 cups finely diced, peeled Granny
    Smith apples

Combine the chopped apples, chilies, vinegar, salt, clove, bay leaf, and cinnamon stick in a large, heavy-duty saucepan over medium heat. Cook, stirring frequently, for about 15 minutes, or until the apples are falling apart and the mixture has reduced by half. Remove from the heat and allow to cool. Remove and discard the bay leaf. Stir in the finely diced apples and pour into a nonreactive container. Cover and refrigerate until ready to use.

SECOND DAY DISH

Barbecued Ham and Pineapple Kabobs

SERVES 2

This is my simple version of the kabobs that were served on the Pupu platters in the "Polynesian" restaurants of my youth. I still try to inject some of that fun into the food I cook today.

1 pineapple, peeled, trimmed, eyes removed, and cut into 1-inch cubes
¾ pound cooked ham, cut into 1-inch cubes
¼ cup honey
¼ cup Dijon mustard
¼ teaspoon ground cloves

2 pieces pita bread
2 large pieces romaine or iceberg lettuce
2 plum tomatoes, cut crosswise into thin slices
10 thin slices cucumber

Preheat and oil the grill.

Alternately, thread the pineapple and ham cubes on each of four skewers so that each skewer has at least 5 pieces of each.

Combine the honey, mustard, and cloves in a small mixing bowl. Set aside.

Lower the grill heat to medium-high. Place the skewers on the grill and grill, turning frequently, for about 5 minutes, or until the juices begin to caramelize. Using a pastry brush, lightly coat the ham and pineapple on each skewer with the honey glaze. Grill, turning occasionally, for an additional 2 minutes, or until the kabobs are nicely glazed and slightly crusty. Remove from the grill.

Slit open each pita to make a pocket. Place a leaf of lettuce into each pocket. Add an equal portion of tomato and cucumber slices to each pita. Slip two ham and pineapple kabobs into each pita, and serve with any leftover honey-mustard mixture on the side.

PORK CHOPS

Everybody always says pork chops are so dry. My answer is, not if they're cooked right. Pork now has so little fat that I agree it can be difficult to cook chops that are still moist in the center, but, as long as you either marinate or brine them for at least thirty minutes and don't overcook them, my recipes for chops will create juicy, tender meat.

Pork chops are cut from the loin and they are sold either fresh or smoked. The meatiest part of the loin provides sirloin (or butterfly) chops that are quite large and extremely tender. Center-cut chops are just as their name implies, cut from the center of the loin. The end chops come from either end of the loin. You can also find rib chops and blade chops.

Chops are cut in varying degrees of thickness, ranging from about ¼ inch to 2 to 2½ inches. The thinner chops are often pounded even thinner to create dishes such as *alla milanese* (coated in a seasoned breading and fried in olive oil). Thick chops are most frequently prepared on the grill or seared and finished in the oven or stuffed and baked. That's a personal choice. I suggest fairly thick chops and low, slow heat for grilling.

With the decrease in fat and cholesterol, pork chops have become more popular than ever. I like to season them well either with herbs, aromatics (garlic and onions), alcohol, or fruit. Because the meat is so much less fatty than it once was, the flavor has also become blander, so I find that introducing other strong flavors, in a marinade or a baste, highlights the texture and accents the taste of the mellow meat.

Grilled Pork Chops with Applesauce and Glazed Carrots

SERVES 6

This simple recipe has the perfect blend of flavors. The slightly salty-sweet carrots are a terrific complement to the mellow pork. The recipe is even better if you take the time to add some fruit wood chips to the fire, which will add an interesting hint of smoke and aroma to the meat.

½ cup olive oil

1 bunch fresh flat-leaf parsley, leaves only, chopped

1 bunch fresh thyme, chopped

3 cloves garlic, cut into slivers

3 leaves fresh sage, chopped

Zest of 1 lemon

6 10-ounce pork chops, excess fat removed, Frenched

Coarse salt and freshly ground black pepper

¾ pound slab bacon, diced

¼ cup water

6 carrots, cut into 2½-inch sticks

¼ cup honey

Approximately 1 cup plain applesauce (see page 154)

Combine the olive oil, parsley, thyme, garlic, sage, and lemon zest in a flat baking dish. Add the pork chops and allow them to marinate, turning them occasionally, for 3 hours.

Preheat and oil the grill.

Shake excess marinade from the pork chops and season them with salt and pepper. Place the chops on the preheated grill and grill, turning them from time to time to keep burning to a minimum, for about 14 minutes, or until an instant-read thermometer inserted into the thickest part of the meat reads 140 degrees.

While the pork chops are grilling, prepare the carrots.

To make the Glazed Carrots, place the bacon in a large sauté pan over medium heat. Add the water and cook the bacon for about 12 minutes, or until the water has evaporated and the bacon has rendered its fat and is crisp and brown. Drain off the excess fat. Return the pan to medium heat. Add the carrots and honey and sauté them for about 6 minutes, or until the carrots are nicely glazed. Taste and, if necessary, adjust the seasoning with additional salt and pepper. Remove the carrots from the heat and keep them warm.

Place an equal portion of the glazed carrots in the center of each of six dinner plates. Place a chop on top of the carrots and spoon a quenelle (see page 132) of applesauce on top of each chop and serve.

CONTEMPORARY

Seared Pork with Chorizo and Garlicky Clams

SERVES 6

This dish could have had its origins in a Spanish or Portuguese seaside village or in the sailing towns in Massachusetts and Rhode Island where immigrant Portuguese fishermen and their families have been making spicy stews for generations. My inspiration for this dish came from a dish prepared by Jasper White at his restaurant, Jasper's, in Boston some years ago.

Chorizo is a wonderfully aromatic, spicy, ground pork sausage that is removed from its casing and crumbled before cooking. You can use either Mexican (made from fresh pork) or Spanish (made from smoked pork) chorizo for this dish. The clam ragout would work well on its own for a warming supper on a chilly day.

1 cup plus 1 tablespoon olive oil

1 rack of pork (at least 6 ribs), trimmed, Frenched, and cut into 6 individual racks

Coarse salt and freshly ground black pepper

10 ounces chorizo sausage, casing removed (see Note)

½ cup diced shallots

3 cloves garlic cut into slivers

48 littleneck clams, washed and scrubbed

3 cups beef (or pork) stock

2 cups dry white wine

2 red bell peppers, cored, seeded, membrane removed, and diced

2 yellow bell peppers, cored, seeded, membrane removed, and diced

2 ripe tomatoes, peeled, seeded, and diced

Zest of 2 lemons

½ cup chopped fresh flat-leaf parsley

½ cup chopped fresh cilantro

½ cup chilled unsalted butter, diced

8 ounces pea shoots (see Note)

Preheat the oven to 400 degrees.

Heat ¼ cup of the olive oil in each of two large sauté pans over high heat. Season the pork racks with salt and pepper and place them in the pans, fat side down. Sear the pork, turning it occasionally, for about 12 minutes, or until all sides are brown and the internal temperature of the meat has reached 140 degrees on an instant-read thermometer. Remove the pork from the pans, tent lightly with aluminum foil to keep it warm, and set aside. (Or, you can place the pork in a very low-heat oven, with the door slightly ajar, to keep warm.)

Heat ½ cup of the remaining olive oil in a large saucepan over medium heat. Add the chorizo and stir to break up the meat. Add the shallots and garlic and sauté the mixture for about 7 minutes, or until the aromatics are beginning to color. Raise the heat and add the clams, stock, and wine. Bring the mixture to a simmer; then, lower the heat and simmer for about 25 minutes or until the liquid has reduced by one-half. Add the bell peppers, tomatoes, and zest and stir to incorporate. Taste and adjust the seasoning with salt and pepper. Simmer for an additional 10 minutes, or just until all of the clams are open. Remove the saucepan from the heat and, using a slotted spoon, lift the clams from the sauce. Discard any clams that do not open. Place the clams in a bowl and tent them lightly with aluminum foil to keep them warm.

Return the saucepan to medium heat. Stir the parsley and cilantro into the clam sauce; then whisk in the chilled butter, at bit at a time, until well-incorporated. Remove from the heat and, if necessary, keep warm until ready to serve.

Heat the remaining 1 tablespoon of olive oil in a large sauté pan over medium heat. Add the pea shoots and sauté for about 4 minutes, or just until wilted. Remove from the heat and season to taste with salt and pepper. (This must be done at the last minute as pea shoots will overcook if they sit too long.) Serve immediately.

Place the individual pork racks in the center of each of six dinner plates. Spoon five or six clams on top of the pork. Ladle the clam sauce over the top and allow it to run down onto the plate. Drape some pea shoots over the top and serve.

Sliced Pork Salad

SERVES 2

Using leftover pork or ham, this combination is a simple one with very direct flavors that complement each other. Just make sure that you get some spicy greens in your salad mix to balance the sweetness of the carrots and apple.

2 tablespoons cider vinegar
2 tablespoons olive oil
Coarse salt and freshly ground black pepper
½ pound mixed salad greens (make sure to include some spicy greens such as arugula, radicchio, or watercress)

1 cup sliced cooked pork
½ cup diced Glazed Carrots (see page 158)
1 Granny Smith apple, peeled, cored, and diced
½ cup toasted pecan halves

Whisk together the vinegar and oil. Season to taste with salt and pepper. Set aside.

Place the salad greens in a large mixing bowl. Add the pork, carrots, apples, and pecans. Sprinkle the reserved vinaigrette over the salad and toss to combine. Serve immediately.

SPARERIBS

Who doesn't love spareribs? We think of them as finger food, slightly sweet and straight off the grill, but in other cuisines they are braised, stuffed, and simmered until the meat falls off the bone, all cooking methods that you rarely see today. Here, I'm sticking to the classic and contemporary barbecue versions.

Spareribs are cut from the front of the rib cage and sold with either the breastbone attached or removed. Baby back ribs are cut from the loin, above the spareribs, and come from younger, smaller pigs. They usually have about ten small ribs on a side. Technically, country-style ribs are three or four large, meaty ribs that are cut from the blade (or shoulder) end of the loin, but the term has come to mean any ribs cut with lots of meat attached. Standard ribs have a bit more fat, baby back have a more delicate flavor, and country-style have much more meat. Use whichever type you prefer.

I like to braise ribs before I barbecue them. The braising period gives the meat a chance to really cook and tenderize. Then the coating of barbecue sauce can quickly caramelize on the grill (or in the oven) without burning. This way you get the crunchy sweetness of the sauce coating the meltingly tender meat. I braise in a soy-based liquid, but you can use a nicely spiced, water-based braise if you don't have the ingredients for the soy braise. The end result will not be quite as tasty but the ribs will be tenderized and take the barbecue sauce nicely.

CLASSIC

Barbecued Coffee Spareribs with Fixings

SERVES 6

Every cook I know is proprietary about their spareribs. Me, too. Between the Soy-Honey Braise and my coffee-flavored Barbecue Sauce and the meaty ribs, you will have a finger-lickin' feast, even without the fixings. You can use any type of rib you like, but I prefer the thick, meaty country-style ribs when I'm at the stove. You can braise the ribs and make the potato salad and the cucumbers early in the day.

2 2½-pound slabs pork spareribs, trimmed of excess fat
Soy-Honey Braise (recipe follows)
Approximately 2 cups Barbecue Sauce (see page 96)

Yukon Gold Potato Salad (recipe follows)
Pickled Cucumbers and Red Onions (recipe follows)

Using a pastry brush, generously coat the spareribs with the Soy-Honey Braise. Place the ribs in a single layer in a deep roasting pan, cover, and allow them to marinate for 6 hours.

Preheat the oven to 350 degrees.

Uncover the ribs and add any remaining Soy-Honey Braise to the pan. Tightly wrap the entire pan with aluminum foil and place the pan over direct high heat on top of the stove to bring the liquid up to a boil. Transfer the pan to the preheated oven and braise the meat for about 2 hours, or until a fork inserted into the meat comes out easily. Check the temperature from time to time as you don't want the braise to boil but merely simmer. If the liquid is boiling, reduce the oven temperature to 325 degrees.

Remove the pan from the oven and carefully lift the spareribs from the braising liquid to a clean baking sheet. Do not turn the oven off. (If you have lowered the temperature, return it to 350 degrees.) Using a pastry brush, generously coat the spareribs with Barbecue Sauce. Place the spareribs in the preheated oven and bake them for about 25 minutes, or until a caramelized crust of Barbecue Sauce has formed. (Alternately, place the ribs on a preheated, oiled grill and grill, turning frequently to prevent the sugar in the sauce from burning, for about 10 minutes, or until the sauce has caramelized.) Serve hot with the Yukon Gold Potato Salad and Pickled Cucumbers and Red Onions on the side.

Soy-Honey Braise

6 cups soy sauce
2 cups honey
2 cups water
6 cloves garlic, smashed

3 star anise
2-inch piece fresh ginger, peeled and smashed
1 cup chopped fresh cilantro leaves

Combine the soy, honey, and water in a nonreactive container. When well-blended, stir in the garlic, star anise, ginger, and cilantro. Cover and refrigerate the braise until you are ready to use it. The braise may be made up to 1 week in advance of its use.

Yukon Gold Potato Salad

4 cups diced, cooked, unpeeled Yukon
   Gold potatoes (about 4 large potatoes)
3 tablespoons minced shallots
1 cup mayonnaise

3 tablespoons Pommery mustard
1 tablespoon fines herbes (see page 65)
1 tablespoon coarse salt or to taste
⅛ teaspoon freshly ground black pepper

Toss the potatoes and shallots together in a medium mixing bowl. Whisk the mayonnaise, mustard, and fines herbes together, and then fold the mixture into the potatoes. Add the salt and pepper and gently fold in the seasoning. Taste and, if necessary, add additional salt and pepper. Cover and refrigerate the potato salad for at least 1 hour. Serve chilled.

Pickled Cucumbers and Red Onions

1 cup red wine, preferably a Burgundy
1 cup red wine vinegar
1 cup sugar
2 tablespoons coarse salt

¼ teaspoon freshly ground black pepper
3 cups diced, seedless, peeled cucumber
1 cup peeled and quartered red pearl
   onions

Combine the wine, wine vinegar, sugar, salt, and pepper in a medium, heavy-duty saucepan over medium heat. Stirring constantly, bring the mixture to a boil. Immediately remove it from the heat and add the cucumbers and onions. Set aside to cool. When cool, pour the mixture into a nonreactive container and refrigerate until you are ready to use it.

CONTEMPORARY

Asparagus-Stuffed Spareribs with Corn Crêpes

SERVES 6

This may be the most creative dish I have ever prepared. It is also a challenging dish to cook. Before preparing the dish for company, I would advise a little practice on some family meals. You will need fairly thick spears of asparagus to fit the bone spaces in the ribs. The Corn Crêpes can be made early in the day and reheated just before using.

2 2½-pound slabs spareribs, trimmed
    of excess fat
Soy-Honey Braise (see page 163)
Approximately thirty 6-inch long, thick
    spears fresh asparagus, blanched

1 cup Barbecue Sauce (see page 96)
Corn Crêpes (recipe follows)
2 cups chopped, toasted, unsalted peanuts

NOTE: Pouring the batter through a sieve twice is a nuisance, but it will ensure that you have a perfectly smooth batter that will create light-as-a-feather crêpes.

Using a pastry brush, generously coat the ribs with the Soy-Honey Braise. Place the ribs in a single layer in a deep roasting pan, cover, and allow them to marinate for 6 hours.

Preheat the oven to 350 degrees.

Uncover the ribs and add any remaining Soy-Honey Braise to the pan. Tightly wrap the entire pan with aluminum foil and place the pan over direct high heat on top of the stove to bring the liquid to a boil. Transfer the ribs to the preheated oven and braise them for about 2 hours, or until a fork inserted into the meat comes out easily. Check the temperature from time to time as you don't want the braise to boil but merely simmer. If the liquid is boiling, reduce the oven temperature to 325 degrees.

Remove the pan from the oven and carefully lift the spareribs from the braising liquid to a clean baking sheet; do not turn off the oven. Working carefully, push the rib bones from the spareribs. You may need to cut the chine bone (backbone) to facilitate this. As quickly as possible, replace each bone with an asparagus spear; then cut the spareribs into individual ribs.

Place the asparagus-stuffed ribs on a clean, nonstick baking sheet. Using a pastry brush, generously coat each rib with Barbecue Sauce. Place them in the preheated oven and bake for about 5 minutes, or until the sauce has caramelized and the ribs are slightly crisp.

Wrap each rib with a Corn Crêpe. Crisscross two ribs in the center of each of six dinner plates. Sprinkle peanuts around the edge of each plate and serve immediately.

Corn Crêpes

3 ears fresh corn, shucked	2 whole large eggs
4 cups heavy cream	2 large egg yolks
1 teaspoon caraway seeds	1¼ cups all-purpose flour
1½ teaspoons coarse salt	¼ cup unsalted butter, melted
¼ teaspoon freshly ground black pepper	

Working with one ear of corn at a time, hold the ear straight upright, and using a sharp knife, carefully slice the kernels from the ears. Place the kernels into a medium saucepan along with the cream, caraway seeds, 1 teaspoon salt, and the pepper. Place the saucepan over medium heat and bring to a simmer. Simmer for about 20 minutes, or until the cream has reduced by one-half. Transfer to a blender and process the mixture to a smooth purée. Pour the purée through a fine sieve into a clean bowl. Set aside.

Combine the whole eggs, egg yolks, and reserved corn cream in a mixing bowl. Slowly add the flour, whisking constantly. Transfer the mixture to a blender and process it to a smooth purée. If necessary, add an additional ½ teaspoon of salt. Pour the mixture through a fine sieve into a clean bowl. Whisk in the melted butter. Cover the bowl with plastic wrap and set it aside for 2 hours.

Place a 6-inch nonstick pan over medium-high heat. When the pan is very hot but not smoking, spray it with nonstick vegetable spray. Ladle about ¼ cup of the batter into the pan, swirling the pan to allow the batter to coat the bottom. Cook it for about 1 minute, or until its bottom is lightly browned. Flip and brown the remaining side. Stack the finished crêpes, separated by wax or parchment paper. When all of the crêpes are cooked and stacked, wrap the stack in aluminum foil and keep it warm until you are ready to use it. (Alternately, reheat the wrapped crêpes in a preheated 300-degree oven for about 15 minutes.)

Barbecued Sparerib Home-Fries with Poached Eggs and Chili Corn Cakes

SERVES 2

This dish is really full of flavor, marvelous for brunch. The crisp potatoes add great crunch to the barbecued meat mixture. The Poached Egg and Hollandaise Sauce top it off. If you want to really put on a show, make your own corn muffins and serve them, hot and fragrant, straight from the muffin pan.

1 tablespoon olive oil

1 medium onion, diced

1 cup diced Red Bliss potatoes

½ red bell pepper, cored, seeded, and finely diced

½ yellow bell pepper, cored, seeded, and finely diced

1 cup finely diced barbecued sparerib meat (see page 162)

½ cup Barbecue Sauce (see page 96)

1 tablespoon minced fresh chives

Coarse salt and freshly ground black pepper

2 poached eggs (see page 7)

¾ cup Hollandaise Sauce (see page 8)

4 Chili Corn Cakes (recipe follows)

Heat the olive oil in a large sauté pan over medium heat. Add the onions and sauté them for 2 minutes. Add the potatoes and red and yellow bell peppers, and continue to sauté for about 10 minutes, or until the vegetables are soft but have not taken on any color. Stir in the rib meat and Barbecue Sauce and cook for 5 minutes, or until the mixture is well-blended and the rib meat has melted into the sauce. Toss the chives into the meat mixture. Season to taste with salt and pepper.

Place equal portions of the meat into the center of each of 2 luncheon plates. Place a poached egg on top of the meat and spoon the sauce over the eggs, allowing some to run down onto the plate. Serve the corn cakes on the side.

Chili Corn Cakes

½ cup unsalted butter, at room temperature
½ tablespoon chili powder
Coarse salt to taste

4 commercially prepared corn
toaster cakes

Preheat the oven to 375 degrees.

Combine the butter, chili powder, and salt in the bowl of a food processor fitted with the metal blade. Process to blend well. (This makes quite a bit more butter than you will need, but it keeps well, covered and refrigerated, and it can be used for spicy French or Italian breads.)

Spread a generous amount of the seasoned butter on each corn cake. Place the corn cakes on a small, nonstick baking pan in the preheated oven and bake them for about 12 minutes, or until they are golden brown and toasty.

LAMB

Perhaps the best lamb I have ever eaten was the famous *pré-salé* lamb of France's Atlantic coast. These lambs graze on the salt marshes that line the coast and their meat is incredibly flavored with salt and sea. This lamb doesn't need much more than a quick turn on the grill.

In America, most of the lamb we eat is labeled "spring lamb," which used to connote that the lamb was born in the fall to be sold in the spring; now it simply means that the lamb was butchered at under a year, preferably between 3 and 5 months for the tenderest lamb. Premium baby lamb can be purchased through select butchers, but mutton, the meat of older sheep, once the only lamb available year-round, is no longer marketed except, occasionally, through Middle Eastern butchers. New Zealand lamb is also now marketed in America and promoted heavily throughout the year. Prime and choice grades are the most frequently available.

Because lamb is butchered at such an early age, the meat does not have an excess of fat. It should have a rosy pink flesh with very smooth, satinlike fat. Lamb that is marked Certified American Lamb must be butchered before one year of age, have no more than ¼ inch of fat trim and a dense, deep pink color. Since lamb has minimal marbling, the leanest cuts, such as the loin, are generally served slightly pink as is the leg, the rack, and most chops. Of course those cuts that are only suitable for braising and stews such as the shoulder or shank are served well-done and falling off the bone.

Lamb has five basic cuts running from the neck to the hind and two basic cuts from the underside. These cuts begin with the neck/shoulder area, with the neck bones and shoulder meat used for stews and other long, slow braises; the rib provides the rack, crown roasts, and rib chops; the loin, as it does with beef, gives the tenderest, most expensive meat used for medallions, saddles, and chops; the leg provides leg of lamb, which can be divided into the shank and the sirloin, or into kabobs. The underside is the source of the shank, the forelegs of the lamb, which are used for stews and the breast, which is usually stuffed and slowly cooked. The latter cuts are the least expensive cuts of lamb.

LEG OF LAMB

Leg of lamb was once enjoyed only in the spring when young lamb was brought to the market and was, therefore, often associated with Easter dinner. Then, improved breeding techniques brought young lamb to the market all year long, and leg of lamb moved from the special occasion treat to the everyday table. And, with the growth of outdoor grilling, a boneless, butterflied leg of lamb even joined the picnic table. However you serve it, leg of lamb is a rich, succulent piece of meat. A three-ounce serving has less than 200 calories and just 78 milligrams of cholesterol.

A leg of lamb usually ranges from six to nine pounds with the smallest legs having the most flavor. To ease carving, you might want to have the aitchbone removed by the butcher. Be sure that all of the silver skin (the smooth, rather shiny outer membrane) is also removed. You may also want to remove the lymph node which is hidden in the center and about halfway down the leg. It is a small, round, fatty-looking node that often contributes the "strong" taste associated with lamb. I don't find it to be a problem.

Roasting a leg of lamb is quite easy. All it really needs is some salt and pepper, a rack to lift it out of its fat as it roasts, and the proper heat. It can also be prepared on a grill, but it is usually best to have it boned for grilling so that you don't risk overcooking the outside before the interior is cooked. A leg usually takes about 15 minutes per pound for rare (140 degrees on an instant-read thermometer) and about 20 minutes per pound for medium (160 degrees on an instant-read thermometer).

Because the leg provides such rich, aromatic meat, it marries well with many pungent flavors. The French wouldn't think of serving a leg without slivers of garlic and sprigs of rosemary inserted into the meat. Greeks add some lemon, oregano, and bay leaf. Middle Easterners use pomegranates, onions, and intense spices. I love a curry and yogurt marinade, which penetrates the lamb right to the bone. I often make a creamy bed of white beans to cradle the juices of a garlicky, rare leg of lamb, a simple dish but perfection.

Roast Leg of Lamb, Stuffed Tomatoes, and Sliced Pan Potatoes

SERVES 6

Here I use a boned leg of lamb but you could also roast a standard leg with the garlic mixture rubbed all over the outside. The tomatoes are a lovely garnish, but if you don't have the time, the recipe will work just as well without them.

¼ cup Roasted Garlic Purée (see page 12)
3 tablespoons finely chopped rosemary
3 tablespoons finely chopped thyme
1 tablespoon coarse salt plus more to taste
¼ teaspoon freshly ground black pepper
    plus more to taste
Zest of 1 lemon

1 8-pound leg of lamb, boned, silver
    skin and excess fat removed
1 cup julienned onion
6 large plum tomatoes
3 tablespoons olive oil
10 ounces soft goat cheese
Sliced Pan Potatoes (recipe follows)

Combine the garlic purée, rosemary, thyme, salt, pepper, and lemon zest in a small bowl. Spoon one-half of the mixture into the interior of the boned lamb and, using a spatula, lightly coat the inside. Roll the meat up and tie it closed with kitchen twine. Rub the remaining garlic mixture on the outside of the lamb. Place the lamb in a shallow roasting pan, cover with plastic wrap, and refrigerate for 24 hours.

Preheat the oven to 350 degrees.

Scatter the onions over the bottom of a shallow roasting pan. Place the leg of lamb on top of the onions. Place the lamb in the preheated oven and roast it for 3 hours, or until an instant-read thermometer inserted into the thickest part of the meat reads 140 degrees. Do not turn off the oven.

About half an hour before the lamb is ready, prepare the tomatoes. Using a sharp knife, cut off and discard the top and bottom of each tomato. With a teaspoon or grapefruit spoon, scoop out and discard the seeds and membrane. Wipe the tomatoes dry, inside and out. Place the tomatoes in a mixing bowl and add the olive oil and salt and pepper to taste. Toss to coat well. Spoon an equal portion of the goat cheese into the hollow of each tomato and place the tomatoes on a nonstick baking sheet. While the lamb is resting, place the tomatoes in the oven and roast for 7 minutes, or until they are just slightly tender. Remove them from the oven.

Place the leg of lamb on a platter and allow it to rest for 10 minutes. Place the tomatoes around the edge of the platter. Transfer the platter to the table, carve the lamb, and serve family style with the potatoes still in their pan.

Sliced Pan Potatoes

2 tablespoons unsalted butter
1 large onion cut crosswise into ⅛-inch-thick slices
1 tablespoon minced fresh rosemary
1 tablespoon minced fresh thyme

5 large potatoes, peeled and cut, crosswise into ¼-inch-thick slices
Coarse salt and freshly ground black pepper
4 cups lamb or beef stock or broth

Preheat the oven to 400 degrees.

Heat the butter in a large, ovenproof sauté pan over medium heat. Add the onion and cook, stirring frequently, for about 7 minutes, or until the onion is golden brown. Stir in one-half of the rosemary and thyme and when the mixture is well combined, spread it over the bottom of the pan.

Remove the pan from the heat and place the potato slices in the pan in slightly overlapping, concentric circles. Season to taste with salt and pepper. Pour the stock over the potatoes and place the pan in the preheated oven. Bake the potatoes for about 1 hour, or until the stock has been absorbed and they are tender when pierced with the point of a very sharp knife. Remove them from the oven and sprinkle with the remaining rosemary and thyme. Serve hot, directly from the pan.

Boneless Leg of Lamb with Citrus-Mint Glaze

SERVES 6

The cut of the lamb may be a little bit different than you are used to, but the cooking method is very straightforward and simple. The savory glaze more than makes up for the simplicity. The glaze can be made a few days in advance of use and stored, tightly covered and refrigerated.

¼ cup vegetable oil

1 8-pound boneless leg of lamb, each muscle removed and seamed

2 tablespoons coarsely ground black pepper

Coarse salt

Citrus-Mint Glaze (recipe follows)

Preheat the oven to 350 degrees.

Heat the oil in a large ovenproof sauté pan over medium-high heat. Season the lamb with the coarse pepper and salt. When the oil is very hot but not smoking, put the seasoned lamb into the pan. Sear it, turning frequently, for about 4 minutes per side, or until nicely browned on all sides. Transfer the lamb to the preheated oven and roast it for 10 minutes, or until an instant-read thermometer inserted into the thickest part of the meat reads 140 degrees.

Remove the lamb from the oven and allow it to rest for 10 minutes. Using a very sharp knife, cut the lamb, across the grain, into very thin slices. Place the slices on a serving platter and serve with Citrus-Mint Glaze.

Citrus-Mint Glaze

¼ cup well-drained, green peppercorns

4 star anise

2 serrano chilies, stemmed, seeded, and finely chopped

2 tablespoons chopped fresh cilantro

2 tablespoons puréed fresh ginger

2 tablespoons coriander seeds

2 tablespoons black peppercorns

1 cup orange marmalade

1 cup mint marmalade

1 cup white wine vinegar

1 cup fresh mint leaf chiffonade (see page 67)

Place the green peppercorns in a small sauté pan over medium heat and cook them, stirring frequently, for about 5 minutes, or until they are dry and toasted. Remove the peppercorns from the heat and transfer to a spice grinder. Process them to a fine grind. Set aside.

Combine the star anise, serrano chilies, cilantro, ginger, coriander, and black peppercorns in a double piece of cheesecloth and using kitchen twine, tie it into a bag. Set aside.

Combine the orange and mint marmalades in a medium, nonstick saucepan over medium-high heat. Add the vinegar along with the reserved ground green peppercorns and the spice bag. Bring the mixture to a boil; then lower the heat and cook, at a bare simmer, for about 20 minutes, or until the liquid has reduced by one-half and is very syrupy. Remove the syrup from the heat and transfer it to a nonreactive container. Cover and refrigerate it for about 2 hours (or up to 3 days), or until well chilled.

When ready to serve, transfer the syrup to a small saucepan and place it over medium heat. Bring it to a simmer; then remove it from the heat. Remove and discard the spice bag. Stir in the mint chiffonade and serve immediately.

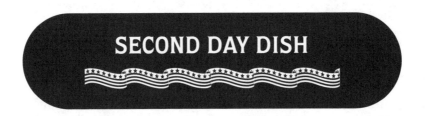

Lamb-Stuffed Pasta Shells with Tomato Broth

SERVES 2

This is the closest I'll get to being Italian! Although it is a very simple Second Day Dish, it has an interesting, and a bit sophisticated, flavor note with the lamb-spinach combination. It can easily be put together early in the day and baked just before dinner.

1 tablespoon olive oil
¼ cup finely diced onion
2 cloves garlic, minced
¼ cup tightly packed basil leaves, chopped
2 cups cored, seeded, and chopped canned tomatoes

1 bay leaf
1½ cups finely diced cooked leg of lamb
2 cups chopped fresh spinach leaves or ½ cup thawed, chopped, frozen spinach, well drained
½ cup heavy cream
Pinch of freshly grated nutmeg

Coarse salt and freshly ground black
   pepper to taste

1 large egg yolk, beaten

4 jumbo pasta shells

Heat the oil in a large saucepan over medium heat. Add the onion and garlic along with half of the basil. Sauté the mixture for 5 minutes. Add the tomatoes and bay leaf and simmer, stirring occasionally, for 15 minutes. Remove the saucepan from the heat. Remove and discard the bay leaf and fold in the remaining basil. Set aside.

Preheat the oven to 375 degrees.

Combine the lamb, spinach, and cream in a large sauté pan. Season with the nutmeg and salt and pepper. Place the pan over medium heat and cook, stirring frequently, for about 10 minutes or until the mixture is quite thick. Remove from the heat and allow it to cool to room temperature. When cool, beat in the egg yolk until well combined.

Cook the shells according to the package directions. Drain well. Generously fill each shell with the lamb-spinach mixture.

Cover the bottom of a small baking pan with a thin layer of the tomato broth. Place the filled shells into the pan and spoon some sauce over the top of them. Tightly cover the pan with aluminum foil and place it in the preheated oven. Bake the shells for about 30 minutes, or until the filling has set and is very hot. Remove the pan from the oven, uncover, and allow to rest for 5 minutes.

Reheat the remaining tomato broth. Place the shells on a shallow serving dish, spoon the remaining broth over the top of them and serve.

LAMB CHOPS

After a big juicy steak, lamb chops are the meat of choice in most steak houses. I think that is because they are always cut, at the least, double thick and are served pink on the inside and slightly salty and crusty on the outside with the little bit of fatty edge nicely crisp. It makes me hungry just thinking about them.

I prefer a chop to be at least 1½ inches thick and well trimmed of fat. The bone can be Frenched, that is, with all of the meat scraped off, presenting a neat handle with which you can hold the chop. I usually season chops with salt and pepper, perhaps some olive oil, lemon, and thyme and grill them over a medium-hot fire. If they aren't too thick, you can also pan-sear chops to seal in the juices and then finish them in a very hot oven.

For both my classic and contemporary lamb chop dishes, I've chosen rack of lamb, which is nothing more than chops kept together. This, to me, is the most elegant presentation of chops. The whole rack is roasted and then individual chops are cut at the time of service. There is nothing that says "fancy" like a couple of racks, bones Frenched, skin crisp and aromatic, interlocking on a platter with roasted vegetables or potatoes as a base. The rib chops can be a bit less succulent than the fatter loin chops but they look marvelous on the plate.

CLASSIC

Rack of Lamb with Bouquet of Vegetables

SERVES 6

This is a very basic recipe except that I have used baby racks of lamb (allowing one per person) in place of the larger racks, and have sautéed rather than roasted the vegetables. If finishing the vegetables on top of the stove seems like too much work at the last minute, feel free to finish them in the oven along with the lamb. Just be sure that you blanch the onions, carrots, and eggplant; otherwise they will not be cooked enough with the quick sauté (or roast). Keep in mind that if you are making the Second Day Dish, you will need extra lamb.

½ cup vegetable oil

6 12-ounce baby lamb racks, Frenched

Coarse salt and freshly ground black pepper

½ cup clarified butter (see page 7)

4 cups diced potatoes

1 tablespoon fines herbes (see page 65)

¼ cup unsalted butter, softened

¼ cup minced shallots

12 pearl onions, peeled and blanched

3 carrots, cut into small sticks, and blanched

3 Japanese eggplants, well trimmed, cut into small sticks, and blanched

2 zucchini, trimmed, seeds removed, and cut into small sticks

2 yellow squash, trimmed, seeds removed, and cut into small sticks

2 red bell peppers, trimmed, seeded, membrane removed, and cut into small sticks

¼ cup chicken stock or broth

Preheat the oven to 500 degrees.

Place ¼ cup of the oil in each of two large ovenproof sauté pans over high heat. Bring the oil up to the smoke point. Season the lamb racks with salt and pepper and immediately put them, skin side down, into the hot pans. Lower the heat to medium and sear the meat for about 3 minutes, or until golden brown. Transfer it to the preheated oven and roast for 8 minutes. Turn the lamb and continue to roast it for an additional 6 minutes, or until an instant-read thermometer inserted into the center of the meat reads 140 degrees. Remove the lamb from the oven and allow it to rest for 5 minutes.

While the lamb is roasting, prepare the vegetables.

Place the clarified butter in a large sauté pan over high heat. When the butter just begins to smoke, add the potatoes. Season to taste with salt and pepper and sauté the potatoes for about 10 minutes, or until they are tender and golden brown. Add the fines herbes and toss to coat.

Melt the softened butter in a large sauté pan over medium heat. Add the shallots and sauté them for about 3 minutes, or until the shallots have sweat their liquid but have not taken on any color. Add the pearl onions, carrots, eggplant, zucchini, yellow squash, and bell pepper. Add the stock and bring to a boil. Lower the heat and cook for about 4 minutes, or until the vegetables are just cooked. Remove them from the heat and season to taste with salt and pepper.

Carve the lamb into chops or medallions and place them on a serving platter. Place the vegetables and potatoes in separate serving bowls and serve, family style, along with the lamb.

Poached Rack of Lamb with Fleur de Sel, Tomato Couscous, and Garlic Pearls

SERVES 6

This is quite a different approach to cooking a rack of lamb. The meat of baby lamb is so tender that I just knew it would lend itself to a quick poach in a lightly seasoned broth. *Fleur de sel* (see Note) has the perfect aromatic bite to highlight the mellow lamb. Even if you don't make the veggies, please do make the Israeli couscous (see Note). It has just the heft to lift the recipe out of the everyday to the sublime.

2 gallons water
2 large onions, diced
2 carrots, diced
2 stalks celery, diced
½ cup tomato purée
6 tablespoons coarse salt plus more to taste
6 12-ounce baby lamb racks, Frenched
2 tablespoons chicken or lamb stock
  (or water)
18 baby carrots with a bit of the green left
  on, blanched

¼ cup unsalted butter
Freshly ground black pepper
2 tablespoons vegetable oil
1 pound fresh spinach leaves, thoroughly
  washed and dried
3 tablespoons *fleur de sel*
Tomato Couscous (recipe follows)
Garlic Confit (recipe follows)

NOTE: *Fleur de sel* is a naturally harvested French sea salt that has a much larger grain and a more aromatic flavor than everyday salt. Because of its delicacy and the fact that it is also very expensive, it is most frequently used to finish a dish.

Israeli couscous is a very large-grained couscous that resembles barley when cooked. It is available from Middle Eastern markets, specialty food stores, and some supermarkets.

Combine the water, onions, carrots, celery, tomato purée, and 6 tablespoons of the salt in a stockpot over high heat. Bring the mixture to a boil. Lower the heat and simmer for 10 minutes. Add the lamb and return to a simmer. Simmer for about 30 minutes, or until an instant-read thermometer inserted into the center reads 130 degrees.

About 10 minutes before the lamb is done, prepare the vegetables.

Heat the stock (or water) in a sauté pan over medium heat. Add the carrots and butter and bring to a simmer. Season to taste with salt and pepper and cook for about 4 minutes, or until the sauce has thickened slightly. Remove the vegetables from the heat and tent them lightly with aluminum foil to keep warm.

Heat the oil in a sauté pan over high heat. Add the spinach and, using tongs, quickly toss the spinach, cooking until just wilted. Remove the spinach from the heat and season to taste with salt and pepper.

Remove the lamb from the poaching liquid and generously season with the *fleur de sel*. Cut each rack in half and interlock the bones between each half. Spoon equal portions of the couscous in the center of each of six dinner plates. Place an interlocked lamb rack over the couscous on each plate. Season the eye of each rack with some additional *fleur de sel* and black pepper. Place three carrots into the rib bones and drape some spinach over the top of them. Lay four confit garlic cloves on top of the spinach and serve.

Tomato Couscous

¼ cup olive oil	3½ cups water or lamb stock
2 medium onions, cut into a ¼-inch dice	3 tablespoons coarse salt plus more
1 cup peeled, seeded, and diced tomatoes	to taste
2 teaspoons Roasted Garlic Purée (see	1 tablespoon chicken or lamb stock
page 12)	1 teaspoon unsalted butter
4 cups Israeli couscous (see Note)	Freshly ground black pepper

Heat the olive oil in a saucepan over medium heat. Add the onions and tomato and sauté them for about 4 minutes, or just until the vegetables have sweat their liquid but have not taken on any color. Stir in the garlic purée and when well blended, stir in the couscous. Remove from the heat.

Combine the water and salt in another saucepan over high heat and bring it to a boil. Immediately pour the salted water over the couscous mixture. Return the couscous to medium-high heat and bring to a boil. Immediately remove the pan from the heat and cover it tightly. Allow the couscous to rest until all of the liquid has been absorbed. This should take no more than 20 minutes. Tightly covered, the couscous should stay quite hot for about 40 minutes. When ready to serve, uncover, add the tablespoon of stock and the butter and toss to fluff. Taste and, if necessary, adjust the seasoning with additional salt and pepper.

Garlic Confit

2 cups chicken stock
Juice of 2 oranges
Juice of 2 lemons

¼ cup sugar
¼ cup (½ stick) unsalted butter
24 large, cloves garlic, peeled

Combine the stock, orange and lemon juices, sugar, and butter in a medium saucepan over medium-high heat and bring to a boil. Lower the heat and simmer for about 15 minutes, or until reduced by one-quarter. Add the garlic and continue to simmer for 30 minutes, or until the garlic is very tender. Remove the mixture from the heat and allow it to cool. You can store the confit, tightly covered and refrigerated, for up to 1 week.

Crisp Goat Cheese, Potato, and Lamb Sandwich

SERVES 2

This is a very elegant use of leftovers. It is about the most delicious sandwich I can imagine.

4 ounces soft goat cheese
¼ teaspoon minced fresh thyme
Coarse salt and freshly ground black
    pepper to taste
Approximately ¼ cup clarified butter
    (see page 7)

1 large Idaho potato, peeled and cut
    crosswise into very thin rounds
4 to 6 thin slices roasted lamb

Using a wooden spoon, combine the goat cheese and thyme with salt and pepper to taste in a small mixing bowl, beating until well combined. Set aside.

Preheat the oven to 275 degrees.

Line a baking sheet with parchment paper. Set aside.

Heat about 2 tablespoons of the clarified butter in a small, heavy-duty, nonstick sauté pan over medium-high heat until it is almost smoking. Lower the heat and place 1 layer of potatoes in concentric circles in the pan until the bottom of the pan is completely covered. Season the potatoes with salt and pepper to taste and cook for about 4 minutes, or until golden. Carefully flip and cook the other side of the potato cake for about 3 minutes, or until golden, adding more butter if necessary. Place them on a double layer of paper towels to drain. Then, transfer them to the prepared baking sheet and make 3 more potato cakes.

Using half of the goat cheese mixture, lightly coat the top of two of the potato cakes. Cover the goat cheese with a layer of sliced lamb and season to taste with salt and pepper. Make a final layer of the goat cheese mixture, and then top the whole stack with a final potato cake, pressing down slightly to hold the sandwich together. Place the sandwiches in the preheated oven and bake them for about 10 minutes or until hot. Serve hot.

LAMB STEW

When I was a kid, lamb was not my favorite meat and I seem to remember lamb stew as slightly watery with overcooked vegetables and fatty meat. I've come to learn that great, old-fashioned, Irish stew hardly needs to be made like that. Use a combination of neck and shoulder meat to get the right degree of flavor, texture, and meatiness; use lots of potatoes, some thinly sliced and some cut into chunks, so that the gravy is thickened without the use of other starch; and throw in a jigger or two of brandy about 15 minutes before you are ready to serve the stew. The alcohol mingles with the rich lamb juices and gives just the tiniest hint of a cold day on the bogs.

When making a lamb stew, the meat you select is the most important element. You need some meaty pieces from the shoulder (or breast or leg, which will be the tenderest but the least compatible to braising) and some flavorful bony pieces from the neck. You can also braise lamb shanks or shoulder chops, which will combine both meatiness and flavor. For a true Irish stew, the meat is not browned before stewing so that the end result is a very pale but complex gravy.

The juices and aromatics in which the meat is stewed need to marry well with the rich, slightly fatty meat. A good defatted lamb stock, or even chicken stock, can be used. The stock can be combined with a hint of fruit (apricot or pear nectars work particularly well), a bit of white wine or brandy, or tomatoes with their juice. Don't add both fruit and tomatoes since their flavors work at cross-purposes. Onions, shallots, and/or garlic provide the aromatic base you will need to meld into the meat juices. Here, I've tried to keep the integrity of the meat-vegetable combination and yet extend the flavors. Sweet root vegetables do it in the classic preparation and the caramelized shallots enfold the rich lamb shanks in the contemporary version.

CLASSIC

Lamb Stew with Root Vegetables and Honey-Thyme Croutons

Serves 6

This is a classic stew, but the variety of root vegetables and the sweet-pungent croutons for dipping bring the braise up-to-date. You may not need to add the roux to thicken the stew at the end because the root vegetables will often release enough starch as they cook to thicken the liquid. Be sure to taste the lamb a couple of times to make certain that it has enough seasoning to accent its meatiness.

½ cup vegetable oil
5 pounds lamb stew meat
Coarse salt and freshly ground black pepper
    to taste
1 cup red wine
2 large onions, diced
2 large carrots, diced
1 head garlic, broken apart, cloves peeled
    and minced
2 cups canned tomato purée

2 large Yukon Gold potatoes, peeled
    and diced
2 celery roots, peeled and diced
2 parsnips, peeled, trimmed, and diced
2 small or 1 large rutabaga, peeled,
    trimmed, and diced
12 cups lamb (or beef) stock
6 ounces (1½ sticks) unsalted butter
1 cup sifted all-purpose flour
Honey-Thyme Croutons (recipe follows)

Preheat the oven to 350 degrees.

Heat the oil in a Dutch oven (or rondeau) over medium-high heat just to the smoke point. Add the lamb, in batches if necessary, to keep from crowding the pot. Season with salt and pepper and sear the lamb, turning it occasionally, for about 10 minutes, or until the meat is nicely browned on all sides. When all the meat has been browned, add the wine and stir to deglaze the pot. Bring to a simmer and cook for about 10 minutes, or until the wine has reduced by one-half. Add the onions, carrots, garlic, and tomato purée and cook for about 10 minutes, or until the onions are translucent but have not browned. Stir in the potatoes, celery root, parsnips, and rutabaga. Add the stock. Taste and, if necessary, adjust the seasoning with salt and pepper. Cover and place the stew in the preheated oven. Bake for about 1 hour, or until the meat and vegetables are very tender.

Using a wooden spoon, blend the flour and butter together in a small bowl.

Remove the stew from the oven. Uncover and place it on top of the stove over low heat. Stir in the flour-butter roux and cook, stirring gently, for about 5 minutes, or until the gravy has thickened slightly. Serve, family style, directly from the Dutch oven with the Honey-Thyme Croutons on the side for soaking up the gravy.

Honey-Thyme Croutons

5 slices home-style white bread, crusts removed
½ cup unsalted butter

3 tablespoons honey
1 tablespoon minced fresh thyme

Line a baking sheet with parchment paper.

Cut the bread into ½-inch-square pieces. Place the bread on the parchment-lined baking sheet and allow it to dry for 24 hours. (If you are in a hurry, you can place the bread on a parchment-lined baking sheet and bake it in a preheated 200-degree oven, turning occasionally, for 30 minutes, or until crisp.) Transfer the croutons to a mixing bowl.

Preheat the oven to 325 degrees.

Combine the butter and honey in a small saucepan over medium heat, stirring to blend well. Add the thyme and remove the mixture from the heat. Pour one-half of the mixture over the croutons and toss to lightly coat. Place the croutons on a baking sheet and into the preheated oven and bake them for 7 minutes. Remove them from the oven, but don't turn off the oven. Using the remaining butter mixture, again toss the croutons in the mixture. Return the croutons to the baking sheet. Place them in the oven, and bake for an additional 7 minutes, or until they are dry and golden. Serve them warm or at room temperature.

CONTEMPORARY

Braised Lamb Shank with Cauliflower-Rosemary Purée

SERVES 6

Here is one of my favorite dishes, a long way from that watery lamb stew I remember. Lamb shanks, with the meat falling off the bone, are absolutely scrumptious. The rich gravy melts into the aromatic, cauliflower purée and glazes the raviolis. Lamb shanks are best made the day before serving so that the flavors have a chance to mellow.

4 medium tomatoes, peeled, cored,
   seeded, and quartered
3 cloves garlic
2 ribs celery, trimmed, peeled, and chopped
1 large carrot, diced
1 large onion, diced
1 sprig fresh rosemary
1 sprig fresh thyme

1 bay leaf
6 lamb shanks, about 1½ pounds each
   with the bone
Coarse salt and freshly ground black pepper
4 cups lamb or beef stock
1 cup canned tomato purée
Cauliflower-Rosemary Purée (recipe
   follows)

Preheat the oven to 350 degrees.

Place the tomatoes, garlic, celery, carrot, onion, rosemary, thyme, and bay leaf in the bottom of a roasting pan. Season the lamb shanks with salt and pepper and place them on top of the vegetables. Place in the preheated oven and roast for 1½ hours, or until the lamb has started to caramelize.

Combine the stock and tomato purée in a medium saucepan over medium heat and bring it to a boil. Remove the shanks from the oven, and immediately pour the boiling liquid over the lamb shanks and vegetables. Return the pan to the oven and continue to braise for an additional 90 minutes, or until the lamb almost falls apart when prodded with a fork.

Using a slotted spoon, transfer the shanks from the braising liquid to a clean plate. Strain the liquid through a medium-fine sieve back into the roasting pan. Place the pan over medium heat on top of the stove and cook, stirring frequently, for about 15 minutes, or until the liquid has reduced by half. Return the shanks to the pan and cook for an additional 10 minutes, or just until the shanks are very hot.

Place a big scoop of cauliflower purée in the center of each of six dinner plates. Place a lamb shank on top of the cauliflower purée and serve.

Cauliflower-Rosemary Purée

3 cups (about 1 pound) cauliflower florets

4 cups water

Coarse salt

2 cups heavy cream

2 sprigs fresh rosemary, needles only, minced

5 tablespoons unsalted butter

Freshly ground black pepper

Combine the cauliflower with the water and just enough salt to season lightly in a medium saucepan over medium-high heat. (The water should just barely cover the cauliflower.) Bring it to a boil; then lower the heat to a simmer. Simmer the cauliflower for 35 minutes, or until the water has reduced by one-half. Raise the heat and add the cream and rosemary. Again, bring to a boil; then lower the heat and simmer for about 30 minutes, or until the liquid has again reduced by one-half.

Transfer the mixture to a blender. Add the butter and process to a smooth, slightly thick purée. Taste and adjust the seasoning with salt and pepper. Serve hot. (The purée may be made up to 2 days in advance of use and stored, covered and refrigerated. Reheat before using.)

Tempura Lamb and Vegetables with Peanut Sauce

SERVES 2

This tasty Second Day Dish calls for peanut sauce, which can be used with rice noodles, as a cocktail dip, or as a stir-fry sauce. Kept tightly covered and refrigerated, it should last for a couple of weeks. You can substitute any vegetable you like for the ones that I have chosen.

4 cups plus 2 tablespoons vegetable oil

4 cloves garlic, minced

2 red chilies, stemmed and thinly sliced

2 tablespoons tomato paste

1 cup chicken stock

½ cup hoisin sauce (see Note)

2 teaspoons chili paste (see Note)

1 teaspoon sugar

½ cup finely chopped, roasted peanuts

¼ cup peanut butter

1 cup all-purpose flour

¼ pound cooked lamb shank meat

¼ pound green beans, trimmed and blanched

2 ounces button mushrooms, cut into ½-inch-thick slices

1 red bell pepper, cored, seeded, and cut into 3 inch × ¼-inch sticks

Tempura batter (see page 89)

> NOTE: Hoisin sauce and chili paste are available from Asian markets, and some specialty food stores and supermarkets.

To make the peanut sauce, heat 2 tablespoons of the vegetable oil in a medium saucepan over medium heat. Add the garlic and chilies and cook for about 3 minutes, or until the vegetables have sweat their liquid but not taken on any color. Stir in the tomato paste and cook, stirring constantly, for 3 minutes. Add the chicken stock, hoisin sauce, chili paste, and sugar and bring to a boil. Lower the heat and simmer for 10 minutes. Stir in the peanuts and peanut butter and cook, stirring constantly, for about 2 minutes, or until the mixture is thick. Remove it from the heat and set aside.

Place the flour in a plastic bag. Add the lamb and the vegetables, a few pieces at a time, hold the bag shut and shake to lightly coat. Shake off the excess flour and set the pieces aside. Continue coating until all of the lamb and the vegetables have been dredged.

Heat the remaining oil in a deep fat-fryer or deep saucepan over high heat to 350 degrees on a candy thermometer.

Working with a few pieces at a time, dip the lamb and vegetables into the tempura batter and immediately drop them into the hot oil. Fry for about 3 minutes, or until the coating is golden brown. Place the pieces on a double layer of paper towels to drain. Season with salt and pepper to taste. (You might want to preheat the oven and keep the finished pieces warm while you are frying up the remaining lamb and vegetables.) Serve hot in takeout-style cartons (such as used for Chinese food), with the peanut sauce on the side for dipping.

FISH AND SHELLFISH

Up until refrigerated shipping was available, only local fish and shellfish was eaten as it was impossible to transport other kind of fresh fish across the country. It was not until after the Second World War that frozen fish was introduced into the supermarket freezers with fish sticks and breaded shrimp the number one sellers. And then there was always canned tuna.

Unless along the shore, restaurants featuring seafood were almost nonexistent until quite recently. Of course, cities like New York, Boston, New Orleans, Baltimore, and San Francisco that had substantial fishing industries always had seafood houses, but the rest of the country was bereft of great seafood restaurants. This all changed as young American chefs took to the stoves in the early 1980s. A desire to expand our culinary horizons, a taste for immigrant cuisines, a focus on lighter, healthier cooking, the introduction of sushi, and consumer demand all came together to bring new and exciting fish and shellfish to the marketplace and to the restaurant and home table.

Where once supermarkets could only offer frozen or canned fish, almost every supermarket of any size now has a fresh fish section and a lobster tank. Farmed fish such as salmon, trout, and catfish are plentiful and relatively inexpensive.

During my career as a chef, the most interesting aspect of this new awareness of seafood has been the way that its preparation has changed. It would have been unthinkable to order salmon (or any other fish) "rare" when I began cooking. "Sushi-grade" was an unknown term. Seviches have moved from the Latin kitchen to haute cuisine. Sashimi, or other raw fish preparations, were never served. All of this has evolved over the last twenty years.

Unfortunately, the demand for seafood has far eclipsed its availability. Overfishing has depleted the wild stock of many, many species. Chilean sea bass and swordfish are but two that have faced near extinction in the wild. Aquaculture in open oceans, that is the farming of fish in their natural setting, is now thought to imperil the balance of the ecosystem. The seas that once provided unending supply are overfished and polluted. The situation changes almost daily. Updating is available through various seafood organizations. For chefs, organizations like Seafood Choices Alliance keep us alert to current issues.

On the other hand, as we strive to allow familiar fish to be replenished, there are many other types that can be served with impunity. Farmed catfish, rainbow trout, tilapia, caviar, mussels, scallops, and crawfish are readily available and many lesser-known species that are plentiful in the wild are being introduced into everyday dining.

COD

Long before cod was eaten fresh, it was the king of the seas by virtue of its vast numbers and its excellence as a salted fish. In fact, up until the nineteenth century cod was almost always sold salted and dried. So important was it to the international economy that treaties were built around its fishing grounds and taxes were placed on its import. And so efficient were the fishermen that the stocks of cod, once the most plentiful fish in the seas, have almost been totally depleted. It is now, for the most part, caught in small numbers by large fishing trawlers, frozen at sea, and processed or salted once the ships land.

The cod family is a large one and comprises such popular fish as cod, scrod (which is actually just the name for young cod), haddock, hake, and pollack. Cod is a rather large fish—a full-blown adult can weigh up to eighty pounds—with succulent flesh that flakes easily when properly cooked. A really fresh fish will have milky residue between the flakes that ensures moisture and flavor. It is the classic fish of chowders and stews, but it can also be poached, baked, or fried.

Salt cod (or stockfish) is a staple of many, many countries and has put its mark on the cuisines of Portugal, Spain, France, Italy, and Scandinavia; *Bacalhau* in Portugal, *bacalao* in Spain, *morue* in France, *baccalà* in Italy, and *lutfisk* in fish puddings, creams, and stews in Scandinavia. The Basques were, it is thought, one of the earliest cultures to fish the waters of the Atlantic. They were known to fish the cod banks of Newfoundland as early as the year 1000 and, as a result, it is said that there are over one-thousand recipes for *bacalao* in Basque cooking with most of them involving garlic, tomatoes, onions, and peppers.

Salt cod is fish that is salted and then dried while stockfish has simply been air-dried. Either one must be soaked in many turns of water to rehydrate the fish and to deplete some of the salt.

Herb-Broiled Cod with Clams, Bacon, Cabbage, and Biscuits

SERVES 6

Here, I've tried to take humble ingredients to new heights. Cabbage when cooked to an almost melting state is sweet and creamy. The bacon adds some smoke and salt to the creaminess and together they make great bedfellows for the delectable cod. There is a touch of the briny in the clams and a nice crunch with the panko crust. For the Second Day Dish, make sure to plan for leftover cod and cabbage.

¾ pound lean bacon, diced
2 tablespoons water
2 heads green cabbage, cored and cut into chiffonade (see page 67)
3 cups fish stock
½ cup (1 stick) unsalted butter
1 teaspoon coarse salt plus more to taste
Freshly ground black pepper
3 tablespoons fines herbes (see page 65)
2½ pounds cod, skin removed

2 cups panko bread crumbs (see Note)
2 teaspoons minced fresh flat-leaf parsley
1 teaspoon minced fresh tarragon
1 teaspoon minced fresh thyme
1 teaspoon minced fresh chives
3 tablespoons clarified butter (see page 7)
1 pound littleneck clams, washed and scrubbed
Buttermilk Biscuits, optional (recipe follows)
Scampi Butter, melted (recipe follows)

> NOTE: Panko bread crumbs are coarse Japanese bread crumbs that create a very crisp coating when cooked. Usually used when frying foods, they are available at Asian markets and specialty food stores.

To make the braised cabbage, place the bacon and water in a large saucepan and set over medium-high heat. Cook, stirring frequently, for about 10 minutes, or until the water has evaporated and the bacon is crisp. Add the cabbage, a few handfuls at a time, and cook, stirring frequently, for about 7 minutes, or until all of the cabbage is wilted. Add the stock, butter, and 1 teaspoon of the salt along with pepper to taste and bring to a boil. Lower the heat and simmer for about 20 minutes, or until the cabbage is almost melting. Stir in the fines herbes and remove from the heat. Taste and, if necessary, adjust the seasoning with additional salt and pepper. Strain the cabbage through a fine sieve, separately reserving the cabbage and 2 cups of the cabbage cooking broth.

Preheat the oven to 500 degrees.

Transfer the cabbage to a large oval casserole, spreading the cabbage out to cover the bottom. Place the cod in the center of the cabbage.

Place the panko, parsley, tarragon, thyme, and chives in a small mixing bowl. Add salt and pepper to taste and drizzle the clarified butter over the top. Toss to combine. Pat the panko mixture on top of the cod. Add the clams to the casserole and pour the reserved 2 cups of cabbage broth around the edge. Place in the preheated oven and bake for about 30 minutes, or until the crust is golden and crisp and the fish flakes easily when poked with a fork. Serve, family style, directly from the casserole with Buttermilk Biscuits and Scampi Butter on the side, if desired.

Buttermilk Biscuits

2 cups all-purpose flour	5 tablespoons vegetable shortening, chilled
1 tablespoon baking powder	2 tablespoons unsalted butter, chilled
½ teaspoon baking soda	1 cup buttermilk
¾ teaspoon salt	¼ cup melted unsalted butter

Preheat the oven to 425 degrees.

Line a baking sheet with parchment paper and set aside.

Combine the flour, baking powder, baking soda, and salt in a medium mixing bowl. Add the shortening and butter and, using your fingertips, work the fat into the dry mixture until large flakes form. Add the buttermilk and stir just until the dough comes together.

Lightly flour a clean, flat surface. Transfer the dough to the floured surface and lightly pat it out to form a circle about ¾ inch thick. Using a biscuit cutter, cut out circles of dough. Gather up all of the trimmings and lightly pat them together. Continue cutting until all of the dough has been used.

Place the biscuits on the prepared baking sheet and bake in the preheated oven for about 15 minutes, or until the dough has risen and the biscuits are golden brown. Remove the biscuits from the oven and, using a pastry brush, lightly coat the tops with the melted butter. Serve hot.

Scampi Butter

1 tablespoon fresh garlic purée
¼ cup white wine
1 cup (2 sticks) unsalted butter, at
    room temperature, cut into pieces

2 teaspoons coarse salt
¼ teaspoon freshly ground black pepper
½ cup chopped fresh flat-leaf parsley
    leaves

Place the garlic in the bowl of a food processor fitted with the metal blade. With the motor running, slowly add the wine. When well combined, add the butter, one piece at a time, blending to a smooth purée. Add the salt and pepper and process to incorporate them. Scrape the butter from the processor bowl into a clean container and very gently fold in the parsley; don't mix too vigorously, or the butter will turn green. Scrape the butter onto a sheet of plastic wrap and pull up the sides to form a neat log shape. Wrap the plastic carefully, twisting the ends to seal tightly, and refrigerate immediately. Keep the butter refrigerated until you are ready to use it.

To serve melted, place in a small saucepan over low heat for about 4 minutes. Do not allow the butter to boil.

Oh, My Cod!

SERVES 6

I've tried to imbue this dish with many of the flavors that I associate with the seashore. It can also satisfy the hearty appetite that a day boating brings. I can speak from experience in saying that it is also a perfect dinner-party dish. The shrimp "hash" and the vinaigrette can be made early in the day, and the dish can be quickly put together before you sit down to eat.

¼ cup clarified butter (see page 7)
1 large potato, peeled and diced
¼ pound bacon, diced

2 tablespoons water
12 large shrimp, peeled, deveined,
    and diced

2 stalks celery, diced
1 medium onion, diced
1 medium carrot, diced
1 red bell pepper, cored, seeded,
    membrane removed, and diced
2 teaspoons Old Bay Seasoning
Coarse salt
2 tablespoons fines herbes (see
    page 65)

2 teaspoons fresh lemon zest
2 tablespoons peanut oil
6 6-ounce cod fillets
Freshly ground black pepper
Tomato Vinaigrette (recipe
    follows)
1 cup celery leaves, optional
½ cup flat-leaf parsley leaves,
    optional

Heat the clarified butter in a medium sauté pan over medium heat. Add the potatoes and sauté for about 15 minutes, or until the potatoes are golden brown. Remove them from the heat and set aside.

Combine the bacon and water in a large sauté pan over medium-high heat. Fry for about 6 minutes, or until the water has evaporated and the bacon is crisp. Stir in the shrimp and sauté them for 3 minutes. Add the celery, onion, and carrot and cook, stirring frequently, for about 7 minutes, or until the vegetables have sweat their liquid but not taken on any color. Stir in the bell pepper and sauté for an additional 3 minutes. Add the Old Bay Seasoning and salt to taste. Add the reserved potatoes along with the fines herbes and sauté for an additional 5 minutes. Stir in 1 teaspoon of the lemon zest and remove the pan from the heat. Set it aside and tent it lightly with aluminum foil to keep it warm.

Heat the peanut oil in a large, nonstick sauté pan over medium-high heat. Season the cod with salt and pepper and lay the cod into the hot pan. Sear it for about 4 minutes, or just until the outside is nicely browned and crisp. Turn and cook it for another 5 minutes, or until the remaining side is crisp and the cod is cooked through but still moist.

Pour a circle of vinaigrette into the center of each of six plates. Mound an equal portion of the "hash" in the center of each plate. Place a piece of cod on the hash on each plate and, if desired, garnish with some celery and parsley leaves and a sprinkle of the remaining lemon zest.

Tomato Vinaigrette

12 plum tomatoes

Coarse salt and freshly ground
  black pepper

2½ cups olive oil

12 garlic slivers

12 sprigs fresh thyme

1 cup red wine vinegar

Preheat the oven to 350 degrees.

Line a baking sheet with parchment paper and set aside.

Cut each tomato in half lengthwise, and place the halves on the prepared baking sheet, cut side up. Season the cut sides with salt and pepper to taste. Using a pastry brush and ½ cup of the olive oil, lightly coat the tomatoes. Place a sliver of garlic and a sprig of thyme on each tomato. Place the baking sheet in the preheated oven and roast the tomatoes for 20 minutes, or until very tender. Remove them from the oven and allow them to cool.

When cool, remove and discard the garlic slivers and thyme. Place the tomatoes in a blender. Add the vinegar and process to a smooth purée. With the motor running on low, slowly add the remaining 2 cups of olive oil. When the mixture is fully emulsified, season to taste with salt and pepper. Pour the vinaigrette into a nonreactive container and cover it. Store at room temperature until ready to serve. (If the vinaigrette is refrigerated, the oil will solidify and break the emulsion. If this happens, simply bring the vinaigrette to room temperature and whisk it to emulsify.)

SECOND DAY DISH

Baked Potato with Cod and Red Pepper Coulis

SERVES 2

This is my take on *brandade de morue,* the classic salt cod mixture of the south of France. It is usually served on crusty baguette slices or on croutons that are the perfect foil for its very rich texture. Sometimes *brandade* is made with only cream and olive oil but, as often as not, it is extended with potatoes. I've used lardons in the potatoes but, if you really want to splurge, add some diced black truffle as is often done in Provence. I've added some cabbage and Red Pepper Coulis to dress up the dish a bit, but you can just serve the potato halves as a handheld snack if you like.

2 slices slab bacon, cut into a medium dice
1 tablespoon water
1 large Idaho potato, scrubbed
1 tablespoon vegetable oil
½ cup Herb-Broiled Cod (see page 196)
1 cup Mashed Potatoes (see page 88)
1 tablespoon chopped chives

Coarse salt and freshly ground black
 pepper to taste
1 tablespoon clarified butter (see page 7)
Red Pepper Coulis, optional (recipe
 follows)
½ cup braised cabbage and bacon, optional
 (see page 196)

Combine the bacon and water in a medium sauté pan over medium heat. Fry the bacon for about 10 minutes, or until all of the water has evaporated and the bacon lardons are crisp. Remove the bacon from the pan and drain it on a double layer of paper towels. Set aside.

Preheat oven to 350 degrees.

Randomly pierce the potato with a fork; this will allow steam to escape while it is baking. Generously rub the potato with vegetable oil to coat it well. Place the potato in the preheated oven and bake it for about 1 hour, or until it is very tender when pierced with the end of a small sharp knife. Remove the potato from the oven and set it aside. Do not turn off the oven.

Flake the cod into the Mashed Potatoes. Add the reserved bacon lardons along with the chopped chives and gently mix them together. Taste and, if necessary, season with salt and pepper.

Cut the baked potato in half lengthwise. Scoop out most of the potato pulp from each half, leaving about a ¼-inch edge. Reserve the scooped-out pulp for another use. Fill the hollows with the mashed potato-cod mixture. Using a pastry brush, lightly brush the tops with clarified butter. Place the filled potato halves on a small baking sheet with sides and bake them in the preheated oven for 15 minutes, or until the filling is hot and the tops have begun to take on some color.

While the potatoes are baking, reheat the coulis and the cabbage. Place each in a small saucepan over medium heat and bring to a simmer. Remove from the heat.

If you are using the cabbage, spoon ¼ cup of it into the center of each of two luncheon plates. Place a baked potato half on top of the cabbage and spoon Red Pepper Coulis around the edge. Serve immediately.

Red Pepper Coulis

6 tablespoons unsalted butter

1 small onion, chopped

⅛ teaspoon saffron

4 red bell peppers, cored, seeded, membrane removed, and chopped

2 cups fish stock or water

1½ teaspoons coarse salt

¼ teaspoon freshly ground black pepper

¼ cup extra virgin olive oil

Melt the butter in a medium saucepan over low heat. Add the onion and saffron, cover, and allow the onion to very slowly sweat its liquid without taking on any color. This should take about 8 minutes. Add the bell peppers and continue to cook slowly, stirring occasionally, for about 20 minutes, or until the peppers have begun to fall apart. Raise the heat and add the fish stock (or water). Bring to a boil; then lower the heat and simmer for 10 minutes. Remove from the heat and pour into a blender. Process to a smooth purée. Pour the purée through a fine sieve into a mixing bowl. Stir in the salt and pepper. Slowly add the olive oil, whisking until the mixture is well emulsified. Set it aside at room temperature until you are ready to use it. If the emulsification breaks, just whisk it back together.

TUNA

Boy, has tuna come a long way from the cans I knew as a kid! I have to say that I still love a tuna salad sandwich, but I also love the meatiness of a big slab of sushi-grade tuna, fresh off the grill and still red in the center.

Tuna is found only in warm waters, where it has been fished for centuries. Because of its size (a bluefin can weigh 1,000 pounds or more) tuna has always been considered a prize catch. Throughout the Mediterranean, beginning in about the fifth century, the bounty of the sea provided an almost inexhaustible supply of tuna. The Greeks learned to catch them with *madragues,* which literally translated means "enclosure for catching tuna." With the coming of international shipping and the arrival of oil tankers, the once teeming sea provides less and less tuna although the Greeks and Italians still have annual festivals celebrating the catch.

I revel in the new appreciation of the beautiful, rich meatlike flavor of tuna. In searching for recipe inspirations for this book, I found that in ancient Greece a famous cook and gastronome, Archestratus, had a well-loved recipe for bonito (a small tuna) wrapped in fig leaves and cooked over an open fire until just barely done. I also found that the great cooks of this period were judged by their ability to prepare fish, particularly tuna. It seems that, at least with tuna, what goes around comes around, as we now barely cook tuna to highlight its color and intense flavor, and great cooks are, once again, measured by their touch with preparing fish.

In Japan, where the Tokyo fish market is an amazing attraction as tourists stand wide-eyed at the enormous prices paid for premium fish, tuna remains the king. The Japanese love of tuna takes their buyers all over the world searching for the best. In America, we have seen a rapid escalation in the price of premium tuna as buyers vie for the firm, pink flesh of the yellowfin and small bluefin and the slightly oily, red flesh of the large bluefin that signifies a great tuna. And, with our appreciation of tuna growing quicker than the seas can provide, the price will continue to escalate, also.

Although much premium tuna is used raw in sushi bars and restaurants, a goodly amount is served just barely cooked. *Nouvelle cuisine* has been blamed for that, but tuna really does need a careful hand as it becomes dry and tasteless very quickly when cooked too much. From my perspective, cooked tuna requires some excellent oil and generous seasoning to stand up to its meatiness. If it is to be cooked through, this should be done with the addition of some type of sauce to enfold the fish and keep it moist. It can be prepared in almost any style, with grilling and oven-searing two of the most satisfactory methods. And, of course, the Japanese style of teriyaki remains one of the best ways to eat tuna.

When purchasing tuna, bluefin is always the best, but it is increasingly difficult to find especially for the home cook, as restaurants and sushi palaces usually get first choice. However, there is still great tuna to be had at fish stores and specialty markets. Always look for firm flesh, clean, clear color, and no dark red marks that would indicate bruising. I generally remove any very dark red flesh as it has a bit stronger flavor.

CLASSIC

Tuna Steak Provençal

SERVES 6

We have gotten so used to eating raw or barely cooked tuna with just a hint of seasoning that I thought it might be interesting to go back to a more traditional recipe that calls for tuna to be cooked all the way through and served with a very savory sauce. This is a very Mediterranean-style recipe that works well, in part because the meaty tuna more than holds its own against the acid and herbescent flavors of the sauce.

¼ cup olive oil
1 cup finely diced onions
4 cloves garlic, minced
1 pound very ripe tomatoes, peeled, cored, seeded, and diced
2 cups white wine
3 tablespoons chopped canned anchovy fillets
2 chopped capers

6 7-ounce tuna steaks
Coarse salt and freshly ground black pepper
½ cup (1 stick) unsalted butter, cut into pieces
Juice of 1 lemon
½ cup chopped fresh basil
1 tablespoon chopped fresh flat-leaf parsley

Heat 2 tablespoons of the olive oil in a large sauté pan over medium-high heat. Add the onions and garlic and sauté them for 5 minutes. Add the tomatoes and cook them, stirring occasionally, for 10 minutes. Stir in the white wine and bring the mixture to a boil. Boil for about 15 minutes, or until the wine has reduced by one-half. Stir in the anchovies and capers. Remove from the heat and tent lightly with aluminum foil to keep warm.

Heat the remaining 2 tablespoons of olive oil in a large sauté pan over medium-high heat. Season the tuna with salt and pepper and place it into the hot pan. Sear it for about 3 minutes per side, or until it is nicely browned and an instant-read thermometer inserted into the center of the fish reads 130 degrees. Using a spatula, lift the tuna from the hot pan to a serving platter and set it aside. Tent lightly with aluminum foil to keep it warm.

Return the tomato mixture to medium heat. When it is hot, whisk in the butter and stir to emulsify the mixture. Add the lemon juice, and then the basil and parsley. Uncover the tuna and pour the pan sauce over the top of it. Serve it, garnished with additional basil and parsley, if desired.

Tuna Steak au Moutarde with Miso Vinaigrette and Shiitake Dumplings

SERVES 6

The great thing about this recipe is that all of the components can stand on their own. You could serve the tuna on top of a bed of spicy greens with a soy vinaigrette. The dumplings can be served as an hors d'oeuvre with a simple tamari dipping sauce, and the vinaigrette can dress up almost any meat, poultry, fish, or salad. When it comes to putting all of these together in one meal, you'll just need a little pre-planning. The dumplings should be started the day before or made in advance and frozen for up to a month. The vinaigrette can be done a couple of days in advance and stored, covered and refrigerated. The tuna can be crusted a few hours in advance and kept chilled. It will all come together in a snap.

½ cup panko bread crumbs (see Note)

½ cup mustard seeds

2 tablespoons plus ¼ teaspoon coarse salt

1 cup Wondra flour (see page 70)

4 large egg whites

2 tablespoons Dijon mustard

6 sheets nori (see Note)

6 8-ounce logs center-cut tuna

Approximately ½ cup olive oil

Miso Vinaigrette (recipe follows)

Shiitake Dumplings (recipe follows)

2 tablespoons sliced scallions

1 tablespoon toasted sesame seeds

NOTE: Panko (see page 196), sesame oil, wonton skins, and miso paste are available from Asian markets, specialty food stores and some supermarkets.

Preheat the oven to 250 degrees.

Line a baking sheet with parchment paper and set aside.

Combine the panko and mustard seeds with 2 tablespoons of salt in a shallow bowl. Place the flour in another shallow bowl.

To make a seasoned egg wash, whisk the egg whites, Dijon mustard, and ¼ teaspoon salt together in another shallow bowl.

Using a pastry brush, lightly coat the nori sheets with just enough water to soften them. Wrap each tuna log with a piece of nori and trim the ends to make an even fit. Place the tuna logs into the flour, turning to coat all sides. Shake off any excess. Then, roll the logs in the seasoned egg wash, allowing the excess to dip off. Roll each log in the panko crust.

Heat 3 tablespoons of oil in a medium sauté pan over medium-high heat until it begins to smoke. Working with two tuna logs at a time, place the tuna in the hot oil and sear it, turning the tuna every 2 minutes, for about 8 minutes, or until all sides are nicely crusted.

As the tuna is cooked, place the logs on the prepared baking sheet and into the preheated oven with the door ajar to just keep the tuna warm while you continue to crust the remaining logs.

Heat the Miso Vinaigrette in a medium saucepan over medium heat. Add the dumplings and bring the mixture to a simmer. Remove it from the heat.

Cut the tuna logs crosswise into ¼-inch-thick slices, keeping each log together. Fan out a tuna log onto the left of, preferably, an oval plate. Place two dumplings in each of six bowls and ladle Miso Vinaigrette over them. Place each bowl on the right side of a plate. Sprinkle the scallions in the vinaigrette and the sesame seeds over the tuna. Serve immediately.

Oh, My Cod!
(Contemporary)

Tuna Steak au Moutarde
with Miso Vinaigrette
and Shiitake Dumplings
(Contemporary)

Poached Salmon with
Tomato-Herb Butter
Sauce and Cucumber
(Classic)

Grilled Lobster
with Rosemary
Oil, Asparagus,
and Tomato-
Garlic Aïoli
(Classic)

Angry Lobster with Lemon Rice
and Crispy Basil (Contemporary)

Lobster-Mango Rolls with Soy-Ginger
Vinaigrette (Second Day Dish)

Sautéed Shrimp with
Spinach-Lasagna Roll
and Crisp Spinach
(Contemporary)

Shrimp Fried Rice
and Sausage
(Second Day Dish)

Miso Vinaigrette

2 cups tomato juice

2 cups Tomato Fondue (recipe follows)

½ cup miso paste

1 tablespoon minced fresh tarragon

½ teaspoon minced fresh ginger

1 cup rice wine vinegar

½ cup soy sauce

½ cup peanut oil

¼ cup mustard oil (see page 50)

2 tablespoons honey

Place the tomato juice, Tomato Fondue, miso paste, tarragon, and ginger in the bowl of a food processor fitted with the metal blade. Process the mixture to a smooth purée. With the motor running, slowly add the vinegar, soy sauce, peanut oil, mustard oil and honey, processing it until well blended. Pour the contents into a nonreactive container and store it, covered and refrigerated, until you are ready to use it.

Tomato Fondue

1 tablespoon olive oil

1 large onion, finely diced

1 clove garlic, thinly sliced

4 cups canned tomato purée

1 tightly packed cup chopped fresh
   basil leaves

Coarse salt and freshly ground black
   pepper

Heat the oil in a medium saucepan over medium heat. Add the onion and garlic and allow them to sweat, stirring frequently, for about 10 minutes, or until translucent. Add the tomato purée and one-half of the basil and bring the mixture to a simmer. Immediately lower the heat and cook it, at a bare simmer, stirring frequently, for about 40 minutes, or until 90 percent of the moisture has evaporated. Stir in the remaining basil and season with salt and pepper to taste. Remove the pan from the heat and allow it to cool. Store the mixture, covered and refrigerated, for up to 5 days, or freeze it, tightly covered and labeled, for up to 3 months.

Shiitake Dumplings

1½ pounds shiitake mushrooms,
    cleaned with stems removed
¼ cup peanut oil
2 cups soy-honey marinade (see
    page 104)
1 teaspoon chopped cilantro

½ teaspoon coarse salt
¼ teaspoon minced fresh ginger
¼ teaspoon sesame oil
¾ teaspoon cornstarch
12 to 14 square wonton skins

Place the mushrooms in a mixing bowl. Drizzle the peanut oil over them and toss to coat.

Preheat and oil the grill or preheat a stove-top grill.

Place the mushrooms on the grill and grill them, turning once, for 2 minutes per side. Return them to the mixing bowl and add the soy-honey marinade. Cover and refrigerate the mixture for 12 hours or overnight.

Drain the mushrooms through a fine sieve, discarding the liquid. Julienne the mushrooms. Add the cilantro, salt, ginger and sesame oil and stir to combine. Add the cornstarch and beat until it is well incorporated into the mixture.

Lay the wonton skins out in a single layer in a diamond shape. Place a small bowl of water close at hand. Spoon about a tablespoon of the mushroom mixture into the center of each wonton skin. Using your fingertips, very lightly coat the edges with water and immediately fold the wontons in half to form a triangle. Wet the folded corners and bring them up and over slightly to make a little, bowl-shaped dumpling.

Bring a large pot of salted water to a boil over high heat. Add the wontons and boil them for about 5 minutes, or until they float to the top. Using a slotted spoon, lift the wontons from the boiling water. Set them aside until you are ready to use them.

SECOND DAY DISH

Tuna Niçoise Salad Hash

SERVES 6

The tuna in the hash can come from either the Provençal or the pepper-crusted tuna. The flavors from either one will work very nicely in this Niçoise presentation. This dish is pretty simple to put together and looks gorgeous on the plate, if you have the hash molded in the 6-inch-round ring mold. However, if you don't have one, a nice, neat circle of hash in the center of the plate will work just fine. You might want to serve some warm, toasty bread with extra virgin olive oil for dipping and a classic Chardonnay to complete the meal.

¼ cup clarified butter (see page 7)
3 Yukon Gold potatoes, peeled and diced
Coarse salt and freshly ground black
    pepper
¼ cup olive oil
1 large onion, finely diced
3 cloves garlic, minced
2 red bell peppers, cored, seeded,
    membrane removed, and diced
2 yellow bell peppers, cored, seeded,
    membrane removed, and diced
½ cup Tomato Fondue (see page 207)

5 large fresh basil leaves, cut into
    chiffonade (see page 67)
1 pound cooked tuna, flaked apart
2 tablespoons extra virgin olive oil
12 cups mixed salad greens
12 large fresh basil leaves
½ cup plus 2 tablespoons David Burke's
    Vinaigrette (see page 107)
6 large, hard-boiled eggs, peeled and
    quartered
1 cup pitted Niçoise olives
Basil Oil (recipe follows)

Heat the butter in a large sauté pan over medium heat. Add the potatoes and fry them, stirring frequently to ensure even cooking, for about 18 minutes, or until they are tender and golden brown. Remove the potatoes from the heat and place in a fine sieve to drain off excess butter. Set the potatoes aside on a double layer of paper towels to drain. Season with salt and pepper to taste.

Heat the olive oil in a large sauté pan over medium heat. Add the onions and cook for about 5 minutes, or until the onions are tender but have not taken on any color. Add the garlic and cook the mixture for an additional 3 minutes. Stir in the bell peppers and continue to sauté the mix for another 7 minutes, or until the peppers have softened. Add the Tomato Fondue and the reserved potatoes and sauté them for another 3 minutes, or just until the mixture is hot. Remove from the heat and toss in the basil. Taste and, if necessary, season with additional salt and pepper.

Place the tuna flakes in a medium bowl and drizzle the extra virgin olive oil over the top. Toss to coat evenly.

Place the salad greens and basil leaves in a mixing bowl and drizzle the dressing over the top. Toss to coat well.

Using a 6-inch-round ring mold, form a circle of hash in the center of each of six dinner plates. Mound some salad on top of the hash on each plate. Sprinkle tuna flakes over the salad. Garnish each plate with hard-boiled egg quarters and olives. Drizzle Basil Oil around the edge of the plate and serve.

Basil Oil

4 tightly packed cups fresh basil leaves
2 cups light olive oil
2 teaspoons salt or to taste

Blanch the basil in boiling salted water for 5 seconds and immediately shock the basil in ice water so that the leaves keep their intense green color. Place the leaves in a paper towels and wrap tightly to dry.

Using a chef's knife, roughly chop the basil. Again, place the basil in a paper towels and wrap it tightly to squeeze out all of the water.

Line a fine sieve with cheesecloth and place it over a mixing bowl. Set aside.

Place the basil and salt in a blender or food processor fitted with the metal blade. Slowly add the oil, processing to make a smooth paste. Scrape the basil purée into the cheesecloth-lined sieve and allow it to drain. Push on the solids from time to time to make sure all of the oil is draining off. Pour the purée into a container with a lid (a squeeze bottle is a perfect receptacle) and let it stand for 1 day before using. Covered tightly and refrigerated, Basil Oil will keep for about 1 week.

SALMON

Salmon, once so abundant, is notable for its ability to survive and procreate under harrowing conditions as well as for its reasonable price and ease of preparation. It is a freshwater fish that spends most of its life in the sea. It is spawned in fresh water to which it always returns to spawn its own offspring. The eggs are hatched in the fall in a shallow streambed, where the tiny fish grow into mature salmon as they make their way up the stream to brackish water that will acclimate them for the sea. This process may take anywhere from one to five years, at which point the salmon return to the sea for no more than six years, and then start the homeward journey as they return to the same streambed to spawn and perpetuate the species.

Very little salmon that comes to the market today is wild salmon. Modern aquaculture has made it possible to farm salmon in the type of water in which it flourishes; that, in turn, has made it inexpensive and bountiful. Salmon farming was developed in Norway in the 1970s in response to the depletion of wild stock and it is now done all over the world. Once only found in the waters of the Atlantic, it is now raised in Norway, Chile, Maine, and even in the Pacific Northwest (which makes its name a bit confusing). It is, in fact, raised almost anywhere there is clean, extremely cold seawater. Farming has been so successful that the consumer can now buy excellent salmon all year round and probably pay less than was charged twenty years ago.

There are a number of different kinds of salmon. Gourmands consider Scottish or Irish wild salmon to be the best. Its fine, pale pink flesh is slightly oily with an almost sweet taste and is perfectly delicious, simply prepared. Unfortunately, about the time that the Norwegians were introducing farmed fish, Scotland encountered an epidemic in its streams that almost totally depleted its stock of wild fish, so its availability is extremely limited.

Salmon is usually tagged Atlantic or Pacific. Pacific salmon is now primarily shipped from Alaska; however, there are farms throughout the Pacific Northwest. Pacific salmon is somewhat darker in color, leaner, and less oily than its Atlantic counterpart. Within the Pacific category you will find chinook or king, coho, keta, and sockeye with chinook having the reddest color and deepest flavor. Virtually all of the Atlantic salmon marketed now is farm raised. Even when farmed, Atlantic salmon is usually thought of as the richer tasting fish.

In my early days of cooking, salmon was found in one of the classic French preparations with which all young chefs had to try their hand. Called *coulibiac au saumon*, it is a complicated dish often likened erroneously to a pâté. It calls for a filling of salmon, rice, mushrooms, hard-boiled eggs, shallots, and dill that was, classically, flavored with the spinal marrow of sturgeon. The filling is first wrapped in crêpes and then in brioche dough. The whole package is baked and served with a rich cream sauce. *Coulibiac* had a resurgence in the sixties when cooks were learning about the French repertoire from Julia Child, but I don't think it has been mentioned often in the past fifteen years.

Salmon is adaptable to almost all types of cooking. If salmon has not been frozen, when cooked it will have a creaminess between its layers that keeps it moist and juicy. It can be cooked whole, usually poached, grilled, or roasted or in steaks or as fillets. Because its skin will crisp beautifully, salmon is frequently cooked with the skin on. It is often served with rich egg- or butter-based sauces such as hollandaise or beurre blanc and fresh herbs such as dill or tarragon, all of which highlight its deep flavorful succulence and delicate pink-orange color. Salmon is now usually cooked to medium-rare with a nicely glazed exterior.

CLASSIC

Poached Salmon with Tomato-Herb Butter Sauce and Cucumber

SERVES 6

This recipe combines some classic complementary salmon flavors—herbs (particularly dill), white wine, cucumber, and sweet butter. The poached salmon is about as simple as you can get when cooking fish. (You can use the recipe for the poaching liquid to cook almost any fish or shellfish.) I don't think there is anything better for a summer lunch than a beautifully poached whole salmon garnished with herbs and cucumber. The poaching liquid, the salad, and the butter can all be made in advance. Baby Red Bliss potatoes boiled in the poaching liquid and served sprinkled with *fleur de sel* and cracked pepper would complete the meal.

6 cups water

1 cup white wine

1 carrot, diced

1 stalk celery, trimmed and diced

½ large onion, diced

½ fennel bulb, trimmed and diced

1 teaspoon peppercorns

1 teaspoon fennel seeds

1 sprig fresh thyme

1 bay leaf

3 tablespoons coarse salt plus more
to taste

¼ cup light olive oil

¼ cup minced shallots

1 large carrot, cut crosswise into
paper-thin disks

3 large cucumbers, peeled, seeded, and
cut into 3 inch × ¼-inch-thick sticks

2 tablespoons minced fresh dill

Freshly ground black pepper to taste

6 7-ounce pieces salmon, skin and
bones removed

Tomato-Herb Butter Sauce (recipe
follows)

To make the poaching liquid, combine the water, wine, carrot, celery, onion, diced fennel, peppercorns, fennel seeds, thyme, and bay leaf in a large roasting pan on top of the stove over high heat. Stir in 3 tablespoons of the salt and bring to a boil. Lower the heat and simmer the liquid for 20 minutes. Remove it from the heat and allow the aromatics to infuse the poaching liquid for at least 1 hour.

Heat the light olive oil in a large sauté pan over medium heat. Add the shallots and sauté for 3 minutes, or until translucent. Add the carrot disks and sauté for 1 minute. Stir in the cucumbers and sauté for an additional 3 minutes, or just until the cucumbers begin to wilt. Stir in the dill and season with salt and pepper to taste. Remove the pan from the heat and set it aside.

Bring the poaching liquid to a boil over high heat. Place the salmon in the poaching liquid and lower the heat to a simmer. Simmer the fish for about 15 minutes, or until an instant-read thermometer inserted into the thickest part of the salmon reads 130 degrees. Using two spatulas, lift the salmon from the poaching liquid and place it on a large, oval serving platter. Spoon the cucumber sauté around the edge of the platter and spoon the Tomato-Herb Butter over the top of it. Serve family style.

Tomato-Herb Butter

¼ cup white wine
1 tablespoon minced shallot
1 cup (2 sticks) unsalted butter, cut
    into pieces
3 tablespoons Tomato Fondue (see
    page 207)

2 tablespoons fines herbes (see
    page 65)
Coarse salt and freshly ground black
    pepper to taste

Combine the wine and shallots in a small nonreactive saucepan over medium heat. Bring the liquid to a simmer; then lower the heat and just barely simmer for about 7 minutes, or until the wine is reduced to 1 tablespoon. Slowly add the butter, a piece at a time, whisking until the butter is emulsified into the wine. Keep the saucepan over the heat only until the butter is completely melted. Whisking constantly, beat in the Tomato Fondue and fines herbes. Season to taste with salt and pepper. Serve lukewarm. (The butter can be made early in the day. When you reheat it, whisk it constantly, in the top half of a double boiler over boiling water.)

CONTEMPORARY

Salmon Leaves Cooked on the Plate with Shrimp, Grapefruit, and Basil

SERVES 6

This is a simple dish to prepare but, you will need six heat-proof dinner plates and you must cut the salmon and shrimp really, really thin so that the fish cooks quickly under the broiler. You can also add a small mound of tender baby salad greens (dressed with the Grapefruit Vinaigrette) to the plate for a more complete dish.

2 large Ruby Red grapefruit
6 7-ounce pieces skinless, boneless salmon
1 tablespoon light olive oil

12 large shrimp, peeled and deveined,
    tails removed
Coarse salt and freshly ground black pepper

Grapefruit Vinaigrette (recipe follows)
10 leaves fresh basil, cut into chiffonade
  (see page 67)

2 tablespoons thinly sliced scallion,
  some green part included

Using a very sharp knife, remove the skin and all pith from the grapefruit. If the ends are uneven, trim them flat. Using the knife, cut down between the membrane on each side of a segment and lift the segments free. Set the grapefruit "*suprêmes*" aside in a small non-reactive bowl.

Move the broiler rack to the slot closest to the heat and preheat the broiler.

Working with one piece of salmon and one heat-proof plate at a time, cut the fish into paper-thin slices and fan the slices out across the plate so that they are smooth and only slightly overlapping. Cover them with plastic wrap while you continue to prepare plates. Place the prepared plates under the preheated broiler and broil for about 4 minutes, or just until the salmon has begun to cook. (Obviously, the size of the broiler will determine how many plates can be done at a time.)

Heat the oil in a medium sauté pan over medium-high heat. Add the shrimp and season with salt and pepper to taste. Sauté for about 4 minutes, or just until the shrimp are cooked through. Add the reserved *suprêmes,* along with the vinaigrette, and stir to just warm the fruit through. Remove the pan from the heat and stir in the basil. Taste and, if necessary, adjust the seasoning with additional salt and pepper. Spoon equal portions of the shrimp mixture over the salmon on each plate. Garnish each plate with some scallions and serve.

Grapefruit Vinaigrette

2 cups fresh grapefruit juice
¼ cup red wine vinegar
2 tablespoons minced shallots
¾ teaspoon coarse salt or to taste

¾ cup light olive oil
¼ cup Basil Oil (see page 210)
Freshly ground black pepper to taste,
  optional

Place the grapefruit juice in a small nonreactive saucepan over medium-high heat and bring it to a boil. Lower the heat and simmer the liquid for about 15 minutes, or until the juice has reduced to 1 cup. Remove the pan from the heat and allow it to cool.

Combine the reduced grapefruit juice with the vinegar, shallots, and salt. Whisk the olive oil and Basil Oil together; then, whisk the oils into the grapefruit juice mixture to just blend.

This is a "broken" vinaigrette, so make sure that you do not whisk long enough to emulsify it. Taste and adjust the seasoning with pepper and, if necessary, additional salt. Serve at room temperature.

SECOND DAY DISH

Roasted Onion Stuffed with Salmon and Tomato Salad

SERVES 2

You can use almost any meat or fish in this recipe but I think salmon works particularly well. The pine nuts and fennel add a nice crunch to an otherwise smooth mix. If you want a more bountiful plate, the tomato slices could be mixed into some salad greens (tossed with David Burke's Vinaigrette {see page 107}) and then placed on each plate to make a nice nest for the onion halves.

2 large red onions, trimmed

½ tablespoon olive oil

Coarse salt and freshly ground black pepper

2 teaspoons chopped cornichons

1 teaspoon capers

Zest of ½ lemon

3 tablespoons mayonnaise

1 teaspoon Dijon mustard

1 teaspoon fresh lemon juice

½ teaspoon Old Bay Seasoning

Pinch of fennel powder

¾ cup flaked, cooked salmon

2 tablespoons finely diced fennel bulb

1 tablespoon toasted pine nuts

1 teaspoon fines herbes (see page 65)

1 large plum tomato, cut crosswise into thin slices

Preheat the oven to 300 degrees.

Generously coat each onion with olive oil and season with salt and pepper to taste. Wrap each onion in heavy-duty aluminum foil and place in a baking pan. Place the pan in the preheated oven and roast the onions for about 1 hour, or until they are tender in the center when pierced with the point of a small sharp knife. Remove them from the oven and unwrap. When the onions are cool enough to handle, cut them in half crosswise and remove and reserve the center rings. Set the onions aside.

Finely chop the onion centers and combine them with the cornichons, capers, and lemon zest in a medium mixing bowl. Add the mayonnaise, mustard, lemon juice, Old Bay Seasoning, and fennel powder, mixing to combine well. Fold in the salmon, diced fennel, pine nuts, and fines herbes. Season the mixture with salt and pepper to taste.

Place the tomato slices in a shallow bowl and season them with salt and pepper to taste. Place a few of the seasoned tomato slices in the center of each of two luncheon plates. Spoon equal portions of the salmon mixture into the hollow of each onion half. Place two filled onion halves on each plate and serve.

LOBSTER

When I talk about lobster, I am talking about those big Maine bruisers although there are certainly other types. As far as I am concerned none can compare to the Maine species. Considered among the world's most luxurious foods along with caviar and foie gras, lobster was once so plentiful that it was an everyday meal and the price was insignificant. This is no longer true as lobsters have fallen victim to the same overfishing that jeopardizes other creatures of the sea.

I always purchase live lobsters, but I know that cooking one is a kitchen chore most people want to avoid. Scientists assure us that lobsters feel no pain either when they hit the boiling water or when a knife pierces them, but I respect people's feelings about this. Still, a live lobster will provide you with the sweetest meat. It helps to put live lobsters in the freezer for a few minutes to put them to sleep so that its muscles don't contract when it is pierced with a knife.

When purchasing lobsters, you want to get the feisty ones. A quiet lobster usually means a lobster that is not at the peak of its form. A live lobster should weigh over one and one-quarter pounds, or it will not have enough meat to make it worth its price. I prefer those that are between two and three pounds; on occasion I've prepared lobsters weighing about ten pounds. When not serving lobster whole (or cut in half) there is no problem with buying "culls," lobsters with only one claw. In the wild, lobsters often lose claws, which will eventually grow back. Store live lobsters in the refrigerator wrapped in seaweed or wet newspapers. Live lobsters placed in tap water will die immediately.

When eating lobster many people covet the green tomalley, or liver. I love it smeared on crackers or crusty bread. The blackish-green roe or coral becomes a solid block of bright red eggs when cooked. It is eaten along with the lobster. There is an ongoing debate about whether the male or female lobster is tastier. The female is distinguished by her soft pliable swimmerets, the small appendages along both sides of the abdomen, which are hard in the male. I don't know that most people could tell the difference, but I have found that female lobsters are a wee bit meatier and their meat is just a bit more tender than that of males. Lobster meat should be very sweet, moist, and tender. If yours is not, it was either too small or it was overcooked.

Lobster is best when boiled, steamed, or grilled. When it is to be served in a sauce or stir-fry, it is usually boiled first and then its meat is removed in chunks. When serving whole or halved lobsters, it is a good idea to offer nutcrackers or lobster crackers and picks to allow every piece of meat to be pulled from the shell.

We now eat more boiled, steamed, or grilled lobster than the old-fashioned richly sauced lobster dishes: Lobster Thermidor, with its overwhelmingly rich cheese, cream, and mushroom sauce; Lobster Américaine with its Provençal leanings; and Lobster Newburg. As you will find in the following recipes, I prefer lobster cooked simply with some terrific accompaniments. And, because I love it so much, there are three extra recipes in this section.

CLASSIC

Boiled Lobster with Drawn Butter and Boiled Potatoes

SERVES 6

Ideally, you would be sitting in a summer shack on the Maine coast when you sit down to this meal. It's a classic and has remained essentially unchanged for generations. Some folks would combine the potatoes with fresh green beans while some would combine the potatoes with new peas in a cream sauce, but no one would change the lobster. Boil or steam it and dip it into some warm, sweet creamery butter—is there anything better? Make a note that if you want to prepare the Second Day Dish, you will need an extra half pound of lobster and twelve more potatoes.

1 pound (4 sticks) unsalted butter
¼ cup minced fresh flat-leaf parsley
1½ cups plus 1 teaspoon coarse salt with more to taste
¼ teaspoon freshly ground black pepper plus more to taste
5 pounds baby Red Bliss or Yukon Gold potatoes
3 2½-pound fresh lobsters
5 gallons water

6 cups white wine
4 stalks celery, chopped
2 large carrots, sliced
2 large onions, diced
3 sprigs fresh flat-leaf parsley
3 sprigs fresh thyme
2 whole lemons, quartered
3 large ripe beefsteak tomatoes, peeled, cored, and cut in half crosswise

Place the butter in a small saucepan over medium heat. Cook it for about 5 minutes, or just until melted. Add 3 tablespoons of the parsley along with 1 teaspoon salt and ¼ teaspoon of pepper. Remove the mixture from the heat and pour it into the top half of a double boiler over very hot water to keep it warm. Do not cover, or the condensation that forms on the lid will drop back into the butter.

Place the potatoes in a large saucepan and add cold, salted water to cover by 1-inch. Place the saucepan over high heat and bring the water to a boil. Lower the heat and simmer the potatoes for 30 minutes, or until a sharp knife can be very easily inserted into the center. Remove them from the heat and drain well. Handling the potatoes carefully to prevent burning yourself, cut the potatoes in half and stir in ¼ cup of the drawn butter along with the remaining 1 tablespoon of parsley and salt and pepper to taste. Tent them lightly with aluminum foil to keep them warm.

Place a skewer straight into each lobster from under the tail through the body. This will hold the lobster straight while it cooks.

To make a shellfish poaching liquid, combine the water, wine, chopped celery, sliced carrots, diced onions, parsley sprigs, thyme, lemons, and the remaining 1½ cups of salt in a large stockpot or lobster pot. Place over high heat and bring the contents to a boil. Immediately add the lobsters and boil them for 18 minutes. Using tongs, lift the lobsters from the water and place them on a large platter. When they are just barely cool enough to handle, pierce into the center of each lobster's head with a sharp chef's knife and, drawing the knife downward, split the lobsters in half lengthwise. Place a lobster half on each of six dinner plates. Pour drawn butter into small ramekins and place one on each plate. Pass around the boiled potatoes and tomatoes.

Poached Lobster with Onion Rings and Basil Ranch Dressing

Serves 6

The finished plate looks quite complicated, but putting it together is quite simple. The lobsters can be cooked and taken apart a couple of hours before serving them and the dressing can be made the day before. You can make the Onion Rings early in the day and reheat them in a 350-degree oven. When you first make them, just be sure to let most of the grease drain out, or reheating will cause them to get soggy. Everything can be put together in a flash.

6 2-pound live lobsters
Fish poaching liquid (see page 213)
¼ cup clarified butter (see page 7)
2 large carrots, julienned
24 stalks fresh asparagus, trimmed, cut into 2-inch pieces, and blanched

Coarse salt and freshly ground black pepper
½ cup finely diced tomatoes
Onion Rings (recipe follows)
Basil Ranch Dressing (recipe follows)

Break the claws from each lobster and place them in a bowl. Remove the head and the tail from each lobster by twisting them away from the body, and place them in another bowl. Form the lobster tails into doughnut-shaped circles, using a metal skewer to hold each firmly in place.

Place the poaching liquid in a large stockpot over high heat and bring it to a boil. Add the claws to the boiling liquid and simmer for 3 minutes. Add the tails and simmer for an additional 7 minutes. Using a slotted spoon or tongs, lift the lobster pieces from the poaching liquid and place them on a large platter to cool slightly. Reserve 2 cups of the poaching liquid.

Using kitchen scissors, cut the body portion of the shell and remove the meat. Crack the claws and remove the meat, trying to keep pieces whole. Save the tail shells for the presentation. Cover the lobster meat lightly with a warm, damp, clean kitchen towel to keep it warm and moist. (If it is necessary to reheat the lobster, combine the reserved 2 cups of poaching liquid with ½ cup of unsalted butter in a large sauté pan over medium-low heat. Add the tail and heat for about 2 minutes; then, add the claws and continue heating for an additional 2 minutes.)

Heat the clarified butter in a large sauté pan over medium heat. Add the carrots and sauté for 4 minutes, or until they just begin to cook. Add the asparagus and salt and pepper to taste and sauté for an additional 4 minutes, or just until the asparagus is heated through. Stir in the diced tomatoes.

Place a lobster "steak" in the center of each of six plates. Pile three Onion Rings on top and place equal portions of the carrot-asparagus mixture in their center. Nestle two claws into the Onion Rings on each plate. Spoon Basil Ranch Dressing around the edge of each plate and serve, garnished with basil leaves, if desired.

Onion Rings

4 large onions
1 cup Wondra flour
Tempura batter (see page 189)

Approximately 8 cups vegetable oil
Coarse salt and freshly ground black
 pepper

Preheat the oven to 200 degrees.

Line two baking sheets with a double layer of paper towels and set aside.

Peel the onions and trim each end from the onions to make an even, flat surface. Cut the onions crosswise into ½-inch-thick rings and pull the rings apart.

Place the flour in a plastic bag. Working with a few onion rings at a time, place them into the flour and, holding the bag closed, shake to coat. Remove the rings from the flour and shake off any excess.

Place the tempura batter in a mixing bowl.

Place the oil in a deep-fat fryer over medium-high heat and bring it to 365 degrees on a candy thermometer.

Working quickly and with a few dredged rings at a time, dip them into the tempura batter and then drop them into the hot oil. Fry them for about 5 minutes, or until the rings are floating and golden brown on all sides. Place them on the paper-towel–lined baking sheets and allow them to drain. Season with salt and pepper to taste. If you need to keep the rings warm, transfer the drained rings to another baking sheet and place them in the preheated oven, with the door ajar, until you are ready to serve.

Basil Ranch Dressing

1¼ cups sour cream
1 cup mayonnaise
½ cup buttermilk
¼ cup Basil Oil (see page 210)
2 cloves garlic, minced

¼ cup sliced scallions, both white and
 green parts
1 tablespoon chopped fresh flat-leaf parsley
1 teaspoon coarse salt
1 tablespoon fresh basil julienne

Combine the sour cream, mayonnaise, buttermilk, and Basil Oil in a medium, nonreactive mixing bowl. When the mixture is well blended, stir in the garlic, scallions, and parsley. Season with salt to taste and fold in the basil. Cover and refrigerate the dressing until you are ready to use it. (The dressing may be made up to 24 hours in advance.)

Mixed Green Salad with Tiny Potatoes Stuffed with Russian-Style Lobster Salad

SERVES 2

If you buy the cooked lobster and boil potatoes in advance, this is a very simple dish to prepare. I've given you a recipe for tartar sauce, but if you really want to speed things up, buy a jar and mix a couple of tablespoons of ketchup into it, toss it with the lobster meat, and the salad is done. When purchasing the salad greens for this recipe, combine some red, green, and white to put some color on the plate. You can easily use the tartar sauce as the dressing for the greens, or you can use my preferred vinaigrette (see page 107).

3 tablespoons mayonnaise
1 tablespoon fresh lemon juice
2 teaspoons ketchup
1½ tablespoons fines herbes (see page 65)
1 teaspoon chopped cornichons
1 teaspoon minced shallots
½ teaspoon chopped capers
½ teaspoon freshly grated lemon zest
Dash of Tabasco sauce

Dash Worcestershire sauce
Coarse salt and freshly ground black pepper
4 cooked, large Red Bliss or medium Yukon
  Gold potatoes
½ pound cooked lobster meat, diced
4 loosely packed cups mixed salad greens
½ cup plus 2 tablespoons David Burke's
  Vinaigrette, optional (see page 107)

To make the tartar sauce, combine the mayonnaise, lemon juice, and ketchup in a small mixing bowl. Stir in the fines herbes, cornichons, shallots, capers, lemon zest, Tabasco, Worcestershire, and salt and pepper to taste. Set the tartar sauce aside.

Using a sharp knife, cut a top and bottom from each potato, taking care that you do not take off too much as you want as much of the potato as possible. Using a melon baller, scoop out and discard the center of each potato, leaving a neat potato shell large enough to hold a hefty portion of the salad.

Place the lobster meat in a mixing bowl and add just enough of the reserved tartar sauce to moisten it lightly. Mound the lobster salad into the center of each potato.

Place the salad greens in a large bowl and lightly drizzle them with tartar sauce or, if you'd rather, my vinaigrette. Toss to coat lightly. Pile equal portions of salad onto each of two plates. Place two potatoes beside the salad and serve.

CLASSIC

Grilled Lobster with Rosemary Oil, Asparagus, and Tomato-Garlic Aïoli

SERVES 6

This recipe could be filling for the first backyard grill of the season with fresh-as-can-be asparagus and the more plentiful and often less expensive spring lobster.

Blanching the lobster before grilling ensures that it cooks quickly and won't dry out with the high heat of the grill. The Tomato-Garlic Aïoli can be made two days in advance. Remember to grill some extra lobster so you can prepare the Second Day Dish.

3 2-pound live lobsters
Fish poaching liquid (see
     page 213)
2 pounds fresh asparagus,
     trimmed and peeled
Rosemary Oil (recipe follows)

Coarse salt and freshly ground black
     pepper
2 tablespoons cracked black pepper
1 teaspoon fresh lemon zest
Tomato-Garlic Aïoli (recipe follows)

Break the claws from each lobster and place them in a bowl. Remove the head from each lobster. Discard the heads and place the bodies in a bowl.

Place the poaching liquid in a stockpot over high heat and bring it to a boil. Add the claws and boil for 1 minute; then add the bodies and boil for an additional 3 minutes. Remove the lobster pieces from the boiling liquid and refresh them under cold running water. Pat them dry. Split the bodies in half lengthwise. Crack the claws and remove the meat in one piece. Set aside.

Place the asparagus on a platter and add about ¼ cup of the Rosemary Oil along with salt and pepper to taste. Toss the asparagus to coat with the oil and set them aside.

Preheat and oil the grill.

Season the lobster with the cracked black pepper and salt to taste. Using a pastry brush, lightly coat the lobster meat with Rosemary Oil.

Place the asparagus on the grill and grill, turning them frequently, for about 4 to 5 minutes, or until they are cooked through and nicely marked. Remove the asparagus from the grill and return them to the platter. Add the lemon zest and, if necessary, additional salt and pepper to taste and toss to coat.

Place the lobster meat on the grill with the bodies flesh side down, and grill for about 4 minutes, or until cooked through and nicely marked. Remove the lobster from the grill and place on a platter. Add the asparagus and serve, family style, with the Tomato-Garlic Aïoli on the side.

Rosemary Oil

2 cups extra virgin olive oil
4 sprigs fresh rosemary

Combine the oil and rosemary in a small saucepan over medium-high heat and bring to a boil. Remove the pan from the heat and set it aside to cool. When the oil is cool, transfer it along with the rosemary into a nonreactive container. Cover and store the oil in a cool spot, but do not refrigerate it. Allow the rosemary to infuse the oil for at least 24 hours before using.

Tomato-Garlic Aïoli

2 cups mayonnaise
3 tablespoons Tomato Fondue (see page 207) or tomato sauce
2 teaspoons Roasted Garlic Purée (see page 12)

1 teaspoon coarse salt
¼ teaspoon freshly ground black pepper

Combine the mayonnaise, Tomato Fondue, garlic purée, salt, and pepper in a small bowl. Whisk to blend the mixture well. Taste and, if necessary, adjust the seasoning with additional salt and pepper.

Angry Lobster with Lemon Rice and Crispy Basil

SERVES 6

This is probably the most requested dish at my restaurant, davidburke&donatella. You can, of course, adjust the heat in this dish to your own palate. I really like it to have a powerful note. It is another terrific dish for entertaining as the rice, basil, and tomatoes can all be made in advance. The rice can be kept warm over hot water or it can be reheated in a microwave. The lobster can be cut up in advance, and then all that is left to do is to put it all together, which should take no more than twenty minutes.

2 cups Wondra flour (see page 70)
¼ cup chili powder
2 tablespoons cayenne pepper
2 tablespoons coarse salt plus more
    to taste
3 2-pound live lobsters
1 cup peanut oil
8 cloves garlic, minced
1 tablespoons hot red pepper flakes

1 cup lobster or chicken stock
2 tablespoons unsalted butter
1 tablespoon fresh lemon juice
½ loosely packed cup fresh basil leaves
½ cup julienned Oven-Dried Tomatoes
    (see page 9)
Freshly ground black pepper
Lemon Rice (recipe follows)
Fried Basil (recipe follows)

Combine the Wondra flour, chili powder, cayenne, and salt in a plastic bag. Set aside.

Cut the live lobsters in half. Remove the claws and break the claws open to expose as much meat as possible. Remove the meat from the lobsters and place it into the seasoned flour. Shake to coat well. Remove the lobster from the flour and shake off any excess.

Preheat the oven to 475 degrees.

Heat the oil in a large sauté pan over high heat until smoking. Add the lobster pieces, cut side down, a few at a time, if necessary, and sear them for about 4 minutes, or until they are golden brown. Transfer the lobster to a baking sheet, and when all of the lobster is seared, place the baking sheet in the preheated oven and bake for 10 minutes.

While the lobster is baking, prepare the sauce. Return the sauté pan to medium heat and add the garlic and red pepper flakes. Sauté for about 3 minutes, or until the garlic is golden brown but not burning. Add the stock and bring to a boil. Lower the heat and simmer for 5 minutes. Whisk in the butter and remove the pan from the heat. Whisk in the lemon juice, basil leaves, and the tomato julienne. Season with salt and pepper to taste.

Remove the lobster from the oven. Place a mound of Lemon Rice in the center of each of six plates. Place equal portions of the lobster over the rice. Spoon the sauce over the top of each mound and garnish with Fried Basil. Serve immediately.

Lemon Rice

1½ tablespoons olive oil plus 2 optional
    tablespoons
½ cup finely diced onions
1 clove garlic, minced
3 cups converted rice
4 cups chicken stock or water

1 cup fresh lemon juice
1½ teaspoons coarse salt plus more to taste
¼ teaspoon freshly ground black pepper
    plus more to taste
1 large zucchini, trimmed, seeded, and
    diced, optional

Heat the oil in a medium saucepan over medium heat. Add the onions and allow them to sweat their liquid for 4 minutes. Add the garlic and sweat for an additional 3 minutes. Stir in the rice and sauté it for 1 minute. Add the stock (or water), lemon juice, salt, and pepper. Raise the heat and bring the stock to a boil. Boil for about 15 minutes, or until the liquid has reduced to about 1½ cups. Lower the heat and tightly cover the rice. (If you don't have a tight-fitting lid, cover the rice with aluminum foil.) Simmer for 30 minutes, or until the rice has absorbed all of the liquid. Remove the pan from the heat and allow the rice to steam for 15 minutes. Do not uncover the pan. When ready to serve, fluff the rice with a fork.

If using the zucchini, while the rice is resting heat the optional 2 tablespoons of olive oil in a large sauté pan over medium-high heat. Add the zucchini and sauté for 4 minutes, or just until slightly softened. Season with salt and pepper to taste. When ready to serve the rice, add the zucchini and fluff it into the rice.

Fried Basil

4 cups vegetable oil
1 large bunch fresh basil, leaves only, well-
    washed and dried

Heat the oil to 350 degrees on a candy thermometer in a large saucepan over high heat. Standing as far back from the pot as possible and wearing an oven mitt, drop the basil leaves into the hot oil. The oil may bubble and splatter. Fry for about 1 minute, or until the leaves are crisp. Using a slotted spoon, transfer the leaves to a double layer of paper towels to drain.

SECOND DAY DISH

Lobster-Mango Rolls with Soy-Ginger Vinaigrette

SERVES 2

This delicious lobster dish is the invention of my friend and fellow chef Neil Murphy. These rolls are terrific for a light lunch or for cocktail fare. All of the components can be put together or prepared in advance, but the rolls have to be assembled at the last minute to keep the filling from getting mushy and the paper from getting soggy. You could also make the rolls with leftover shrimp, crab, chicken, or pork. If you don't have mesclun on hand, almost any light greens will do, even chopped iceberg lettuce. The vinaigrette makes quite a bit more than you need for this dish, but it is a very tasty seasoning for grilled fish, poultry, or pork.

½ cup diced seedless cucumber
½ cup peeled, seeded, and diced tomato
½ cup diced mango
Soy-Ginger Vinaigrette (recipe follows)
½ large seedless cucumber, peeled and
    julienned
1 medium tomato, peeled, cored,
    seeded, and julienned
1 medium mango, peeled, seeded,
    and julienned

8 sheets rice paper
4 cups mesclun
4 fresh cilantro leaves
4 fresh basil leaves
1 cup julienned or diced, cooked
    lobster meat
2 sprigs cilantro

Combine the diced cucumber, tomato, and mango in a small mixing bowl. Add enough Soy-Ginger Vinaigrette to just moisten. Set aside.

Combine the julienned cucumber, tomato, and mango in a small mixing bowl and set aside.

Fill a large shallow bowl with warm water and lay out 2 clean kitchen towels.

Working with 2 sheets of rice paper at a time, soak the paper in the warm water for about 1 minute, or until soft. Place 1 sheet on one of the towels and the other on top of the first sheet, with the edges slightly overlapping. Use the remaining towel to absorb any excess water and to force the edges together. Mound about 1 cup of the mesclun into the center of the rice paper. Add 2 leaves each of the cilantro and basil. Top with a spoonful of the lobster and a spoonful of the julienned cucumber, tomato, and mango mixture. Roll the rice paper up and around the filling, pulling slightly to make a tight roll once you have rolled it about halfway. Continue rolling to make a tight cigarlike roll. Continue making rolls until you have made four. Cut each roll into thirds and place two rolls on each of two plates. Spoon the diced vegetable/fruit mixture over the rolls, and garnish with a sprig of cilantro. Drizzle some vinaigrette around the plate and serve immediately.

Soy-Ginger Vinaigrette

1 cup soy sauce
1 cup sherry wine vinegar
3 tablespoons minced fresh ginger

2 tablespoons minced shallots
2 cups light olive oil

Combine the soy sauce, vinegar, ginger, and shallots in a medium mixing bowl. Slowly whisk in the olive oil until it is well emulsified. Store the vinaigrette at room temperature until you are ready to serve it. It may be made up to 24 hours in advance. Whisk to re-emulsify before using.

SHRIMP

Did you ever notice that the shrimp platter at a cocktail party is always the first to disappear? Everybody seems to love a shrimp fest. Shrimp did not become widely available until well into the twentieth century because it is highly perishable and, until the advent of refrigerated fishing trawlers in the late 1920s, could not be brought to market quickly enough. There were, of course, coastal areas where local fisherman could speedily bring their catch directly to the cook. Charleston, South Carolina, has long been famous for its early morning shrimp criers announcing their briny catch and the New Orleans shrimp boil is part and parcel of American culinary lore. Shrimp dishes are also an integral part of coastal or island cuisines in areas as diverse as Chile, China, Japan, Africa, and Scandinavia.

Shrimp is most often used as a generic term for prawns, langoustines, crawfish and small lobsters as well as the ten-legged crustacean that is the true shrimp. Prawns are often sold as large shrimp, but this is not scientifically correct. However, the name "prawn" has also come to mean the largest commercially available shrimp. All pretty confusing, eh? The true shrimp ranges in size from microscopically tiny to a giant species found in the Gulf of Mexico and along the Pacific Northwest coast of the United States. Shrimp are found in fresh or salty water, icy cold or warm waters, in the muddy bottom of the shallows and floating along in the deep water. Wherever its home, shrimp is a superb, low-fat, low-calorie source of protein, vitamins, and minerals though high in cholesterol.

Raw shrimp are sized according to the number required to make a pound. In "restaurant speak," shrimp are always ordered by number such as U10, meaning 10 per pound, which is the largest (also called giant). Jumbo offers approximately 15 per pound, large about 20 and so forth. The size of shrimp will not necessarily determine its taste. However, the color frequently does, as the pink color that we associate with a cooked shrimp is caused by its iodine content. Therefore, the deeper the color the more intense the iodine flavor. The most commonly available shrimp are either a creamy white or a very pale pink color, but you will now also find exotic varieties that might be spotted, striped, or variegated. Recently huge, heads-on shrimp have been introduced into the marketplace, and they make quite a spectacular presentation.

One of the major questions when preparing shrimp is whether to devein or not. This is really a matter of aesthetics rather than necessity. The black vein running down the back of the shrimp is its digestive track and can be quite gritty. I always remove it with a small paring knife. Then, I rinse the shrimp under cold running water to make sure that all of the grit has been washed away. Of course, if you are cooking whole shrimp in the shell, it is almost impossible to remove the vein so aesthetics have to take a backseat.

Shrimp can be cooked either before or after shelling, although it is usually most economical to purchase uncooked shrimp in the shell. Shelling and cooking will, of course, cause significant weight loss, so plan accordingly. I usually allow from 6 to 8 shrimp per person for an entrée serving. Raw shrimp should be cooked on the day of purchase. Brief storage is okay if the shrimp are rinsed under cold running water and patted dry, wrapped in a cool, damp paper towels, and refrigerated in an airtight nonreactive container for no more than a few hours.

Shrimp is truly one of the sea's most versatile foods. It is prepared using almost every cooking method and in almost every cuisine. When from pristine waters and extremely fresh, it is also eaten raw. It is easy to prepare, either steamed, boiled, or broiled for a quick and simple meal, and it lends itself to exotic curries, stir-fries, stews, and salads. It's hard to go wrong with shrimp.

CLASSIC

Broiled Shrimp with Scampi Butter and Tomato-Rice Pilaf

SERVES 6

When serving this very aromatic dish, be sure you have plenty of crusty bread to sop up the delicious, garlicky butter. If you add a tossed salad and a great white wine, you will have close to a perfect meal. If you can't find giant shrimp, jumbo will do. You just don't want them to be too small or they will cook too fast to absorb the garlic-butter flavor. For the Second Day Dish (terrific fried rice) you will need some extra shrimp and 4 cups of pilaf, so cook accordingly.

3 pounds giant (10 per pound) shrimp,
     peeled and deveined
Scampi Butter, chilled (see page 198)
Tomato-Rice Pilaf (recipe follows)

1 large ripe tomato, peeled, cored, seeded,
     and cut into small dice
2 tablespoons chopped fresh flat-leaf
     parsley

Preheat the broiler.

Place the shrimp in a pan large enough to fit them in a single layer and small enough to fit under the broiler. Cut the chilled Scampi Butter into tablespoon-size pieces and place 1 piece on top of each shrimp. Place the shrimp under the preheated broiler and broil, basting and turning them occasionally, for about 7 minutes, or until the shrimp is bright pink and cooked through. Remove from the oven.

Place the Tomato-Rice Pilaf in the center of a serving platter. Spoon the shrimp along with the cooking juices around the edge of the platter. Garnish it with diced tomato and chopped parsley.

Tomato-Rice Pilaf

3 tablespoons olive oil
1 cup finely diced onion
3 cloves garlic, minced
1 medium tomato, peeled, cored,
     seeded, and diced

3 cups converted rice
4 cups hot shrimp or fish stock or water
2 cups canned tomato sauce
Coarse salt and freshly ground black
     pepper

Preheat the oven to 450 degrees.

Place the oil in a heat-proof casserole (with a lid) over medium heat. Add the onion and sauté it for about 4 minutes, or until the onion has begun to sweat its liquid but has not taken on any color. Stir in the garlic and sauté for an additional 3 minutes. Stir in the diced tomato and continue to sauté for about 5 minutes, or until the tomato begins to break apart. Add the rice and sauté for 3 minutes more. Stir in the stock and then the tomato sauce. Season with salt and pepper to taste and bring to a boil. Cover the pilaf, place it in the preheated oven, and bake it for 35 minutes. Remove the casserole from the oven and allow it to rest for 15 minutes. Uncover, fluff the pilaf with a fork, and serve.

Sautéed Shrimp with Spinach Lasagna Roll and Crisp Spinach

SERVES 6

This is a dynamite dish for entertaining. The simple lasagna can be made the day before and stored, tightly covered and refrigerated. The Crisp Spinach can be made early in the day. All you have to do at the last minute is place the lasagna in the oven and broil the shrimp.

10 sheets lasagna noodles

6 pounds fresh spinach, stems removed, thoroughly washed

½ cup (1 stick) unsalted butter

¾ cup all-purpose flour

3 cups very hot milk

¼ teaspoon freshly grated nutmeg

Coarse salt and freshly ground black pepper

¼ cup ricotta cheese

¼ cup freshly grated Parmesan cheese

¼ cup melted unsalted butter

3 pounds jumbo (10 per pound) shrimp, peeled, and deveined

1 cup olive oil

1 tablespoon minced shallots

½ teaspoon minced garlic

½ teaspoon hot red pepper flakes

¼ cup white wine vinegar

Crisp Spinach (recipe follows)

Bring a large pot of salted water to a boil over high heat. Add the lasagna noodles and blanch them according to the package directions. Drain the noodles well and lay them out on clean kitchen towels to cool. When cool, cut each lasagna sheet in half crosswise. Set aside.

Bring another large pot of salted water to a boil over high heat. Add the spinach and cook for 20 seconds, or just until the spinach has wilted but is still bright green. Immediately drain and refresh the spinach under cold running water. Again, drain it well, pushing out as much of the excess water as possible. Using your hands, squeeze out any remaining water from the spinach. Transfer the spinach to a chopping block and, using a chef's knife, finely chop it. Set aside.

Line a baking sheet with parchment paper. Set aside.

Preheat the oven to 375 degrees.

Place the butter in a medium saucepan over medium heat. When the butter has melted, stir in the flour with a wooden spoon. Lower the heat and cook, stirring constantly, for 5 minutes, or until the flour taste has cooked out but the mixture has not browned. Whisk in the hot milk and nutmeg. Season the mixture with salt and pepper to taste and cook, stirring constantly, for about 5 minutes more, or until the bechamel is the consistency of very thick cream. Remove it from the heat and beat in the ricotta and Parmesan cheeses along with the reserved spinach, taking care that the spinach is very dry.

Spoon equal portions (about ½ cup) of the spinach mixture onto each piece of lasagna. Roll the pasta around the filling to make a firm, neat roll. Place the rolls on the prepared baking sheet. Using a pastry brush, lightly coat the rolls with the melted butter. Season the tops with salt and pepper to taste and cover the entire pan with aluminum foil.

Place the rolls in the preheated oven and bake for about 25 minutes, or until the filling begins to plump and a skewer inserted into the center comes out hot. Remove the foil and return the rolls to the oven for an additional 5 minutes. Remove the rolls from the oven and lightly tent with aluminum foil (you can use the piece that covered the pan while baking) to keep hot.

About 15 minutes before the lasagna rolls are done, prepare the shrimp.

Heat ¼ cup of the olive oil in a large sauté pan over medium-high heat until it just begins to smoke. Add the shrimp and season with salt and pepper. Sauté the shrimp for about 8 minutes, or until they are bright pink and cooked through. Using a slotted spoon, transfer the shrimp to a platter. Tent them lightly with aluminum foil to keep warm.

Lower the flame to medium-low. Add the shallots and garlic and sauté for about 4 minutes, or just until the shallots are translucent. Stir in the red pepper flakes. Add the vinegar and stir to deglaze the pan. Whisk in the remaining olive oil and remove the pan from the heat. Season with salt and pepper to taste.

Place two lasagna rolls on each of six dinner plates. Shingle 5 shrimp around the front of the lasagna. Spoon the vinegar pan juices over the shrimp and lasagna. Garnish each plate with Crisp Spinach and serve.

Crisp Spinach

4 cups vegetable oil
½ pound spinach, stemmed, thoroughly
    washed and dried

Heat the oil to 350 degrees on a candy thermometer. Add the spinach leaves and fry them for about 1 minute, or just until the spinach is crisp and no bubbles are forming around the leaves. Using a slotted spoon, remove the leaves from the oil and drain them well on paper towels. Serve at room temperature.

SECOND DAY DISH

Shrimp Fried Rice and Sausage

SERVES 2

The secret to great fried rice is the dryness of the mixture. It is very important that you keep the fat and liquid to a minimum and that you keep tossing and turning the ingredients to help the moisture evaporate. No matter what kind of fried rice you are making, it is always best to start with leftover rice that has had some time to loose its moisture. You might even let it set out in the open air for a couple of hours. Any ingredient that needs to keep its crispness should be added at the very last minute.

2 tablespoons peanut oil (or any unflavored oil)
1 large egg
2 tablespoons finely diced onion
1 sweet Italian sausage, removed from the casing
2 cups Tomato-Rice Pilaf (see page 232)
½ cup diced cooked shrimp

2 tablespoons soy sauce
2 tablespoons cooked fresh peas or thawed and drained frozen petite peas
1 tablespoon sliced scallions, white and some green parts
½ tablespoon chopped fresh cilantro
Coarse salt and freshly ground black pepper

Place the oil in a wok over high heat and bring it to the smoke point. Add the egg and scramble it until it is very dry and golden brown. Add the onion and stir-fry it for about 2 minutes, or until translucent. Add the sausage and sauté for about 5 minutes, or until the fat has rendered out. Pour off any excess fat. Stir in the rice and stir-fry, scraping the bottom of the pan from time to time to lift up any browned bits that have formed, for about 15 minutes, or until the ingredients are quite dry and slightly brown. Add the shrimp and stir-fry for an additional 2 minutes. Stir in the soy sauce and continue to cook, lifting the rice slightly up and out of the wok to keep the drying process in motion. Remove the wok from the heat, and toss in the peas, scallions, and cilantro. Season with salt and pepper to taste. Transfer the rice mixture to a large serving bowl and serve immediately.

CRAB

Although there are many different types of crab, almost all are only available fresh locally. This is because it is extremely difficult to keep crab alive during shipment and, like lobster and other shellfish, crab must be cooked when alive. A few species are shipped, live, for sale in fine fish markets across the country, but the most common types of crab—king, snow, and Dungeness—are generally precooked, frozen, and shipped. They are sold either frozen or thawed in supermarkets and fish markets.

Because of the difficulty in obtaining live fresh crabs, I have used only crabmeat for the recipes in the section. Refrigerated, packaged crabmeat is available all across the country with the finest, lump crabmeat, usually available from fine fish markets or specialty food stores. This crabmeat, sold most often in 1-pound plastic containers, usually comes from the blue crab found along both the Atlantic and Gulf coasts. It can take up to 10 crabs to yield 1 pound of meat. Packaged, refrigerated crabmeat is quite often pasteurized for safe storage, but the pasteurization depletes the flavor somewhat, so it is best to purchase crabmeat labeled "freshly-picked" whenever possible. I don't recommend purchasing canned crabmeat.

If you can find live crabs, of course, they make absolutely succulent eating. They can be cooked any way you would cook lobster, or prepared in an old-fashioned "crab boil" (be sure to use Old Bay Seasoning). On the East Coast, smaller blue crabs are the most readily available while the larger Dungeness is the crab of choice on the West Coast. King crab, which can weigh twenty or more pounds, can only be eaten fresh in Alaska. Florida is home to fresh stone crab legs that can only be found cooked and frozen elsewhere. When stone crab are caught, one claw is snapped off and then the crab is quickly returned to the water where it will, in time, regenerate a replacement claw.

Crab may be a component of some singularly fantastic classic preparations such as cioppino, the Italian-flavored stew of San Francisco; Louisiana's rich, savory gumbos; or the base for great bisques and other soups. But crab cakes are the only crab dish in the classic culinary lexicon. Sweet and mellow with just a hint of zest, they make a perfectly delicious classic dish.

Crab Cakes with Baltimore-Spiced Tomato Vinaigrette

SERVES 6

These are truly classic crab cakes, light, moist, buttery, and rich. The secret is to not overmix the blend and to gently form the cakes so that the crab is not compressed. If you want to fancy up the dish, make a little salad of celery and flat-leaf parsley leaves tossed with some fresh lemon juice and extra virgin olive oil (and, of course, a taste of salt and pepper) and mound it in the center of the platter. The crab cakes and vinaigrette can be put together early in the day. Only the crab cakes will need last-minute cooking.

1 tablespoon peanut oil	Pinch of cayenne pepper
¾ cup finely diced onion	2 large eggs
½ cup finely diced celery	¼ cup water
1 cup unsalted butter, softened	2 cups Wondra flour
1 cup mayonnaise	4 cups fresh bread crumbs
2 pounds lump crabmeat, picked clean of all shell and cartilage	Approximately 1 cup clarified butter (see page 7)
3 tablespoons minced fresh chives	Baltimore-Spiced Tomato Vinaigrette (recipe follows)
1 tablespoon freshly grated lemon zest	
2 teaspoons Old Bay Seasoning	

Heat the oil in a small sauté pan over medium heat. Add the onion and celery and sauté the vegetables for about 4 minutes, or until they are soft and translucent. Remove them from the heat and drain off and discard the excess oil. Set aside.

Combine the butter and mayonnaise in a large mixing bowl. Using a handheld electric mixer or a wooden spoon beat until the mixture is well blended and very smooth. Fold in the crabmeat, chives, lemon zest, Old Bay Seasoning, and cayenne along with the reserved onions and celery. Cover and refrigerate the crab cake mixture for 15 minutes to chill slightly.

To make an egg wash, combine the eggs and water in a shallow dish and whisk to combine.

Place the Wondra flour in a shallow dish and the bread crumbs with salt and pepper to taste in another.

Line a baking sheet with parchment paper and set aside.

Remove the crab cake mixture from the refrigerator. Using about ¼ cup per cake, form the crab mixture into cakes. Do not firmly press or squish the mixture together, as you want a lightly textured cake. Dip each cake into the egg wash, allowing the excess to drip off. Coat each cake in Wondra, shaking off the excess, and then finally in the bread crumbs. Place the coated cakes on the prepared baking sheet. Lightly cover with plastic wrap and refrigerate for about 30 minutes, or until the cakes are firm.

Heat the clarified butter in a large sauté pan over medium heat until it begins to smoke. In batches, using additional butter as needed, fry the crab cakes for 3 minutes per side, or until they are golden brown. Place them on paper towels to drain. (If it is necessary to keep the crab cakes warm, place them on the parchment-lined baking sheet in a preheated 200-degree oven with the door slightly ajar, so that they don't continue to cook.)

Place the crab cakes on a serving platter and serve the Baltimore-Spiced Tomato Vinaigrette on the side.

Baltimore-Spiced Tomato Vinaigrette

> Tomato Vinaigrette (see page 200)
> 1 tablespoon Old Bay Seasoning
> ¼ teaspoon cayenne pepper

Combine the Tomato Vinaigrette with the Old Bay Seasoning and cayenne, whisking to blend well.

You can store the vinaigrette, covered and refrigerated, until you are ready to use it. Bring it to room temperate and whisk to blend before using.

Crab Cakes with
Baltimore-Spiced
Tomato Vinaigrette
(Classic)

Grilled Soft-Shell Crabs
with Curry-Yogurt Cream
(Contemporary)

Grand Marnier
Cheesecake Soufflé
(Contemporary)

Coconut Cheesecake
Beignets with Red Fruit
Sorbet and Berries
(Second Day Dish)

ew logs at a time, sear them, turning to brown the logs on all sides, for about 5 min-
hen the logs are brown, transfer them to the parchment-lined baking sheet, and con-
earing the remaining logs with fresh butter. When all of the chicken has been seared,
e baking sheet in the preheated oven and bake the chicken for 17 minutes, or until
ernal temperature reaches 160 degrees on an instant-read thermometer. Reserve the
an along with any juices and fat remaining in the pan.

ile the chicken is baking, prepare the pasta. Cook the orecchiette according to the
e directions. Drain well. Add the extra virgin olive oil, minced garlic, parsley, and salt
pper to taste. Toss to combine.

r off all but about 2 tablespoons of the liquid in the sauté pan. Return the pan to
m heat and add the shallots. Sauté for about 4 minutes, or until the shallots have
to sweat their liquid but have not taken on any color. Stir in the lemon juice and
, stirring constantly to scrape up any browned bits in the bottom of the pan. Bring the
to a boil and slowly whisk in the cold butter, one piece at a time, until the sauce is
y thick and creamy. Season with salt and pepper to taste and stir in the chopped chives.
ace equal portions of the pasta into each of six shallow pasta bowls. Cut each chicken
to about 6 pieces and fan one log out on top of the pasta in each bowl. Spoon some
over the chicken in each bowl and serve.

b Clubs on Crackers

SERVES 2

nk this recipe is fun because I've elevated Ritz crackers to grand status. The rich, sweet,
cake filling, the spicy arugula, the salty bacon, and the crunch of the crumbs all come
ther to make a very elegant brunch, lunch, or late-night dish.

¼ cup mayonnaise

½ teaspoon minced fresh tarragon

¾ cup crab cake mixture (see page 237)

1 tablespoon olive oil

Warm Apple-Blueberry Cobbler with
Butterscotch Ice Cream (Second Day Dish)

All-American Chocolate Chip Cookies (Classic)

Chocolate Chip Tacos
with Chocolate Mousse
(Contemporary)

Chocolate Chip UFOs
(Second Day Dish)

Chicken Breast Stuffed "Crab Francese"

This dish is inspired by the classic, homey, veal Francese prepa
ian restaurants. I've added a little touch of rollatini by formi
hint of saltimbocca with the crab replacing the prosciutto, ch
top of a lightly seasoned bowl of pasta, this contemporary ve
together for a delicious meal.

2 large eggs
2 tablespoons water
6 large skinless, boneless chicken breast
  halves, rinsed and patted dry
1½ cups crab cake mixture (see page 237)
Coarse salt and freshly ground black pepper
2 cups all-purpose flour
Approximately 1 cup clarified butter (see
  page 7)
1 pound dried orecchiette pasta

¼ cup extra v
4 cloves garlic
¼ cup choppe
3 shallots, peel
¼ cup plus 2 ta
  juice
3 tablespoons
1 cup (2 sticks)
  cut into piec
3 tablespoons c

Preheat the oven to 350 degrees.

Line a baking sheet with parchment paper and set it aside.

To make an egg wash, combine the eggs with the water in a shall

Using a very sharp knife, split the chicken breasts down the cen
through them to the opposite side. Open the breast up into a butte
flat side of a large knife or a cleaver, lightly pound the breast to
about ¼ cup of the crab mixture into the center of each chicken piec
neat log. Season with salt and pepper. Roll each log in the flour a
Then, roll in the egg wash, allowing the excess to drip off.

Heat about ¼ cup of the clarified butter in a large sauté pan over

Fi

24

Season the crabs with salt and pepper and place them on the preheated grill. Grill them, turning once, for 3 minutes on each side, or until the crab is just cooked through.

Remove them from the grill and serve with the remaining Curry-Yogurt Cream on the side.

SECOND DAY DISH

Soft-Shell Crab Sandwich

SERVES 2

This doesn't have to be a Second Day Dish. You could fry up some fresh soft shells and make a new batch of the Tartar Sauce, or even your own version of tartar sauce. However, if you do have leftovers, this is a terrific way to use them up. The soft bun is a welcome home for the crisply fried crabs, and the salad adds just the right crunch. You could also make this sandwich using any baked, grilled, or fried fish.

2 fried soft-shell crabs (see page 242)
2 romaine lettuce leaves
2-inch-thick slices ripe tomato
¼ cup thinly sliced seedless cucumber
2 tablespoons David Burke's Vinaigrette
   (see page 107)

¼ cup Olive-Tomato Tartar Sauce
   (see page 244)
2 large hamburger buns or other rolls,
   split and toasted

Preheat the oven to 350 degrees.

Line a baking sheet with parchment paper and place the soft-shell crabs on it. Place it in the preheated oven and reheat the fried crabs for 10 minutes.

Combine the lettuce, tomato, and cucumber in a mixing bowl. Drizzle with the vinaigrette and toss to combine.

Smear tartar sauce on both cut sides of each bun. Mound some of the salad (making sure each sandwich has a tomato slice) on the lid side of each bun. Remove the crab from the oven and place a warm soft-shell crab on the other side of each bun. Serve open or closed.

MEATLESS MAIN COURSE

This is just a one-recipe section. Although there are, of course, many, many meatless main courses, I have not devoted much of my cooking time to their exploration. However, there is one that I particularly love, and since it is an American tradition, I felt that had to include it. Macaroni and cheese it is—I hope that my three versions will satisfy.

MACARONI AND CHEESE

I don't think there is any dish that spells home and Mom like macaroni and cheese. Until I started working on this book, I had no idea that this dish was as classic as I found it to be. Americans started eating a version of macaroni and cheese in the early 1800s and a formal recipe was printed in the Mary Randolph's original, 1824 *The Virginia House-wife*. This first recipe was quite simple: layers of cooked buttered noodles, which were sprinkled with grated cheese and then baked. From that point forward, almost every printed cookbook had a version of macaroni and cheese. It wasn't until the late 1800s that a cream sauce came into play in recipes and, as far as I can tell, cheese sauce was not introduced until around World War I.

There was a period of time when macaroni and cheese bake-offs were held in communities, large and small. All kinds of variations developed as new ingredients were added: a hint of heat with a pinch of cayenne, extra-cheesy with layers of grated cheese added to the dish along with the cheese sauce, additional protein with ham or sausage bits, and even some chopped celery and onion for a little more flavor.

With the introduction of Kraft's now-famous "blue box" in the 1930s, more and more cooks forgot how to make the homemade dish. And, with women leaving the kitchen for the workplace during the Second World War, the Kraft macaroni and cheese dinner became the number one seller in the marketplace. Even with today's reduced-fat–reduced-calorie consciousness, the Kraft dinner remains one of the top sellers in the supermarket aisle.

For my recipes, I've thrown caution to the wind and heaped on the richness. I figure that we don't eat homemade macaroni and cheese every day, so we might as well enjoy it at its best.

CLASSIC

Baked Horseradish-Cheddar Macaroni and Cheese

SERVES 6

This is my classic macaroni and cheese with just a bit of a bite from the horseradish to offset the richness. It is, as it has always been, easy to put together. My mom used to do it early in the morning and then throw the casserole in the oven just as we began asking "When's dinner?" I can still remember the browning cheesy smell that would fill the house.

3 tablespoons melted unsalted butter

½ pound dried elbow macaroni

1 cup milk

2 large eggs, beaten

¼ teaspoon freshly grated nutmeg

Coarse salt and freshly ground black pepper

1 pound horseradish Cheddar cheese, grated

Preheat the oven to 350 degrees.

Using 2 tablespoons of the melted butter, lightly coat a 6-quart casserole. Set aside.

Cook the macaroni according to the package directions. Drain it well and pour into a mixing bowl. Add the remaining butter and toss to coat.

Mix the milk, eggs, and nutmeg with salt and pepper in a medium mixing bowl. Add half of the cheese and stir to combine.

Spoon half of the buttered macaroni into the prepared casserole. Pour one half of the milk mixture over the macaroni and toss to combine. Sprinkle half of the remaining cheese over the macaroni. Combine the remaining macaroni with the remaining milk mixture. When well combined, pour it into the casserole. Sprinkle the remaining cheese on top. Place in the preheated oven and bake it for about 35 minutes, or until the top is crusty and golden brown and the edges are bubbling. Remove it from the oven and serve, family style.

CONTEMPORARY

Macaroni and Cheese Tartlette with Mushroom and Truffle Oil

SERVES 6

You have a choice: either go shopping for the specialty ingredients and make everything from scratch or take some shortcuts. You could purchase frozen pastry shells, use whatever mushrooms you have on hand, use regular bread crumbs, and chop some parsley. It's your call.

½ cup unsalted butter

1 pound button mushrooms, cleaned, stemmed, and cut into ¼-inch-thick slices

½ pound oyster mushrooms, cleaned, stemmed, and pulled apart

¼ pound shiitake mushrooms, cleaned, stemmed, and cut into ¼-inch thick slices

¼ pound chanterelle mushrooms, cleaned, stemmed, and pulled apart

2 tablespoons minced shallots

Mushroom Velouté (recipe follows)

4 cups hot, cooked elbow macaroni

½ pound fontina cheese, grated

Coarse salt and freshly ground black pepper

Pâte Brisée (recipe follows)

½ cup panko bread crumbs (see page 196)

1 tablespoon truffle oil

3 tablespoons fines herbes (see page 65)

Brown the butter in a large sauté pan over medium-high heat, taking care that it remains golden brown and does not burn. Add the button mushrooms and sauté for 4 minutes. Stir in the oyster mushrooms and sauté for 2 minutes, or just until they have wilted slightly. Stir in the shiitake and chanterelle mushrooms and sauté for 3 minutes. Add the shallots and sauté the mixture for another 4 minutes. Stir in the Mushroom Velouté. Add the macaroni. When well combined, stir in the cheese and season with salt and pepper to taste.

Prepare the tart shells as directed in the Pâte Brisée recipe.

Preheat the broiler.

Generously fill each tart shell with the macaroni mixture. Sprinkle the bread crumbs over the top and place the filled shells under the preheated broiler. Broil for about 1 minute, or until the tops are crusty and golden brown. Remove from the broiler and drizzle the tops with truffle oil. Garnish with the fines herbes and serve.

Mushroom Velouté

6 tablespoons unsalted butter
½ pound button mushrooms, cleaned
    and chopped
½ cup finely diced onion

1½ teaspoons salt plus more to taste
4 cups heavy cream
2 tablespoons all-purpose flour
Freshly ground black pepper to taste

Heat 4 tablespoons of the butter in a medium saucepan over medium-low heat. Add the mushrooms and onions and season with salt to taste. Cover and allow the mushrooms and onions to sweat their liquid for 10 minutes, taking care that they do not brown. Raise the heat to medium and stir in the cream. Cook for about 25 minutes, or until the liquid has reduced by one quarter. Remove the pan from the heat, and strain the contents through a fine sieve, discarding the vegetables and reserving the cream.

Heat the remaining butter in a medium saucepan over medium heat. Stir in the flour and cook, stirring constantly, for about 4 minutes, or until the mixture has formed a pale golden roux. Whisk in the reserved cream mixture and cook, stirring constantly, for 5 minutes or until the mixture is thickened. Strain it through a fine sieve into a clean container. Taste and adjust the seasoning with salt and pepper to taste. Set it aside until you are ready to use it. The velouté may be made up to 2 days in advance and stored, tightly covered and refrigerated.

Pâte Brisée

⅓ cup ice water
1 teaspoon sugar
1 teaspoon salt

2½ cups all-purpose flour, sifted
1 cup (2 sticks) unsalted butter, cut
    into cubes and chilled

Place the water in a small bowl. Add the sugar and salt and stir to dissolve. Set aside. Combine the flour and butter in a medium mixing bowl. Using your fingers, a fork or a pastry blender work the butter into the flour until the mixture is the consistency of cornmeal. Add the reserved water mixture and stir to just combine; try not to overmix as the dough will toughen as it is worked. Form the mixture into a ball and wrap it in plastic wrap. Refrigerate it for at least 15 minutes to chill slightly.

Preheat the oven to 350 degrees.

Lightly flour a clean, flat surface and roll out the chilled dough to a ¼-inch thickness. Using a 5-inch-round cookie or biscuit cutter or your own template, cut out 6 circles. Fit the dough into each of six 4-inch tart shells, pushing on the sides to make a firm fit. Trim off any excess dough, and prick the pastry with a fork. Refrigerate the tart shells for 15 minutes to set.

Place the pastry shells in the preheated oven and bake them for 15 minutes, or until golden brown. Remove the shells from the oven and place them on a wire rack to cool. The shells may be made up to 24 hours in advance and stored, lightly covered, at room temperature.

Macaroni and Cheese Fritters

SERVES 6

I used to call this dish *cromesquis* but it scared everyone. *Cromesqui* is simply French for a savory fritter. They don't sound nearly as exotic when called fritters. If you can't find panko bread crumbs or don't have them on hand, you can use regular bread crumbs, but the coating won't be as crackling crisp. You can serve these fritters as a brunch dish, cut in half with some poached quail eggs on top, or for lunch on top of a green salad.

4 cups Baked Horseradish-Cheddar
    Macaroni and Cheese (see page 251)
    or other macaroni and cheese
4½ cups all-purpose flour
2 tablespoons chopped fresh chives

¼ pound cooked ham, cut into small pieces
8 cups panko bread crumbs (see page 196)
4 large eggs
½ cup water
Approximately 6 cups peanut or vegetable oil

Combine the macaroni and cheese with ½ cup of the flour and chives in a medium mixing bowl, stirring to mix well. Measure out about ¼ cup at a time. Flatten the mixture out in the palm of your hand and place a piece of ham in the center. Form the mixture around the ham into golf ball-size rounds. Continue making balls until you have used all of the mixture.

Place the remaining flour and the panko in two large shallow dishes.

To make an egg wash, combine the eggs with the water in another shallow dish.

Working with one ball at a time, dredge each ball in the flour, then in the egg wash, and finally in the panko. Repeat the process for each ball to give it a thick coating.

Heat the oil to 350 degrees on a candy thermometer in a deep-fat fryer over high heat. Add the coated balls, a few at a time, and fry for about 3 minutes, or until they are golden brown and crisp. Using a slotted spoon, transfer the fried *cromesqui* to a double layer of paper towels to drain. Serve hot.

DESSERTS

I truly love sweets and preparing desserts—the flourish to finish a meal. Classic desserts, to me, are those sweets that say home and Mom's kitchen. They are simple to make, often steeped in tradition, with taste-evoking memories of good times. They are about family and friends and holidays and celebrations. Rice and bread puddings; warm plain cakes served with cream; baked fruit desserts, such as pies, cobblers, dumplings, and crisps; custards, puddings, and fruitcakes are just a few of the classics that you will find interwoven in many, many cuisines.

I've chosen just a few classic desserts—classics that everyone knows and almost everyone eats. I've done chocolate cake for the chocoholics, cheesecake for the New York crowd, apple pie for Mom, and finally chocolate chip cookies for the kid in all of us.

CHOCOLATE CAKE

Who doesn't love chocolate cake? I would guess that cooks have been making some kind of cake featuring chocolate ever since the Aztecs found that the bitter cocoa bean could be turned into something sweet. However, written recipes for chocolate cakes did not begin appearing until the late 1880s when chocolate and cocoa powder became available to home bakers.

It is amazing how quickly a repertoire of chocolate cakes developed both commercially and in home kitchens. There are now so many types of chocolate cake that it is hard to come up with the most classic. In New York, my choice would be a Brooklyn Brownout Cake, in other areas of the country it might be German Chocolate Cake, Chocolate Pudding Cake, Chocolate Decadence, Devil's Food Cake, or even the basic and rich Chocolate Fudge Cake.

In this section, I look at a tried-and-true New York classic, fiddle with one of the classic restaurant cakes of the 1980s, a baked-to-order, hot, soufflélike little cake oozing molten chocolate from its center, and end with delicious truffles.

CLASSIC

Brooklyn Brownout Cake

MAKES ONE 9-INCH CAKE

This is a classic New York cake, but I don't know why it is called Brooklyn Brownout. I know that Blackout cake was the specialty of Ebinger's, a much-loved Brooklyn bakery, so perhaps this is just a twist on that old favorite. It is fairly simple to make, keeps well in the refrigerator, and satisfies every chocoholic's craving. Since the filling has to set in the freezer for an hour, you might want to make it before you make the cake. You can use the rich chocolate filling as an icing for almost any layer cake.

2⅔ cups all-purpose flour

2½ cups sugar

½ cup plus 2 tablespoons unsweetened
   cocoa powder

1½ teaspoons baking soda

½ teaspoon salt

3 large eggs, at room temperature

⅔ cup sour cream

2 teaspoons pure vanilla extract

½ cup plus 2 tablespoons unsalted
   butter, melted

½ cup plus 2 tablespoons corn oil

1¼ cups ice water

Chocolate Filling (recipe follows)

Preheat the oven to 350 degrees.

Grease and flour a 9-inch round × 3-inch deep cake pan. Set aside.

Sift the flour, sugar, cocoa, baking soda, and salt together into a medium bowl.

Whisk the eggs, sour cream, and vanilla together until they are very smooth. Set aside.

Combine the butter and oil in the large bowl of an electric mixer. Slowly beat in the ice water to make a creamy emulsion. This should take about 3 minutes. Begin adding the flour mixture, about one-third at a time, mixing to blend well. Finally, beat in the reserved egg mixture to make a smooth batter, scraping down the sides of the bowl to make sure all of the ingredients are blended in. Pour the batter into the prepared cake pan, shaking lightly to settle. Place the cake pan on a baking sheet, place in the preheated oven, and bake for about 1 hour, or until a tester inserted in the middle comes out clean. Remove the cake from the oven and place it on a wire rack to cool.

When the cake has cooled and the filling has set, using a serrated knife, carefully cut off and reserve the uneven top of the cake. You want both the top and the bottom to be perfectly flat. Then, cut the cake into three even layers. This is best done by lightly marking the edge with the knife before making the final cuts.

If you want to decorate the cake with crumbs, preheat the oven to 190 degrees. Place the piece of cake that you have cut off in the bowl of a food processor fitted with the metal blade and process, using quick on and off turns, to make rough crumbs. Place the crumbs on a baking sheet with sides and into the preheated oven. Bake for about 30 minutes, or just until the crumbs have dried. Return the crumbs to the food processor and process to make fine crumbs, taking care that you don't overprocess and create a powder, which will be useless.

Spray the bottom of a 9-inch round × 3-inch deep cake pan with nonstick vegetable spray. Place a piece of parchment paper cut to fit into the bottom of the pan.

Lay the cake layers out on a flat surface, reversing the layers so that the smooth bottom will be the top of the finished cake. Place the smooth bottom layer into the bottom of the prepared pan with the smoothest side facing down. Cover it with a smooth, even ¼-inch-thick layer of Chocolate Filling. (It is easy to smooth out using an offset spatula warmed in hot water and dried well.) Follow with the second cake layer and another layer of Chocolate Filling. Place the final layer on top and place a piece of plastic wrap over the pan. Refrigerate for 1 hour.

Remove the cake from the refrigerator and run a sharp knife around the edge to slightly loosen the cake. Invert the cake onto a cake plate and tap lightly on the bottom to loosen the cake from the pan, slowly lifting the pan as you tap. Using a warm, offset spatula, lightly cover the sides of the cake with some of the remaining Chocolate Filling to make a smooth, even coating. Finish the top with a covering of the filling, smoothing it out to make an even coating. If using the crumbs, sprinkle them on the top and around the sides of the cake. Refrigerate until ready to serve.

Chocolate Filling

1⅔ cups plus 6 tablespoons heavy cream	2 tablespoons rum, optional
6 ounces fine-quality, semisweet chocolate, chopped	4 large egg whites, at room temperature
6 ounces fine-quality, bittersweet chocolate, chopped	¾ cup sugar
	¼ teaspoon cream of tartar

Place 6 tablespoons of the heavy cream in a small saucepan over medium heat and bring it to a simmer. Remove from the heat.

Place the semisweet and bittersweet chocolate in a stainless steel bowl set over a pan of boiling water. The bottom of the bowl should not touch the water. Heat, stirring constantly, just until the chocolate has melted. Immediately whisk in the hot cream and then the rum, if using. When well incorporated, remove from the heat and set aside.

Combine the egg whites, sugar, and cream of tartar in the top half of a double boiler over high heat. Heat, stirring constantly, for about 5 minutes, or until the mixture reaches 140 degrees on a candy thermometer. Transfer the mixture to the large bowl of an electric mixer and beat, on high, for about 5 minutes, or until the meringue has doubled in volume and is very glossy and cool to the touch. Set aside.

Using a handheld electric mixer, beat the remaining 1⅔ cups of heavy cream until it holds a medium peak. Set aside.

Fold the cool meringue into the chocolate mixture, folding to just combine. When nicely blended, fold the whipped cream into the mixture. Cover it lightly with plastic wrap and place in the freezer for about 1 hour to firm. Use as directed in the recipe or as a filling and frosting for any layer cake.

Molten Chocolate Cake

SERVES 6

In the 1980s, this was the restaurant cake of the moment. Everyone had a version, and, no wonder—it is deliciously decadent and irresistible. This is extremely easy to make at home and, if you are serving it to guests, put the cakes together and bake them while you clear the entrée from the table. Whipped cream is a perfect match, but melting vanilla or coffee ice cream is pretty sensational also. Place some cocoa powder in a fine sieve and tap it gently over the plates for a beautiful presentation.

12 ounces semisweet chocolate

1 cup (2 sticks) unsalted butter, cut into pieces

4 large eggs, at room temperature

4 large egg yolks, at room temperature

½ cup sugar

¼ cup almond flour

2 cups whipped cream, optional

Preheat the oven to 425 degrees.

Lightly coat six 4-inch-round × 2-inch-high molds with nonstick vegetable spray. Set aside.

Combine the chocolate and butter in a stainless steel bowl set over a pan of boiling water. The bottom of the bowl should not touch the water. Heat, stirring constantly, just until the chocolate and butter has melted. Remove the mixture from the heat but keep warm.

Place the eggs and egg yolks in the large bowl of an electric mixer. Begin beating the eggs and, with the motor running, add the sugar in thirds, beating to incorporate well between each addition. Continue beating on high for about 7 minutes, or until the mixture has doubled in size and is a soft pale yellow. Lower the speed of the mixer and add the almond flour in thirds, beating to incorporate well between each addition. Slowly beat the reserved melted chocolate-butter mixture into the batter, beating for 1 minute. Fill the prepared molds with the batter. Place them in the preheated oven and bake for 10 minutes, or until the top is just set with a slight crater in the center. Remove from the oven and quickly invert onto six dessert plates. Serve hot with whipped cream on the top, if desired.

Chocolate Cake "Truffles" in a Chocolate Bag

MAKES 30 TRUFFLES

This dessert will bring oohhs and aahhs when you place it on the table. Quite simple in concept, the chocolate bags are, however, very fragile and might test your patience when trying to peel the paper off of the chocolate. I suggest that you make some extra bags, so that if you break a few, you'll still be ahead of the game. You will need a bunch of small paper bags to make the Chocolate Bags. You can usually pick them up in the supermarket where they are sold as lunch or sandwich bags. If you can't find them in your local market, try a mall candy shop, which almost always has small paper bags on hand. And, you get to eat Brooklyn Brownout Cake again!

½ Brooklyn Brownout Cake, icing
    scraped off (see page 258) or
    other rich chocolate cake

1½ pounds semisweet chocolate,
    finely chopped

Line a baking sheet with parchment paper. Set aside.

Using a small melon baller, scoop out 30 small balls of cake. Set aside.

Place 1 pound of the chocolate in a stainless steel bowl set over a pan of boiling water. The bottom of the bowl should not touch the water. Heat, stirring constantly, until the chocolate has melted and has reached 120 degrees on a candy thermometer. Stir in the remaining ½ pound of chocolate, stirring constantly and heating until it reaches 89 degrees to 93 degrees on a candy thermometer. (This is called tempering, a process that stabilizes chocolate so that it can be easily worked with and remain smooth and shiny.) Remove from the heat.

Stick a skewer into each chocolate cake ball and then dip it into the melted chocolate. Tap it off the skewers onto the parchment-lined baking sheet. Continue coating the chocolate cake balls until all are covered. Place in the refrigerator to chill for about 45 minutes.

Open up six small paper bags and line them up in a row. Working with one bag at a time, ladle about 3 ounces of the melted chocolate into each bag and, gently moving the the bag around, thoroughly coat the entire inside of the bag with chocolate. Pour out any excess. Set the coated bags on a flat plate and refrigerate them for about 1 hour, or until firm. Working with one bag at a time, carefully peel the paper bag away from the chocolate leaving a small chocolate bag.

Place five truffles in each bag, place the bags on decorative dessert plates, and serve.

CHEESECAKE

This is the quintessential New York dessert. Throughout the twentieth century, some of New York's greatest delicatessens and Jewish restaurants laid claim to serving the finest cheesecake. Competing were Reuben's (of the equally famous sandwich), Leonard's, Junior's (still in operation in Brooklyn), Lindy's, and the classic delis like the Stage and the Carnegie. Lindy's came to be seen as serving the best, as theirs was an unbelievably rich and eggy cake with a hint of lemon in the crust.

Cheesecakes have a long culinary history beginning with the early Greeks. However, from time to time, they have disappeared from recipe books only to resurface years or generations later even more complex than when last seen. I have found references to cheesecake in almost every cuisine I have studied. One of my favorites is the light, airy, Italian cheesecake made with fresh ricotta cheese and a hint of lemon and extra virgin olive oil.

More than any other basic cake, cheesecakes seem to inspire invention. Firmly established as an American dessert, we have seen cheesecakes in almost every flavor imaginable; marbled and plain, glazes of every taste and color, toppings ranging from simple sour cream to exotic fruits. The cheese is usually cream cheese, but I have seen Cheddar cheesecakes, tofu cheesecakes, and cottage cheesecakes among others.

CLASSIC

New York Cheesecake

MAKES ONE 9-INCH CAKE

Here is my version of the New York favorite. Not quite the same as Lindy's—I use a graham cracker crust instead of a pastry crust and add a little sour cream to the batter. The secret to a perfect cheesecake is steady and complete mixing, slow, quiet baking, and undisturbed cooling. If a crack appears in the top, it usually means that the cake was baked in too hot an oven. However, the cake will still be delicious, if not as pretty as a picture. If it cracks badly, just place some berries in an attractive pattern on the top and serve with a smile.

1 cup graham cracker crumbs	½ teaspoon freshly grated
2 tablespoons melted unsalted butter	lemon zest
2½ pounds cream cheese, at room	⅛ teaspoon salt
temperature	5 large eggs, at room temperature
1¼ cups superfine sugar	¼ cup heavy cream
6 tablespoons sour cream	¼ cup milk

Preheat the oven to 300 degrees.

Lightly coat the sides and bottom of a 9-inch-round springform pan with butter. Set aside.

Combine the graham cracker crumbs and the melted butter in a medium mixing bowl, using your fingertips to blend the mixture well. Pour it into the prepared pan and, using your fingertips, press it firmly into the bottom to cover smoothly. Place the pan in the refrigerator while you prepare the batter.

Place the cream cheese and sugar in the large bowl of an electric mixer and beat it for about 5 minutes, or until the mixture is quite pale and fluffy and the sugar is well-incorporated. Beat in the sour cream, lemon zest, and salt and beat to combine. Add the eggs, one at a time, beating to incorporate after each addition. Add the cream and milk and beat just to blend.

Remove the prepared pan from the refrigerator. Pour the batter into the pan and smooth out the top with an offset spatula. Place the pan in a baking pan large enough to hold it leaving space on all sides. Pour in water to come halfway up the springform pan and place it in the preheated oven. Bake, without opening the oven door, for 50 minutes, or until a sharp knife inserted into the center comes out clean. Turn off the oven, open the oven door, and allow the cake to cool in the oven.

When the cake is cool, open the springform and transfer the cake to a cake platter, leaving it on the pan bottom. Serve it at room temperature or chilled with fresh fruit or berries, if desired.

CONTEMPORARY

Grand Marnier Cheesecake Soufflés

SERVES 6

This is the opposite end of the cheesecake spectrum. As rich as you might find the classic, these delicate soufflés are light, fluffy, and sweetly aromatic with all the flavor of the original. You can put them together and refrigerate for an hour or two before baking. However, once baked, they must be served immediately, or you will have pancakes rather than soufflés!

2 tablespoons unsalted butter, at room
   temperature
½ cup plus 2 tablespoons sugar
2 tablespoons cornstarch
½ pound cream cheese, at room
   temperature

Pastry Cream (recipe follows)
3 large egg yolks
3 tablespoons Grand Marnier
6 large egg whites

Preheat oven to 375 degrees.

Lightly coat the inside of each of six 6-ounce molds or ramekins with the butter. Using 2 tablespoons of the sugar, lightly dust the buttered interiors, shaking out any excess. Refrigerate the molds while making the batter.

Combine the remaining sugar with the cornstarch and sift them together into a clean bowl. Set aside.

Combine the cream cheese and Pastry Cream in the bowl of an electric mixer and beat them for about 5 minutes, or until the mixture is very pale and smooth. Beat in the egg yolks, one at a time, beating well after each addition. Add the Grand Marnier and beat to blend.

Place the egg whites in a separate bowl and, using clean beaters, beat the egg whites for about 3 minutes, or until loose peaks form. Slowly add the reserved cornstarch mixture and beat for about 3 minutes or until soft peaks form. Fold about one-third of the egg white mixture into the cheese mixture, folding gently until well incorporated. Fold in the remaining egg white mixture until just blended, taking care not to overmix and deflate the egg whites.

Spoon the batter into the prepared molds or ramekins. Place them in the preheated oven and bake for about 12 minutes or until the soufflé has risen and set and the top is golden brown. Remove the soufflés from the oven and serve immediately.

Pastry Cream

2 large egg yolks	⅔ cup milk
2 tablespoons cornstarch	1 vanilla bean
2½ tablespoons sugar	

Combine the egg yolks, cornstarch, and sugar in a small bowl and beat with an electric mixer for about 5 minutes, or until the mixture makes a light ribbon when lifted from the bowl.

Place the milk in a small saucepan over medium heat. Split the vanilla bean in half lengthwise, and scrape the seeds into the milk. (Save the bean to flavor confectioners' or granulated sugar.) Heat the milk just until bubbles appear around the edge of the pan. Remove it from the heat and very slowly whisk the hot milk into the egg mixture. (It is important that the milk is added very slowly, or the heat will cause the eggs to cook slightly and curdle.) Return the pan to medium heat and cook, whisking constantly, for about 3 minutes, or until the cream has thickened. Remove it from the heat and place a piece of plastic wrap over the top. Allow it to cool to room temperature. Once cooled, the cream can be placed in an airtight container and refrigerated for up to 2 days.

Coconut Cheesecake Beignets with Red Fruit Sorbet and Berries

SERVES 6

Rich, sweet cheesecake deep-fried to a meltingly soft center with a crisp, crunchy, coconut-flavored crust. Yes, I know, I've let myself go here, but this is such a perfect use for any left-over cheesecake. The acidic sorbet and the slightly tart fruit make a nice balance for the richness of the beignets. If you don't have time to make the sorbet, just use a fine-quality, store-bought raspberry, lemon, or passion fruit sorbet. Don't pass over the berries though, as they really do complete the dish.

½ New York Cheesecake (see page 264)

1 cup cornstarch

2½ cups confectioners' sugar

4 large eggs, at room temperature

2½ cups freshly grated coconut or
packaged unsweetened coconut

Approximately 6 cups vegetable oil

Red Fruit Sorbet (recipe follows)

1 pint fresh raspberries

1 pint fresh strawberries, hulled

Using a medium melon baller, scoop out 24 balls of cheesecake. Refrigerate them until ready to coat.

Sift the cornstarch and 1 cup of the confectioners' sugar together into a large shallow bowl.

Place the eggs in another large shallow bowl and whisk until frothy.

Place the coconut in a third shallow bowl.

Finally, place the remaining confectioners' sugar in another shallow bowl or in a plastic or brown paper bag.

Remove the cheesecake balls from the refrigerator and roll each ball in the cornstarch mixture to coat well. Shake off any excess.

Next, dip the coated balls into the eggs, allowing the excess to drip off.

Finally, roll the balls in the coconut.

Heat the oil to 350 degrees in a deep-fat fryer over high heat. Add the coated cheesecake balls, a few at a time, and fry until golden brown. Using a slotted spoon, lift the beignets from the oil and place them on a double layer of paper towels to drain. When well drained, either roll (if the sugar is in a shallow bowl) or toss (if the sugar is in a paper bag) in the remaining confectioners' sugar. Serve warm with a scoop of Red Fruit Sorbet, garnished with raspberries and strawberries.

Red Fruit Sorbet

¾ cup sugar

¾ cup water

1 pint fresh raspberries

1 pint fresh strawberries, hulled

1 tablespoon fresh lemon juice, optional

Combine the sugar and water in a small saucepan over high heat. Bring the mixture to a boil and boil for about 4 minutes, or until the sugar has melted and the liquid is somewhat viscous. Remove from the heat and allow it to cool. (To test the viscosity of the liquid, when

your apple pie, feel free to add or subtract sugar, lemon juice, and spices. If you want to make the Second Day cobbler dish, you will need a couple of extra cups of the cooked apple filling, so plan accordingly.

1¾ cups all-purpose flour

1¼ cups plus 1 tablespoon granulated sugar

½ teaspoon salt

¾ cup (1½ sticks) unsalted butter, cut into small pieces and chilled

¼ cup ice water

¼ cup firmly packed light brown sugar

3 Granny Smith apples, peeled, cored, and sliced

3 Golden Delicious apples, peeled, cored, and sliced

½ cup melted unsalted butter

¾ teaspoon ground cinnamon

¼ teaspoon freshly grated nutmeg

2 tablespoons cornstarch

5 tablespoons water

Juice of 1 lemon

1 large egg

Combine the flour, 1 tablespoon of the granulated sugar, and the salt in a medium mixing bowl. Add the butter and, using your fingertips or a fork, blend the butter into the flour to make coarse flakes, taking care not to overwork the dough. Sprinkle the water over the flour mixture and mix it with your hands or a fork just until the dough comes together. Do not knead the dough or it will toughen. Divide the dough into 2 pieces. Pat the dough out to form a circle. Wrap each circle in plastic wrap and refrigerate them for about 45 minutes, or until well chilled.

Combine ¼ cup of the granulated sugar with the brown sugar in a small bowl. Set aside.

Combine the apples with the remaining 1 cup of granulated sugar and the melted butter, cinnamon, and nutmeg in a medium saucepan over medium heat. Cook for 5 minutes. Combine the cornstarch with 3 tablespoons of the remaining water and, when well-blended, stir the mixture into the apples along with the lemon juice. Remove from the heat and allow to cool to room temperature.

To make an egg wash, whisk the egg and remaining 2 tablespoons of water together in a small bowl. Set aside.

Remove the dough from the refrigerator and unwrap it. On a lightly floured board, roll out each piece of dough to a circle about ⅛-inch thick and 12 inches round. Carefully lift 1 dough circle over a 9-inch pie pan and gently place it into the pan. Fit the dough into the pan, pushing against the sides to make a firm fit. You should have about a 2-inch overhang of dough around the edge. Spoon the filling into the dough-lined pan, slightly mounding in the center. Using a pastry brush, lightly coat the edge with some of the egg wash. Carefully lay the remaining piece of dough over the top and crimp the edges together, cutting off and discarding excess dough. Using a sharp knife, make even (and decorative, if you desire) cuts in the top so that steam can escape while the pie is baking. Using the pastry brush, lightly brush the top of the pie with the egg wash and sprinkle with the reserved sugar mixture. Place the pie in the preheated oven and bake for about 40 minutes, or until the pie is steaming and the top is golden brown. Remove the pie from the oven and cool it on a wire rack for about 30 minutes before cutting. Serve warm, at room temperature, or chilled.

Apple Tart with Tahitian Vanilla Ice Cream

SERVES 6

This could not be a simpler contemporary version of the classic apple pie. Frozen puff pastry is usually of excellent quality and certainly saves a lot of time in the kitchen. You can bake the tarts early in the day but since they should be served warm, you will have to reheat them in a preheated 325-degree oven for about 5 minutes. Of course, there is nothing more delicious than homemade vanilla ice cream, but if time is not on your side, don't hesitate to use a fine-quality, commercial variety.

¼ cup granulated sugar
¼ cup firmly packed light brown sugar
3 sheets frozen puff pastry
3 large Granny Smith apples, peeled, cored, and cut lengthwise into ⅛-inch-thick slices

¼ cup clarified butter, melted (see page 7)
Tahitian Vanilla Ice Cream (recipe follows)

Preheat the oven to 325 degrees.

Line a baking sheet with parchment paper.

Combine the granulated and brown sugars in a small bowl. Set aside.

Cut the puff pastry into six 6-inch circles. Place six 6-inch-round × 2-inch-high ring molds on the prepared baking sheet. Spray each ring mold with nonstick vegetable spray. Fit a puff pastry round into each ring mold, allowing the edges to come up slightly around the interior of the mold. Randomly prick the pastry with a fork.

Place the apple slices on top of the pastry, fanning them out to make a neat circular pattern. Using a pastry brush, lightly coat the apples with some clarified butter. Sprinkle their tops with the reserved sugar mixture. Place them in the preheated oven and bake for 15 minutes. Remove the tarts from the oven and again brush the apples with the remaining clarified butter. Return the tarts to the oven and bake them for an additional 15 minutes, or until the apples are glazed and the pastry is golden brown. Remove the tarts from the oven and allow to rest for 5 minutes before lifting off the molds. Place each tart on a dessert plate. Place a scoop of Tahitian Vanilla Ice Cream on top and serve.

Tahitian Vanilla Ice Cream

1½ cups whole milk
½ cup heavy cream
1 Tahitian vanilla bean

6 large egg yolks
¾ cup sugar

Combine the milk and cream in a medium nonreactive saucepan over medium heat. Split the vanilla bean in half lengthwise, and scrape the beans into the milk. Heat the milk mixture just until bubbles appear around the edge of the pan. Remove from the heat.

Combine the egg yolks and sugar in a medium mixing bowl and whisk together until thoroughly combined. Whisking constantly, slowly pour about one-half of the hot milk mixture into the eggs. (It is important that the milk is added very slowly, or the heat will cause the eggs to cook slightly and curdle.) Whisk in the remaining hot milk. When well blended, return the mixture to the saucepan and place it over medium heat. Cook, whisking constantly, for about 3 minutes, or until the mixture thickens slightly and coats the back of a wooden spoon. Remove the mixture from the heat and allow it to cool.

When cool, pour it into an ice cream machine and freeze it following the manufacturer's directions. Store it, in the freezer, in an airtight container.

SECOND DAY DISH

Warm Apple-Blueberry Cobbler with Butterscotch Ice Cream

SERVES 6

Another simple dessert take on apple pie using filling from my Flaky Apple Pie. Baking in crème brûlée dishes makes an elegant finale, I think, out of very basic ingredients. If you don't have time to make the ice cream, purchase any fine-quality, commercial ice cream. You could even buy rich vanilla ice cream and stir some store-bought butterscotch sauce into it.

1 cup all-purpose flour
1 cup firmly packed light brown sugar
¼ teaspoon ground cinnamon
¼ teaspoon freshly grated nutmeg
½ cup (1 stick) unsalted butter, cut
    into pieces and chilled

2 cups cooked apple pie filling
    (see page 270)
1 pint fresh blueberries
Butterscotch Ice Cream (recipe
    follows)

Preheat the oven to 325 degrees.

Lightly butter six 6-ounce crème brûlée dishes. Set aside.

To make the streusel topping, combine the flour, brown sugar, cinnamon, and nutmeg in a small mixing bowl. Add the butter and, using your fingertips, incorporate the butter into the flour mixture to make coarse crumbs. Set aside.

Combine the apple pie filling and blueberries in a medium mixing bowl. Spoon the mixture into the reserved dishes, smoothing out the tops. Place in the preheated oven and bake for 15 minutes, or just until the fruit begins to boil. Remove from the oven and generously cover the top of each cobbler with some of the reserved streusel topping. Return the cobblers to the oven and bake them for about 25 minutes, or until the topping is crunchy and golden brown. Remove from the heat and then serve hot with a scoop of Butterscotch Ice Cream on top.

Butterscotch Ice Cream

1 cup sugar
¼ cup cold water
2 tablespoons light corn syrup
½ cup (1 stick) unsalted butter,
    at room temperature

½ cup heavy cream
Tahitian Vanilla Ice Cream base
    (see page 273)

Combine the sugar, water, and corn syrup in a medium saucepan over medium heat. Bring the mixture to a boil and boil it for about 10 minutes, or until the water begins to evaporate and the sugar begins to caramelize. Continue cooking until the syrup reads 320 degrees on a candy thermometer. Immediately whisk in the butter to stop the cooking process. Whisk in the cream and return the mixture to a boil. Cook, stirring constantly, for 2 minutes. Remove from the heat and allow to cool.

Prepare the Tahitian Vanilla Ice Cream as directed. When it is frozen, remove it from the ice cream maker and swirl the reserved butterscotch mixture into it. Transfer it to an airtight container and store in the freezer.

CHOCOLATE CHIP COOKIES

Chocolate chip cookies originated in the *Toll House Cook Book* written in 1930 by a Bostonian cook and inn owner (Toll House Inn in Whitman, Massachusetts), Ruth Wakefield. Her recipe called for Nestlé Yellow Label chocolate to be chopped into pea-size pieces to make what she called "Chocolate Crispies." The book was so popular throughout New England that Nestlé's sales skyrocketed. The company eventually contracted with Ruth Wakefield to use her recipe on the back of their chocolate package and to call the cookies Toll House.

It wasn't until some years later that the company invented the chocolate chips that made the cookies a breeze to make. Wakefield's original recipe, updated and changed from time to time by Nestlé but still called "The Original Toll House Cookie," is the mother of all chocolate chip cookies. Most children use the recipe from the Nestlé package to do their first baking.

The original recipe did not call for nuts, but I always add them to my chocolate chip cookies. The choice is yours. By the way, it is estimated that chocolate chip cookies account for more than half of the home-baked cookies made in America every year.

CLASSIC

All-American Chocolate Chip Cookies

MAKES ABOUT 2 DOZEN COOKIES

An all-time classic favorite with kids of all ages. I personally like my cookies with big pieces of walnuts or pecans, but I've made them an optional ingredient, so it's up to you to decide. Use really good chips such as Ghirardelli—they do make a difference. You can also use chocolate chunks for really chocolatey cookies.

2½ cups all-purpose flour

1 teaspoon baking soda

1 teaspoon salt

1½ cups (3 sticks) unsalted butter, at room temperature

1½ cups firmly packed light brown sugar

1½ teaspoons pure vanilla extract

2 large eggs

2 cups semisweet chocolate chips

1½ cups toasted walnut or pecan pieces, optional

Preheat the oven to 375 degrees.

Line 2 cookie sheets with nonstick silicone liners or parchment paper. Set aside.

Sift the flour, baking soda, and salt together and set aside.

Place the butter in the bowl of an electric mixer and beat until smooth. Add the sugar and vanilla and beat for about 5 minutes, or until the mixture is light and creamy. Add the eggs, one at a time, beating well to incorporate after each addition and scraping down the sides of the bowl to include every bit of the ingredients. Add the flour mixture, beating to blend well. Fold the chocolate chips and nuts, if using, into the dough.

Spoon about 2 tablespoons of dough per cookie onto the prepared cookie sheets, taking care not to crowd them since the cookies will expand. Place them in the preheated oven and bake for 15 minutes, or until they are golden brown and set in the middle. Using a spatula, lift the cookies onto wire racks to cool for about 10 minutes. You can store them, tightly covered, for up to 3 days.

CONTEMPORARY

Chocolate Chip Taco with Chocolate Mousse

SERVES 6

These playful "tacos" make a spectacular dessert with not too much effort. The tacos, which are really a version of the classic French *tuile,* can be made a day or two in advance. If you do make them in advance, be sure to store them in a dry spot as any humidity will soften them.

To make them, you need to cut a 6-inch-round stencil, which is best done out of a large plastic lid. It is simple to do, particularly with a grade-school compass and a good pair of scissors. You can use cardboard, but it gets very soggy very quickly so you will need to make a few. The Chocolate Mousse can be made early in the day and you can put the "tacos" together just before serving them.

1½ cups confectioners' sugar

1⅜ cups all-purpose flour

2 tablespoons unsweetened cocoa powder

¾ cup (1½ sticks) unsalted butter, at room temperature

⅜ cup honey

3 large egg whites

½ cup semisweet chocolate chips

Chocolate Mousse (recipe follows)

Sift the confectioners' sugar, flour, and cocoa together. Set aside.

Combine the butter and honey in the bowl of an electric mixer and beat for about 4 minutes, or until the mixture is very smooth. Add the egg whites, one at a time, beating well to incorporate after each addition. Add the dry ingredients and beat the mixture for 5 minutes. Cover it lightly with plastic wrap and place in the refrigerator for 2 hours.

Preheat the oven to 300 degrees.

Line 2 cookie sheets with nonstick silicone liners or parchment paper.

Place the stencil down on the prepared cookie sheet and, one at a time, spread cookie dough on the stencil to make thin, smooth-topped, 6-inch-round cookies. Sprinkle the top of each "taco" with chocolate chips. Place the "tacos" in the preheated oven and bake for 15 minutes, or just until the cookie has set. Remove from the oven and, working quickly, lift the "tacos" to a rolling pin (or bottle) and drape the soft cookies over the rolling pin to form a taco shape. Let them rest for about 10 minutes. If the cookies get too firm to fold over the rolling pin, place them back in the oven for about 15 seconds to soften.

Fill each Chocolate Chip Taco with a generous helping of the Chocolate Mousse and serve immediately. If desired, place some cocoa powder in a fine sieve and gently tap the sieve over the plates to cover them with a light dusting of cocoa.

Chocolate Mousse

1½ cups chopped semisweet chocolate or chocolate chips

½ cup (1 stick) unsalted butter, at room temperature

2 large egg yolks

½ tablespoon sugar

2 cups heavy cream, whipped

Combine the chocolate and butter in a stainless steel bowl set over boiling water. Do not allow the bottom of the bowl to touch the water. Heat the mixture, stirring constantly, for about 5 minutes, or just until the chocolate and butter have melted and are blended. Do not cook. Remove the mixture from the heat and set aside.

Combine the egg yolks and sugar in the bowl of an electric mixer and beat them until they are pale yellow and very light. Slowly whisk in the chocolate mixture until very well blended. Fold in one-third of the whipped cream to lighten the base. Slowly fold in the remaining whipped cream until just blended. Do not overmix, or the mixture will lose its airiness. Cover the mixture lightly and place in the refrigerator until you are ready to use it.

Chocolate Chip UFOs

SERVES 6

These ice cream sandwiches are the best using leftover cookies. If you want to get fancy, use one of the more exotically flavored ice creams. For adults, use a dark coffee, cappuccino, or latte ice cream with some chopped, chocolate-covered coffee beans folded in.

18 All-American Chocolate Chip Cookies (see page 276)

2 cups Tahitian Vanilla (or other vanilla) Ice Cream, softened slightly (see page 273)

4 ounces semisweet chocolate chips

Place 6 of the cookies in the bowl of a food processor fitted with the metal blade. Process, using quick on and off turns, to make loose crumbs. Transfer them to a shallow dish and set aside.

Place the ice cream in a bowl and fold in the chocolate chips. If it gets too soft to work with, return it to the freezer to firm up slightly.

Using a spatula and working quickly, smooth about ¼ cup of ice cream on the flat, baked side of each of 6 cookies. Place another cookie, baked side down, on top of the ice cream. Roll the edges in the reserved crumbs to coat well. Place the sandwiches in the freezer to firm for at least 1 hour. Wrap them individually in plastic wrap and freeze until you are ready to serve them.

Mail Order and Web Site Sources

Perona Farms
Smoked fish, Game, David Burke's Pastrami Salmon
350 Andover-Sparta Road
Andover, New Jersey 07821
(800) 750-6190
www.peronafarms.com

David Burke's Flavor Sprays
Sean Pomper
Director of Operations
Flavor Spray Diet
(718) 793-7772
Fax: (718) 261-2114
seanpomper@flavorspraydiet.com

Les Chateaux
David Burke's Savory Lollipops
1 Craft Avenue
Inwood, New York 11096
(516) 239-6795
www.gourmetpops.com

D'Artagnan
Wild game, Meats, Foie gras
280 Wilson Avenue
Newark, New Jersey 07105
(800) 327-8246
www.dartagnan.com

Browne Trading Corporation—Fish and Shellfish
260 Commercial Street
Portland, Maine 04101
(800) 944-9848
www.browne-trading.com

www.realchef.com—David Burke's Table Sauce

Citarella—Meats, Game, Fish, Specialty Food Products
2135 Broadway
New York, New York 10024
(212) 874-0383
www.citarella.com

Dean and Deluca—Specialty food products, Kitchenware, Meats, Game, Fish
Mail Order Department
560 Broadway
New York, New York 10012
(800) 221-7714
www.deandeluca.com

Sahadi's
Spices, Middle Eastern Products, Nuts, Grains
187 Atlantic Avenue
Brooklyn, New York 11201
(718) 624-4550
www.sahadis.com or Sahadis@aol.com

Zingerman's
Specialty Foods of all Types
620 Phoenix Drive
Ann Arbor, Michigan 48108
(888) 636-8162
www.zingermans.com

Katagiri
Japanese Food Products and Kitchenware
224 East 59th Street
New York, New York 10022
(212) 755-3566
www.katagiri.com

Adriana's Caravan
Mail Order Spices, Condiments, and Asian Products
404 Vanderbilt Street
Brooklyn, New York 11218
(800) 316-0820
www.adrianascaravan.com

Kalustyan Oriental Export Trading Company
East Indian and Middle Eastern Products
123 Lexington Avenue
New York, New York 10016
(212) 685-3451
www.kalustyans.com

Bridge Kitchenware
Specialty Kitchenware and Appliances
711 Third Avenue
New York, New York 10017
(212) 688-4220
www.bridgekitchenware.com

Acknowledgments

First, I'd like to thank my editor, Jon Segal, and my coauthor, Judie Choate. I'd also like to thank everyone in both the kitchens and offices who have helped me in this process, including my chefs—Scott Ubert, Steve Charron, Pat Trama, Whitey, Chris Shea, Jason Tillman, Doran Wong, and Carissa Waechter; my assistants, Christa Weaving, Autumn Simas, Jill Castellini, and Ruthie Rousso; and, of course, Cristina LaVerde, for her patience and understanding.

Index

A

aïoli:
  Tomato-Garlic Aïoli, 225
  Tomato-Roasted Garlic Aïoli, 42–3
almonds:
  Almond, Praline, and Banana Pancakes with
      Orange Syrup and Yogurt, 16–17
  Almond Oatmeal Crème Brûlée with Orange
      Essence, 31–2
  Stuffed Doughnuts with Whipped Cream and
      Berries, 28–9
anchovies, in The Famous Caesar Salad, 68–9
Angry Lobster with Lemon Rice and Crispy Basil,
      226–8
appetizers, 37–51
  shellfish cocktails, 37, 39–44
    Chopped Seafood Salad with Tomato and Onion
        in Avocado Halves, 43–4
    Hot Shellfish Cocktail with Tomato-Roasted
        Garlic Aïoli, 41–3
    Shrimp, Lobster, and Crab with Cocktail Sauce
        and Old Bay Mayonnaise, 40–1
  smoked salmon, 45–51
    Pastrami Salmon and Smoked Salmon with
        Potato Pancakes, Honey-Mustard Vinaigrette,
        and Apple Salad, 47–50
    Smoked Salmon Lollipops, 50–1
    Smoked Salmon with Horseradish Mousse and
        Corn Blini, 46–7
  see also hors d'oeuvres
apples:
  apple pie filling, 270–5
    Apple Tart with Tahitian Vanilla Ice Cream,
        272–3
    Flaky Apple Pie, 270–2
    Warm Apple-Blueberry Cobbler with
        Butterscotch Ice Cream, 274–5

Apple Salad, 47–8
applesauce
    Firecracker Applesauce, 155–6
    plain applesauce, 154
    Cinnamon-Brown Sugar and Apple Syrup, 19–20
Asian-Style Pot Roast, 139–40
asparagus:
    Asparagus Salad, 243
    Asparagus-Stuffed Spareribs with Corn Crêpes,
        165–6
    Grilled Asparagus, 224–5
    Roasted Asparagus, 126
Aureole, New York, 83
avocados:
    Chopped Seafood Salad with Tomato and Onion in
        Avocado Halves, 43–4
    Classic Cobb Salad, 58–60
    preventing discoloration of, 59
    Spiced Cobb Salad "Summer Roll" with Blue
        Cheese Dipping Sauce, 62

B

bacon:
    Bacon, Potato, and Eggs Strudel, 12–13
    Cobb salad
        Classic Cobb Salad, 58–60
        Spiced Cobb Salad "Summer Roll" with Blue
            Cheese Dipping Sauce, 62
        "Stacked" Chopped Cobb Salad with Chipotle
            Vinaigrette, 60–1
    Herb-Broiled Cod with Clams, Bacon, and
        Cabbage, 196–7
    see also Canadian bacon
Baltimore-Spiced Tomato Vinaigrette, 238
bananas, in Almond, Praline, and Banana Pancakes
        with Orange Syrup and Yogurt, 16–17

barbecued:
  barbecued chicken, 93–100
    Barbecued Chicken Parts with Corn on the Cob and Grilled Vegetables, 94–6
    Barbecued Chicken Sticky Buns, 99–100
    Pretzel-Onion Crusted Barbecued Chicken with Pretzel Latkes, Corn, and Mustard, 96–8
  Barbecued Ham and Pineapple Kabobs, 156
  barbecued spareribs
    Asparagus-Stuffed Spareribs with Corn Crêpes, 165–6
    Barbecued Coffee Spareribs with Fixings, 162–4
    Barbecued Sparerib Home-Fries with Poached Eggs and Chili Corn Cakes, 167–8
Barbecue Sauce, 96
basil:
  Basil Oil, 210
  Basil Ranch Dressing, 222
  Fried Basil, 227–8
beef, 119–46
  Carpaccio of Chef's Salad, 65–6
  Classic Chef's Salad Bowl, 64
  cuts of, 119–20, 121, 129
  grades of, 119
  judging prime piece of, 120
  meatloaf, 141–6
    Meatloaf Bundt Cake, 144–5
    Meatloaf Pancakes with Goat Cheese Salad and Fried Eggs, 145–6
    Not-So-Basic Meatloaf, 142–4
  pot roast, 136–40
    Asian-Style Pot Roast, 139–40
    Pot Roast Sloppy Joes, 140
    Yankee Pot Roast with Brown Bread Dumplings and Melted Vegetables, 137–8
  roast prime rib of beef, 129–35
    Red Chili in a Potato Boat with Minced Crisp Onion, 134–5
    Roasted Spice-Crusted Rib with Wild Mushroom-Vegetable Stew, Horseradish-Mustard Mousse, and Popovers, 131–3
    Roast Prime Rib with Gratin Potato, 130–1
  steak and potatoes, 121–8
    Cracked Pepper Sirloin with Shrimp-Potato Pancake and Roasted Asparagus, 124–6
    Grilled Sirloin Steak with Garlicky Spinach, 123
    Sirloin and Horseradish Knish with Mustard-Russian Sauce, 126–8
Beignets, Coconut Cheesecake, 267–8

berries:
  Coconut Cheesecake Beignets with Red Fruit Sorbet and Berries, 267–9
  Honey-Tossed Raisins and Berries, 30–1
  Stuffed Doughnuts with Whipped Cream and Berries, 28–9
  see also specific berries
biscuits:
  Buttermilk Biscuits, 197
  Cheddar Biscuits, 56
  Cornbread Biscuits, 88–9
blini, in Smoked Salmon with Horseradish Mousse and Corn Blini, 46–7
blueberries:
  Honey-Tossed Raisins and Berries, 30–1
  Warm Apple-Blueberry Cobbler with Butterscotch Ice Cream, 274–5
blue cheese:
  Cobb salad
    Classic Cobb Salad, 58–60
    Spiced Cobb Salad "Summer Roll" with Blue Cheese Dipping Sauce, 62
    "Stacked" Chopped Cobb Salad with Chipotle Vinaigrette, 60–1
  Roquefort Dressing, 59–60
Bouquet of Vegetables, 178–9
brandade de morue, 200
bread:
  bread puddings
    Bread Pudding, 114
    Clam Chowder Bread Pudding with Tomato and Watercress Salad, 56–7
    French Toast with Bread Pudding Brûlée, 22–4
  Brown Bread Dumplings, 138
  Chef's Salad Bruschetta, 66–7
  Cornbread and Sausage Stuffing, 111
  Duck Pithiviers, 105–7
  Honey-Thyme Croutons, 186
  Popovers, 133
  see also biscuits; French toast
breakfast and brunch, 3–34
  bacon and eggs, 6–13
    Bacon, Potato, and Eggs Strudel, 12–13
    Canadian Bacon and Onion Potato Cake with Poached Eggs and Spicy Tomato Salsa, 10–12
    Eggs Benedict with Hash Brown Potatoes and Oven-Dried Tomatoes, 6–9
    Barbecued Sparerib Home-Fries with Poached Eggs and Chili Corn Cakes, 167–8

Crab Clubs on Crackers, 240–1
doughnuts, 25–9
    Drunken Fortune Doughnuts, 27–8
    Simple Sugar-and-Spice Doughnuts, 26–7
    Stuffed Doughnuts with Whipped Cream and
        Berries, 28–9
French toast, 19–24
    French Toast with Bread Pudding Brûlée, 22–4
    French Toast with Cinnamon-Brown Sugar and
        Apple Syrup, 19–20
    Titanic French Toast with Three Jams, 21–2
oatmeal, 30–2
    Almond Oatmeal Crème Brûlée with Orange
        Essence, 31–2
    Oatmeal *Gougères,* 33–4
    Oatmeal with Cinnamon-Brown Sugar and
        Honey-Tossed Berries and Raisins, 30–1
pancakes, 14–18
    Almond, Praline, and Banana Pancakes with
        Orange Syrup and Yogurt, 16–17
    Buttermilk Pancakes with Whipped Butter and
        Maple Syrup, 14–16
    Smoked Salmon Pancake Roll-up with Onions
        and Capers, 17–18
Brooklyn Brownout Cake, 258–60
Brown Bread Dumplings, 138
Brown Sugar-Cinnamon and Apple Syrup,
    19–20
brunch, *see* breakfast and brunch
Bruschetta, Chef's Salad, 66–7
butter:
    clarified butter, 7
    salted whipped butter, 15
    Scampi Butter, 198
    Tomato-Herb Butter, 214
    Worcestershire Compound Butter, 125
buttermilk:
    Buttermilk Biscuits, 197
    buttermilk pancakes, 14–18
    Almond, Praline, and Banana Pancakes with
        Orange Syrup and Yogurt, 16–17
    Buttemilk Pancakes with Whipped Butter and
        Maple Syrup, 14–16
    Meatloaf Pancakes with Goat Cheese Salad and
        Fried Eggs, 145–6
    Smoked Salmon Pancake Roll-up with Onions
        and Capers, 17–18
    Southern Buttermilk-Fried Chicken, 86–7
Butterscotch Ice Cream, 275

C

cabbage:
    Chicken and Cabbage Spring Rolls, 91–2
    Coleslaw, 87
    Herb-Broiled Cod with Clams, Bacon, and
        Cabbage, 196–7
Caesar salad, 68–72
    Chopped Caesar Salad with Crab Cake Croutons,
        70–1
    The Famous Caesar Salad, 68–9
    Spicy Spaghetti with Sausage and Caesar Sauce,
        71–2
cakes:
    cheesecake, 264–9
        Coconut Cheesecake Beignets with Red Fruit
            Sorbet and Berries, 267–9
        Grand Marnier Cheesecake Soufflés, 266–7
        New York Cheesecake, 264–5
    chocolate cake, 258–63
        Brooklyn Brownout Cake, 258–60
        Chocolate Cake "Truffles" in a Chocolate Bag,
            262–3
        Molten Chocolate Cake, 261
Canadian bacon:
    Bacon, Potato, and Eggs Strudel, 12–13
    Canadian Bacon and Onion Potato Cake with
        Poached Eggs and Spicy Tomato Salsa, 10–12
    Eggs Benedict, 6–8
canard à l'orange, 102
Candied Lemon Peel, 115
Cappuccino, Chestnut-Turkey, 114–15
Carpaccio of Chef's Salad, 65–6
Carrots, Glazed, 158–9
casseroles:
    Baked Horseradish-Cheddar Macaroni and
        Cheese, 251
    Herb-Broiled Cod with Clams, Bacon, and
        Cabbage, 196–7
Cauliflower-Rosemary Purée, 188
Charles' Southern-Style Kitchen, New York, 85
Cheddar cheese:
    Baked Horseradish-Cheddar Macaroni and
        Cheese, 251
    Cheddar Biscuits, 56
    chef's salad
        Carpaccio of Chef's Salad, 65–6
        Chef's Salad Bruschetta, 66–7
        Classic Chef's Salad Bowl, 64
    Oatmeal *Gougères,* 33–4

cheese, *see* blue cheese; Cheddar cheese; goat cheese;
    macaroni and cheese; Swiss cheese
cheesecake, 264–9
    Coconut Cheesecake Beignets with Red Fruit
        Sorbet and Berries, 267–9
    Grand Marnier Cheesecake Soufflés, 266–7
    New York Cheesecake, 264–5
chef's salad, 63–7
    Carpaccio of Chef's Salad, 65–6
    Chef's Salad Bruschetta, 66–7
    Classic Chef's Salad Bowl, 64
Chestnut-Turkey Cappuccino, 114–15
chicken, 75–6, 78–100
    barbecued chicken, 93–100
        Barbecued Chicken Parts with Corn on the Cob
            and Grilled Vegetables, 94–6
        Barbecued Chicken Sticky Buns, 99–100
        Pretzel-Onion Crusted Barbecued Chicken with
            Pretzel Latkes, Corn, and Mustard, 96–8
    Bresse chickens, 75–6
    brining technique for, 80–1
    buying, 78
    Chicken Breast Stuffed "Crab Francese,"
        239–40
    Cobb salad, 58–62
        Classic Cobb Salad, 58–60
        Spiced Cobb Salad "Summer Roll" with Blue
            Cheese Dipping Sauce, 62
        "Stacked" Chopped Cobb Salad with Chipotle
            Vinaigrette, 60–1
    fried chicken, 85–92
        Chicken and Cabbage Spring Rolls,
            91–2
        Southern Buttermilk-Fried Chicken, Coleslaw,
            Cornbread Biscuits, Home-Style Green Beans,
            and Mashed Potatoes, 86–9
        Soy-Soaked Tempura Chicken with Vegetable
            Stir-Fry, 89–90
    gauging doneness of, 78–9
    roast chicken, 78–84
        Chicken-Potato Pancakes with Apple-Sour
            Cream Sauce, 83–4
        Roast Chicken "Farmhouse Style" with Potatoes,
            Mushrooms, Bacon, Onions, and Apple Cider
            Gravy, 79–80
        Seawater-Soaked Chicken with Thyme and
            Poppy Seed Gnocchi, 80–3
chiffonade, 67
Child, Julia, 212

chili:
    Chili Corn Cakes, 168
    Red Chili in a Potato Boat with Minced Crisp
        Onion, 134–5
Chipotle Vinaigrette, 60
chocolate:
    chocolate cake, 258–63
        Brooklyn Brownout Cake, 258–60
        Chocolate Cake "Truffles" in a Chocolate Bag,
            262–3
        Molten Chocolate Cake, 261
    chocolate chip cookies, 276–9
        All-American Chocolate Chip Cookies, 276–7
        Chocolate Chip Taco with Chocolate Mousse,
            277–9
        Chocolate Chip UFOs, 279
    Chocolate Filling, 260
    Chocolate Mousse, 278–9
chopped salads:
    Chopped Caesar Salad with Crab Cake Croutons,
        70–1
    Chopped Seafood Salad with Tomato and Onion in
        Avocado Halves, 43–4
chorizo, in Seared Pork with Chorizo and Garlicky
    Clams, 159–60
chowders, 52–7
    Clam Chowder Bread Pudding with Tomato and
        Watercress Salad, 56–7
    New England Clam Chowder with Oyster
        Crackers, 53–4
    Sweet Potato-Turkey Chowder, 116
    Two Soups—New England and Manhattan Clam
        Chowders with Cheddar Biscuits, 54–6
cinnamon:
    Cinnamon-Brown Sugar and Apple Syrup, 19–20
    filling house with smell of sugar scented with, 25
Citrus-Mint Glaze, 175–6
clams:
    chowders
        Clam Chowder Bread Pudding with Tomato and
            Watercress Salad, 56–7
        New England Clam Chowder with Oyster
            Crackers, 53–4
        Two Soups—New England and Manhattan
            Clam Chowders with Cheddar Biscuits, 54–6
    Herb-Broiled Cod with Clams, Bacon, and
        Cabbage, 196–7
    Hot Shellfish Cocktail with Tomato-Roasted Garlic
        Aïoli, 41–3

Seared Pork with Chorizo and Garlicky Clams, 159–60
clarified butter, 7
cobbler: Warm Apple-Blueberry Cobbler with Butterscotch Ice Cream, 274–5
Cobb salad, 58–62
    Classic Cobb Salad, 58–60
    Spiced Cobb Salad "Summer Roll" with Blue Cheese Dipping Sauce, 62
    "Stacked" Chopped Cobb Salad with Chipotle Vinaigrette, 60–1
Cocktail Sauce, 41
Coconut Cheesecake Beignets with Red Fruit Sorbet and Berries, 267–9
cod, 195–202
    Baked Potato with Cod and Red Pepper Coulis, 200–2
    Herb-Broiled Cod with Clams, Bacon, Cabbage, and Biscuits, 196–8
    Oh, My Cod!, 198–200
coffee:
    Barbecued Coffee Spareribs with Fixings, 162–4
    Barbecue Sauce, 96
Coleslaw, 87
Compote, Cranberry-Pineapple, 112–13
condiments:
    Basil Oil, 210
    Crisp Spinach, 234
    Fried Basil, 227–8
    Rosemary Oil, 225
    see also butter; dressings; sauces; vinaigrettes
cookies, chocolate chip, 276–9
    All-American Chocolate Chip Cookies, 276–7
    Chocolate Chip Taco with Chocolate Mousse, 277–9
    Chocolate Chip UFOs, 279
corn:
    Chili Corn Cakes, 168
    Corn Crêpes, 166
    Corn on the Cob, 94–5
    Smoked Salmon with Horseradish Mousse and Corn Blini, 46–7
cornbread:
    Cornbread and Sausage Stuffing, 111
    Cornbread Biscuits, 88–9
coulibiac au saumon, 212
Coulis, Red Pepper, 202
couscous:
    Israeli, 180
    Tomato Couscous, 181–2

crab, 236–45
    crab cakes
        Chicken Breast Stuffed "Crab Francese," 239–40
        Chopped Caesar Salad with Crab Cake Croutons, 70–1
        Crab Cakes with Baltimore-Spiced Tomato Vinaigrette, 237–8
        Crab Clubs on Crackers, 240–1
        Shrimp, Lobster, and Crab with Cocktail Sauce and Old Bay Mayonnaise, 40–1
    soft-shell crabs, 242–5
        Grilled Soft-Shell Crabs with Curry-Yogurt Cream, 244–5
        Soft-Shell Crab Sandwich, 245
        Soft-Shell Crabs with Olive-Tomato Tartar Sauce and Asparagus Salad, 242–4
Cracked Pepper Pineapple Rings, 105
Cracked Pepper Sirloin, 124
Crackers, Crab Clubs on, 240–1
Crackling Pork Shank with Firecracker Applesauce, 154–6
Cranberry-Pineapple Compote, 112–13
crème brûlée:
    Almond Oatmeal Crème Brûlée with Orange Essence, 31–2
    French Toast with Bread Pudding Brûlée, 22–4
Crêpes, Corn, 166
cromesqui, 254
croutons:
    Crab Cake Croutons, 70–1
    Honey-Thyme Croutons, 186
Cucumbers and Red Onions, Pickled, 164
Curry-Yogurt Cream, 244–5

D

David Burke's Vinaigrette, 107
desserts, 257–79
    Almond Oatmeal Crème Brûlée with Orange Essence, 31–2
    apple pie filling, 270–5
        Apple Tart with Tahitian Vanilla Ice Cream, 272–3
        Flaky Apple Pie, 270–2
        Warm Apple-Blueberry Cobbler with Butterscotch Ice Cream, 274–5
    cheesecake, 264–9
        Coconut Cheesecake Beignets with Red Fruit Sorbet and Berries, 267–9

desserts (*continued*)
  cheesecake (*continued*)
    Grand Marnier Cheesecake Soufflés, 266–7
    New York Cheesecake, 264–5
  chocolate cake
    Brooklyn Brownout Cake, 258–60
    Chocolate Cake "Truffles" in a Chocolate Bag, 262–3
    Molten Chocolate Cake, 261
  chocolate chip cookies, 276–9
    All-American Chocolate Chip Cookies, 276–7
    Chocolate Chip Taco with Chocolate Mousse, 277–9
    Chocolate Chip UFOs, 279
  French Toast with Bread Pudding Brûlée, 22–4
  Stuffed Doughnuts with Whipped Cream and Berries, 28–9
doughnuts, 25–9
  Drunken Fortune Doughnuts, 27–8
  Simple Sugar-and-Spice Doughnuts, 26–7
  Stuffed Doughnuts with Whipped Cream and Berries, 28–9
dressings:
  Basil Ranch Dressing, 222
  Roquefort Dressing, 59–60
  see also vinaigrettes
Drunken Fortune Doughnuts, 27–8
duck, 76–7
  roast Long Island duckling, 101–7
    Classic Roast Duck with Oranges, 102–3
    Duck Pithiviers, 105–7
    Soy-Honey Roast Duck, 103–5
dumplings:
  Brown Bread Dumplings, 138
  Shiitake Dumplings, 208

E

eggs:
  Bacon, Potato, and Eggs Strudel, 12–13
  Barbecued Sparerib Home-Fries with Poached Eggs and Chili Corn Cakes, 167–8
  Canadian Bacon and Onion Potato Cake with Poached Eggs and Spicy Tomato Salsa, 10–12
  Classic Cobb Salad, 58–60
  Eggs Benedict with Hash Brown Potatoes and Oven-Dried Tomatoes, 6–9

The Famous Caesar Salad, 68–9
French toast, 19–24
  French Toast with Bread Pudding Brûlée, 22–4
  French Toast with Cinnamon-Brown Sugar and Apple Syrup, 19–20
  Titanic French Toast with Three Jams, 21–2
Meatloaf Pancakes with Goat Cheese Salad and Fried Eggs, 145–6
poaching, 6–8
safety concerns and, 7

F

Firecracker Applesauce, 155–6
fish, 193–216
  cod, 195–202
    Baked Potato with Cod and Red Pepper Coulis, 200–2
    Herb-Broiled Cod with Clams, Bacon, Cabbage, and Biscuits, 196–8
    Oh, My Cod!, 198–200
  tuna, 203–10
    Tuna Niçoise Salad Hash, 208–10
    Tuna Steak au Moutarde with Miso Vinaigrette and Shiitake Dumplings, 205–8
    Tuna Steak Provençal, 204–5
  see also salmon; shellfish
framboise, in Drunken Fortune Doughnuts, 27–8
French toast, 19–24
  French Toast with Bread Pudding Brûlée, 22–4
  French Toast with Cinnamon-Brown Sugar and Apple Syrup, 19–20
  Titanic French Toast with Three Jams, 21–2
fried:
  Fried Basil, 227–8
  fried chicken, 85–92
    Chicken and Cabbage Spring Rolls, 91–2
    Southern Buttermilk-Fried Chicken, Coleslaw, Cornbread Biscuits, Home-Style Green Beans, and Mashed Potatoes, 86–9
    Soy-Soaked Tempura Chicken with Vegetable Stir-Fry, 89–90
  Shrimp Fried Rice and Sausage, 235
frisée, in Goat Cheese Salad, 145–6
Fritters, Macaroni and Cheese, 254

G

garlic:
  Garlic Confit, 182
  Garlicky Spinach, 123
  Roasted Garlic Purée, 12
  Tomato-Garlic Aïoli, 225
  Tomato-Roasted Garlic Aïoli, 42–3
Ginger-Soy Vinaigrette, 89, 229
Glaze, Citrus-Mint, 175–6
Gnocchi, Thyme and Poppy Seed, 80–3
goat cheese:
  Crisp Goat Cheese, Potato, and Lamb Sandwich,
    182–3
  Goat Cheese Salad, 145–6
  Stuffed Tomatoes, 173–4
Gougères, Oatmeal, 33–4
Grand Marnier:
  Grand Marnier Cheesecake Soufflés, 266–7
  Titanic French Toast with Three Jams, 21–2
Grapefruit Vinaigrette, 215–16
Gratin Potato, 130–1
Green Beans, Home-Style, 87–8
grilled:
  Barbecued Ham and Pineapple Kabobs, 156
  Grilled Lobster with Rosemary Oil, Asparagus, and
    Tomato-Garlic Aïoli, 224–5
  Grilled Pork Chops with Applesauce and Glazed
    Carrots, 158–9
  Grilled Soft-Shell Crabs with Curry-Yogurt Cream,
    244–5
  Grilled Vegetables, 94–5
  Pretzel-Onion Crusted Barbecued Chicken with
    Pretzel Latkes, Corn, and Mustard, 96–8
  steaks, 122
    Grilled Sirloin Steak with Garlicky Spinach, 123
  see also barbecued

H

ham:
  chef's salad
    Carpaccio of Chef's Salad, 65–6
    Chef's Salad Bruschetta, 66–7
    Classic Chef's Salad Bowl, 64
  cured or processed, 151
  fresh ham, 151–6
    Barbecued Ham and Pineapple Kabobs, 156
    Crackling Pork Shank with Firecracker
     Applesauce, 154–6

    Roast Fresh Ham with Pineapple Tarte Tatin,
     152–3
    Sliced Pork Salad, 161
hamburger, 120
Hash, Tuna Niçoise Salad, 208–10
Hash Brown Potatoes, 9
Herb-Broiled Cod with Clams, Bacon, Cabbage, and
    Biscuits, 196–8
Hollandaise Sauce, 7, 8
Home-Fries, Barbecued Sparerib, 167
honey:
  Honey-Mustard Vinaigrette, 49–50
  Honey-Thyme Croutons, 186
  Honey-Tossed Berries and Raisins, 30–1
  Soy-Honey Braise, 163–4
  Soy-Honey Roast Duck, 103–5
hors d'oeuvres:
  Bacon, Potato, and Eggs Strudel, 12–13
  Chef's Salad Bruschetta, 66–7
  Chicken and Cabbage Spring Rolls, 91–2
  Oatmeal *Gougères,* 33–4
  Shiitake Dumplings, 208
  Smoked Salmon Lollipops, 50–1
  Smoked Salmon Pancake Roll-up with Onions and
    Capers, 17–18
  Soy-Soaked Tempura Chicken, 89–90
  see also appetizers
horseradish:
  Baked Horseradish-Cheddar Macaroni and
    Cheese, 251
  Horseradish Mousse, 46
  Horseradish-Mustard Mousse, 133
  Sirloin and Horseradish Knish, 126–7

I

ice cream:
  Butterscotch Ice Cream, 275
  Chocolate Chip UFOs, 279
  Tahitian Vanilla Ice Cream, 273

K

Kabobs, Barbecued Ham and Pineapple,
    156
Kentucky Fried Chicken, 85
knishes: Sirloin and Horseradish Knish
    with Mustard-Russian Sauce,
    126–8

L

lamb, 169–90
  cuts of, 171
  lamb chops, 178–83
    Crisp Goat Cheese, Potato, and Lamb Sandwich, 182–3
    Poached Rack of Lamb with *Fleur de Sel,* Tomato Couscous, and Garlic Pearls, 180–2
    Rack of Lamb with Bouquet of Vegetables, 178–9
  lamb stew, 184–90
    Braised Lamb Shank with Cauliflower-Rosemary Purée, 187–8
    Lamb Stew with Root Vegetables and Honey-Thyme Croutons, 185–6
    Tempura Lamb and Vegetables with Peanut Sauce, 189–90
  leg of lamb, 172–7
    Boneless Leg of Lamb with Citrus-Mint Glaze, 175–6
    Lamb-Stuffed Pasta Shells with Tomato Broth, 176–7
    Roast Leg of Lamb, Stuffed Tomatoes, and Sliced Pan Potatoes, 173–4
  rack of, 178
Lasagna Roll, Spinach, 233–4
Latkes, Pretzel, 98
lemon:
  Candied Lemon Peel, 115
  Lemon Rice, 227
lobster, 218–29
  Angry Lobster with Lemon Rice and Crispy Basil, 226–8
  Boiled Lobster with Drawn Butter and Boiled Potatoes, 219–20
  buying, 218
  Grilled Lobster with Rosemary Oil, Asparagus, and Tomato-Garlic Aïoli, 224–5
  Lobster-Mango Rolls with Soy-Ginger Vinaigrette, 228–9
  male vs. female, 218
  Mixed Green Salad with Tiny Potatoes Stuffed with Russian-Style Lobster Salad, 223–4
  Poached Lobster with Onion Rings and Basil Ranch Dressing, 220–2
  Shrimp, Lobster, and Crab with Cocktail Sauce and Old Bay Mayonnaise, 40–1

M

macaroni and cheese, 250–4
  Baked Horseradish-Cheddar Macaroni and Cheese, 251
  Macaroni and Cheese Fritters, 254
  Macaroni and Cheese Tartlette with Mushroom and Truffle Oil, 252–4
mango, in Lobster-Mango Rolls with Soy-Ginger Vinaigrette, 228–9
Manhattan clam chowder, in Two Soups—New England and Manhattan Clam Chowders with Cheddar Biscuits, 54–6
Mashed Potatoes, 88
mayonnaise:
  Mustard-Russian Sauce, 128
  Old Bay Mayonnaise, 41
  Tomato-Garlic Aïoli, 225
  Tomato-Roasted Garlic Aïoli, 42–3
meatloaf, 141–6
  Meatloaf Bundt Cake, 144–5
  Meatloaf Pancakes with Goat Cheese Salad and Fried Eggs, 145–6
  Not-So-Basic Meatloaf, 142–4
Mint-Citrus Glaze, 175–6
Miso Vinaigrette, 207
Mixed Green Salad with Tiny Potatoes Stuffed with Russian-Style Lobster Salad, 223–4
Molten Chocolate Cake, 261
Mousse, Chocolate, 278–9
Murphy, Neil, 228
mushrooms:
  Macaroni and Cheese Tartlette with Mushroom and Truffle Oil, 252–4
  Mushroom Velouté, 253
  porcini powder, 115
  Shiitake Dumplings, 208
  Wild Mushroom-Vegetable Stew, 131–2
mussels, in Hot Shellfish Cocktail with Tomato-Roasted Garlic Aïoli, 41–3
mustard:
  Honey-Mustard Vinaigrette, 49–50
  Horseradish-Mustard Mousse, 133
  Mustard-Russian Sauce, 128

N

New England clam chowder:
  New England Clam Chowder with Oyster Crackers, 53–4

Two Soups—New England and Manhattan Clam
    Chowders with Cheddar Biscuits, 54–6
New York Cheesecake, 264–5

O

oatmeal, 30–2
    Almond Oatmeal Crème Brûlée with Orange
        Essence, 31–2
    Oatmeal *Gougères,* 33–4
    Oatmeal with Cinnamon-Brown Sugar and
        Honey-Tossed Berries and Raisins, 30–1
Oh, My Cod!, 198–200
oils, flavored:
    Basil Oil, 210
    Rosemary Oil, 225
Old Bay Seasoning:
    Baltimore-Spiced Tomato Vinaigrette, 238
    Old Bay Mayonnaise, 41
Olive-Tomato Tartar Sauce, 242–4
onions:
    Canadian Bacon and Onion Potato Cake, 10–11
    Onion Rings, 222
    Pickled Cucumbers and Red Onions, 164
    Roasted Onion Stuffed with Salmon and Tomato
        Salad, 216–17
orange:
    Almond Oatmeal Crème Brûlée with Orange
        Essence, 31–2
    Classic Roast Duck with Oranges, 102–3
    Orange Syrup, 16–17

P

Palmer, Charlie, 83
pancakes:
    buttermilk pancakes, 14–18
        Almond, Praline, and Banana Pancakes with
            Orange Syrup and Yogurt, 16–17
        Buttermilk Pancakes with Whipped Butter and
            Maple Syrup, 14–16
        Meatloaf Pancakes with Goat Cheese Salad and
            Fried Eggs, 145–6
        Smoked Salmon Pancake Roll-up with Onions
            and Capers, 17–18
    corn pancakes
        Corn Crêpes, 166
        Smoked Salmon with Horseradish Mousse and
            Corn Blini, 46–7

potato pancakes
    Canadian Bacon and Onion Potato Cake, 10–11
    Chicken-Potato Pancakes with Apple-Sour
        Cream Sauce, 83–4
    Pastrami Salmon and Smoked Salmon with
        Potato Pancakes, Honey-Mustard Vinaigrette,
        and Apple Salad, 47–50
    Pretzel Latkes, 98
    Shrimp-Potato Pancakes, 125
Paris-Brest, 28
Park Avenue Café, New York City, 12
Parker House rolls:
    Barbecued Chicken Sticky Buns, 99–100
    Parker House Roll Dough, 100
pasta:
    Lamb-Stuffed Pasta Shells with Tomato Broth,
        176–7
    macaroni and cheese, 250–4
        Baked Horseradish-Cheddar Macaroni and
            Cheese, 251
        Macaroni and Cheese Fritters, 254
        Macaroni and Cheese Tartlette with Mushroom
            and Truffle Oil, 252–4
    Spicy Spaghetti with Sausage and Caesar Sauce,
        71–2
    Spinach Lasagna Roll, 233–4
    Thyme and Poppy Seed Gnocchi, 80–3
Pastrami Salmon and Smoked Salmon with Potato
    Pancakes, Honey-Mustard Vinaigrette, and
    Apple Salad, 47–50
pastry:
    Apple Tart with Tahitian Vanilla Ice Cream, 272–3
    Bacon, Potato, and Eggs Strudel, 12–13
    Flaky Apple Pie, 270–2
    Macaroni and Cheese Tartlette with Mushroom
        and Truffle Oil, 252–4
    Oatmeal *Gougères,* 33–4
    Pâte Brisée, 253–4
    Pineapple Tarte Tatin, 153
    Sirloin and Horseradish Knish with Mustard-
        Russian Sauce, 126–8
Pastry Cream, 267
Pâte Brisée, 253–4
pâtés, 141–2
Peanut Sauce, 189
pepper:
    Cracked Pepper Pineapple Rings, 105
    Cracked Pepper Sirloin, 124
peppers, in Red Pepper Coulis, 202

phyllo, in Bacon, Potato, and Eggs Strudel, 12–13
Pickled Cucumbers and Red Onions, 164
Pie, Flaky Apple, 270–2
pineapple:
    Barbecued Ham and Pineapple Kabobs, 156
    Cracked Pepper Pineapple Rings, 105
    Cranberry-Pineapple Compote, 112–13
    Pineapple Tarte Tatin, 153
Pithiviers, Duck, 105–7
poaching:
    eggs, 6–8
    liquids for
        for salmon, 213
        for shellfish, 220
Popovers, 133
Poppy Seed and Thyme Gnocchi, 80–3
porcini powder, 115
pork, 149–68
    cuts of, 149–50
    fresh ham, 151–6
        Barbecued Ham and Pineapple Kabobs, 156
        Crackling Pork Shank with Firecracker
            Applesauce, 154–6
        Roast Fresh Ham with Pineapple Tarte Tatin,
            152–3
    pork chops, 157–61
        Grilled Pork Chops with Applesauce and Glazed
            Carrots, 158–9
        Seared Pork with Chorizo and Garlicky Clams,
            159–60
        Sliced Pork Salad, 161
    safe internal temperature for, 150
    spareribs, 162–8
        Asparagus-Stuffed Spareribs with Corn Crêpes,
            165–6
        Barbecued Coffee Spareribs with Fixings,
            162–4
        Barbecued Sparerib Home-Fries with Poached
            Eggs and Chili Corn Cakes, 167–8
    see also bacon; Canadian bacon; ham; sausage
potatoes:
    Bacon, Potato, and Eggs Strudel, 12–13
    Baked Potato with Cod and Red Pepper Coulis,
        200–2
    Barbecued Sparerib Home-Fries, 167–8
    Boiled Potatoes, 219–20
    Crisp Goat Cheese, Potato, and Lamb Sandwich,
        182–3

Gratin Potato, 130–1
Hash Brown Potatoes, 9
Mashed Potatoes, 88
Mixed Green Salad with Tiny Potatoes Stuffed with
    Russian-Style Lobster Salad, 223–4
potato pancakes
    Canadian Bacon and Onion Potato Cake, 10–11
    Chicken-Potato Pancakes with Apple-Sour
        Cream Sauce, 83–4
    Pastrami Salmon and Smoked Salmon with
        Potato Pancakes, 47–50
    Pretzel Latkes, 98
    Shrimp-Potato Pancakes, 125
Red Chili in a Potato Boat with Minced Crisp
    Onion, 134–5
shrimp "hash," 198–9
Sirloin and Horseradish Knish, 126–7
Sliced Pan Potatoes, 174
Thyme and Poppy Seed Gnocchi, 80–3
Tuna Niçoise Salad Hash, 208–10
Yukon Gold Potato Salad, 164
pot roast, 136–40
    Asian-Style Pot Roast, 139–40
    Pot Roast Sloppy Joes, 140
    Yankee Pot Roast with Brown Bread Dumplings
        and Melted Vegetables, 137–8
poultry, 75–116
    selecting, 76
    see also chicken; duck; turkey
praline, in Almond, Praline, and Banana Pancakes
    with Orange Syrup and Yogurt, 16–17
pretzels:
    Pretzel Latkes, 98
    Pretzel-Onion Crusted Barbecued Chicken with
        Pretzel Latkes, Corn, and Mustard, 96–8
prime rib, see beef
puddings:
    bread puddings
        Bread Pudding, 114
        Clam Chowder Bread Pudding with Tomato and
            Watercress Salad, 56–7
        French Toast with Bread Pudding Brûlée,
            22–4
    Chocolate Mousse, 278–9
purées:
    Cauliflower-Rosemary Purée, 188
    Roasted Garlic Purée, 12
    Sweet Potato and Vanilla Purée, 112

R

Raisins, Honey-Tossed Berries and, 30–1
Ranch Dressing, Basil, 222
Randolph, Mary, 250
raspberries:
    Honey-Tossed Raisins and Berries, 30–1
    Red Fruit Sorbet, 268–9
    Stuffed Doughnuts with Whipped Cream and
        Berries, 28–9
raspberry jam, in Drunken Fortune Doughnuts, 27–8
Red Chili in a Potato Boat with Minced Crisp Onion,
    134–5
Red Fruit Sorbet, 268–9
Red Pepper Coulis, 202
rice:
    Lemon Rice, 227
    Shrimp Fried Rice and Sausage, 235
    Tomato-Rice Pilaf, 232
rice paper, in Lobster-Mango Rolls with Soy-Ginger
    Vinaigrette, 228–9
rillettes, 149
Roquefort Dressing, 59–60
Rosemary Oil, 225

S

salads:
    Apple Salad, 47–8
    Asparagus Salad, 243
    Caesar salad, 68–72
        Chopped Caesar Salad with Crab Cake
            Croutons, 70–1
        The Famous Caesar Salad, 68–9
        Spicy Spaghetti with Sausage and Caesar Sauce,
            71–2
    chef's salad, 63–7
        Carpaccio of Chef's Salad, 65–6
        Chef's Salad Bruschetta, 66–7
        Classic Chef's Salad Bowl, 64
    Chopped Seafood Salad with Tomato and Onion in
        Avocado Halves, 43–4
    Cobb salad, 58–62
        Classic Cobb Salad, 58–60
        Spiced Cobb Salad "Summer Roll" with Blue
            Cheese Dipping Sauce, 62
        "Stacked" Chopped Cobb Salad with Chipotle
            Vinaigrette, 60–1
    Coleslaw, 87

Goat Cheese Salad, 145–6
Mixed Green Salad with Tiny Potatoes Stuffed with
    Russian-Style Lobster Salad, 223–4
Roasted Onion Stuffed with Salmon and Tomato
    Salad, 216–17
salades composées, 63
Sliced Pork Salad, 161
Tomato and Watercress Salad, 57
Tuna Niçoise Salad Hash, 208–10
Yukon Gold Potato Salad, 164
salmon, 211–17
    Pastrami Salmon, 49
    Poached Salmon with Tomato-Herb Butter Sauce
        and Cucumber, 212–14
    Roasted Onion Stuffed with Salmon and Tomato
        Salad, 216–17
    Salmon Leaves Cooked on the Plate with Shrimp,
        Grapefruit, and Basil, 214–16
    smoked salmon, 45–51
        curing and smoking techniques for, 37, 45–6
        Pastrami Salmon and Smoked Salmon with
            Potato Pancakes, Honey-Mustard Vinaigrette,
            and Apple Salad, 47–50
        Smoked Salmon Lollipops, 50–1
        Smoked Salmon Pancake Roll-up with Onions
            and Capers, 17–18
        Smoked Salmon with Horseradish Mousse and
            Corn Blini, 46–7
    types of, 211–12
Salsa, Spicy Tomato, 11–12
salt cod, 195
Sanders, Colonel Harland, 85
sandwiches:
    Crisp Goat Cheese, Potato, and Lamb Sandwich,
        182–3
    Duck Pithiviers, 105–7
    French toast principles and, 19
    Meatloaf Pancakes with Goat Cheese Salad and
        Fried Eggs, 145–6
    Pot Roast Sloppy Joes, 140
    Soft-Shell Crab Sandwich, 245
sauces:
    Barbecue Sauce, 96
    Citrus-Mint Glaze, 175–6
    Cocktail Sauce, 41
    Curry-Yogurt Cream, 244–5
    Hollandaise Sauce, 7, 8
    Horseradish Mousse, 46

sauces (*continued*):
    Horseradish-Mustard Mousse, 133
    Mushroom Velouté, 253
    Mustard-Russian Sauce, 128
    Old Bay Mayonnaise, 41
    Olive-Tomato Tartar Sauce, 242–4
    Peanut Sauce, 189
    Red Pepper Coulis, 202
    Soy-Honey Braise, 163–4
    Spicy Tomato Salsa, 11–12
    tartar sauce, 223
    Tomato Fondue, 207
    Tomato-Garlic Aïoli, 225
    Tomato-Herb Butter, 214
    Tomato-Roasted Garlic Aïoli, 42–3
    Tomato Sauce, 135
    see also butter; dressings; vinaigrettes
sausage:
    Cornbread and Sausage Stuffing, 111
    Seared Pork with Chorizo and Garlicky Clams,
        159–60
    Shrimp Fried Rice and Sausage, 235
    Spicy Spaghetti with Sausage and Caesar Sauce,
        71–2
Scampi Butter, 198
Seawater-Soaked Chicken with Thyme and Poppy
        Seed Gnocchi, 80–3
shellfish, 193–4
    shellfish cocktails, 37, 39–44
        Chopped Seafood Salad with Tomato and Onion
            in Avocado Halves, 43–4
        Hot Shellfish Cocktail with Tomato-Roasted
            Garlic Aïoli, 41–3
        Shrimp, Lobster, and Crab with Cocktail Sauce
            and Old Bay Mayonnaise, 40–1
    see also clams; crab; lobster; shrimp
Shiitake Dumplings, 208
shrimp, 230–45
    Broiled Shrimp with Scampi Butter and Tomato-
        Rice Pilaf, 231–2
    deveining and shelling, 231
    Hot Shellfish Cocktail with Tomato-Roasted Garlic
        Aïoli, 41–3
    Salmon Leaves Cooked on the Plate with Shrimp,
        Grapefruit, and Basil, 214–16
    Sautéed Shrimp with Spinach Lasagna Roll and
        Crisp Spinach, 233–4
    Shrimp, Lobster, and Crab with Cocktail Sauce and
        Old Bay Mayonnaise, 40–1

Shrimp Fried Rice and Sausage, 235
shrimp "hash," 198–9
Shrimp-Potato Pancakes, 125
side dishes:
    Apple Salad, 47–8
    asparagus
        Asparagus Salad, 243
        Grilled Asparagus, 224–5
        Roasted Asparagus, 126
    Bouquet of Vegetables, 178–9
    Bread Pudding, 114
    Brown Bread Dumplings, 138
    Cauliflower-Rosemary Purée, 188
    Chili Corn Cakes, 168
    Cornbread and Sausage Stuffing, 111
    Firecracker Applesauce, 155–6
    Garlic Confit, 182
    Garlicky Spinach, 123
    Glazed Carrots, 158–9
    Grilled Vegetables, 94–5
    Home-Style Green Beans, 87–8
    Lemon Rice, 227
    Onion Rings, 222
    Oven-Dried Tomatoes, 9
    Pickled Cucumbers and Red Onions, 164
    Pineapple Tarte Tatin, 153
    Popovers, 133
    potatoes
        Boiled Potatoes, 219–20
        Gratin Potato, 130–1
        Hash Brown Potatoes, 9
        Mashed Potatoes, 88
        shrimp "hash," 198–9
        Shrimp-Potato Pancakes, 125
        Sliced Pan Potatoes, 174
        Yukon Gold Potato Salad, 164
    Shiitake Dumplings, 208
    Spinach Lasagna Roll, 233–4
    Stuffed Tomatoes, 173–4
    Sweet Potato and Vanilla Purée, 112
    Tomato and Watercress Salad, 57
    Tomato Couscous, 181–2
    Tomato-Rice Pilaf, 232
    Vegetable Stir-Fry, 90
    Wild Mushroom-Vegetable Stew, 131–2
    wild rice, 102–3
    see also biscuits
sirloin steak, *see* beef
slicing meats thinly, 65

Sloppy Joes, Pot Roast, 140
smoked salmon, *see* salmon
soft-shell crabs, *see* crab
Sorbet, Red Fruit, 268–9
Soufflés, Grand Marnier Cheesecake, 266–7
soups, *see* chowders
Southern Buttermilk-Fried Chicken, Coleslaw,
    Cornbread Biscuits, Home-Style Green Beans,
    and Mashed Potatoes, 86–9
soy:
    Soy-Ginger Vinaigrette, 89
    Soy-Honey Braise, 163–4
    Soy-Honey Roast Duck, 103–5
    Soy-Soaked Tempura Chicken with Vegetable Stir-
        Fry, 89–90
Spaghetti with Sausage and Caesar Sauce, Spicy, 71–2
spareribs, 162–8
    Asparagus-Stuffed Spareribs with Corn Crêpes,
        165–6
    Barbecued Coffee Spareribs with Fixings, 162–4
    Barbecued Sparerib Home-Fries with Poached
        Eggs and Chili Corn Cakes, 167–8
Spiced Cobb Salad "Summer Roll" with Blue Cheese
    Dipping Sauce, 62
Spicy Spaghetti with Sausage and Caesar Sauce, 71–2
Spicy Tomato Salsa, 11–12
spinach:
    Crisp Spinach, 234
    Garlicky Spinach, 123
    Lamb-Stuffed Pasta Shells with Tomato Broth,
        176–7
    Spinach Lasagna Roll, 233–4
Spring Rolls, Chicken and Cabbage, 91–2
"Stacked" Chopped Cobb Salad with Chipotle
    Vinaigrette, 60–1
steak, *see* beef
stews:
    lamb stew
        Braised Lamb Shank with Cauliflower-
            Rosemary Purée, 187–8
        Lamb Stew with Root Vegetables and Honey-
            Thyme Croutons, 185–6
        Tempura Lamb and Vegetables with Peanut
            Sauce, 189–90
    Red Chili in a Potato Boat with Minced Crisp
        Onion, 134–5
    Wild Mushroom-Vegetable Stew, 131–2
Stir-Fry, Vegetable, 90
stock, turkey, 110

strawberries:
    Honey-Tossed Raisins and Berries, 30–1
    Red Fruit Sorbet, 268–9
Strudel, Bacon, Potato, and Eggs, 12–13
Stuffing, Cornbread and Sausage, 111
sugar:
    Brown Sugar-Cinnamon and Apple Syrup,
        19–20
    cinnamon-scented, filling house with smell
        of, 25
    Simple Sugar-and-Spice Doughnuts,
        26–7
sweet potatoes:
    Sweet Potato and Vanilla Purée, 112
    Sweet Potato-Turkey Chowder, 116
Swiss cheese:
    Carpaccio of Chef's Salad, 65–6
    Chef's Salad Bruschetta, 66–7
    Classic Chef's Salad Bowl, 64
syrups:
    Cinnamon-Brown Sugar and Apple Syrup,
        19–20
    Orange Syrup, 16–17

                    T
Tahitian Vanilla Ice Cream, 273
tartar sauce, 223
    Olive-Tomato Tartar Sauce, 242–4
tarts:
    Apple Tart with Tahitian Vanilla Ice Cream,
        272–3
    Macaroni and Cheese Tartlette with Mushroom
        and Truffle Oil, 252–4
    Pineapple Tarte Tatin, 153
tempura:
    Soy-Soaked Tempura Chicken with Vegetable
        Stir-Fry, 89–90
    Tempura Lamb and Vegetables with Peanut
        Sauce, 189–90
terrines, 141
thyme:
    Honey-Thyme Croutons, 186
    Thyme and Poppy Seed Gnocchi, 80–3
Titanic French Toast with Three Jams, 21–2
tomatoes:
    Baltimore-Spiced Tomato Vinaigrette, 238
    Lamb-Stuffed Pasta Shells with Tomato Broth,
        176–7

tomatoes (*continued*):
    Olive-Tomato Tartar Sauce, 242–4
    Oven-Dried Tomatoes, 9
    Spicy Tomato Salsa, 11–12
    "Stacked" Chopped Cobb Salad with Chipotle
        Vinaigrette, 60–1
    Stuffed Tomatoes, 173–4
    Tomato and Watercress Salad, 57
    Tomato Couscous, 181–2
    Tomato Fondue, 207
    Tomato-Garlic Aïoli, 225
    Tomato-Herb Butter, 214
    Tomato-Rice Pilaf, 232
    Tomato-Roasted Garlic Aïoli, 42–3
    Tomato Sauce, 135
    Tomato Vinaigrette, 200
tourtes, 141, 144
truffles: Chocolate Cake "Truffles" in a Chocolate
        Bag, 262–3
tuna, 203–10
    Tuna Niçoise Salad Hash, 208–10
    Tuna Steak au Moutarde with Miso Vinaigrette and
        Shiitake Dumplings, 205–8
    Tuna Steak Provençal, 204–5
turducken, 77
turkey, 76
    Classic Chef's Salad Bowl, 64
    roast turkey, 108–16
        Roast Half Turkey with Bread Pudding,
            Chestnut-Turkey Cappuccino, and Candied
            Lemon Peel, 113–15
        Sweet Potato-Turkey Chowder, 116
        Traditional Roast Turkey with Condiments,
            109–13
    smoked turkey
        Carpaccio of Chef's Salad, 65–6
        Chef's Salad Bruschetta, 66–7
    turkey stock, 110
Two Soups—New England and Manhattan
        Clam Chowders with Cheddar Biscuits,
        54–6

V

vanilla:
    Sweet Potato and Vanilla Purée, 112
    Tahitian Vanilla Ice Cream, 273
vegetables:
    Bouquet of Vegetables, 178–9
    Grilled Vegetables, 94–5
    Tempura Lamb and Vegetables with Peanut Sauce,
        189–90
    Vegetable Stir-Fry, 90
    see also side dishes; *specific vegetables*
vinaigrettes:
    Baltimore-Spiced Tomato Vinaigrette, 238
    Basic Vinaigrette, 60
    Caesar salad vinaigrette, 69
    Chipotle Vinaigrette, 60
    David Burke's Vinaigrette, 107
    Grapefruit Vinaigrette, 215–16
    Honey-Mustard Vinaigrette, 49–50
    Miso Vinaigrette, 207
    Soy-Ginger Vinaigrette, 89, 229
    Tomato Vinaigrette, 200
Virginia House-wife, The (Randolph), 250

W

Watercress and Tomato Salad, 57
Whipped Cream, Stuffed Doughnuts with Berries
    and, 28–9
Wild Mushroom-Vegetable Stew, 131–2
wild rice, 102–3
    Duck Pithiviers, 105–7
Worcestershire Compound Butter, 125

Y

Yankee Pot Roast with Brown Bread Dumplings and
    Melted Vegetables, 137–8
Yogurt-Curry Cream, 244–5
Yonah Schimmel's, New York, 126
Yukon Gold Potato Salad, 164

A Note About the Authors

DAVID BURKE, a graduate of the Culinary Institute of America, was the first American to be awarded the prestigious Meilleurs Ouvriers de France Diplome d'Honneur, given to the chef who shows unparalleled skill in his native cuisine. His other awards include Japan's Nippon Award for Excellence, the Robert Mondavi Award of Excellence, and the Culinary Institute of America's August Escoffier Award. In New York City he was chef at the River Café, opened the Park Avenue Café with Alan Stillman, CEO of the Smith and Wollensky group, and is now executive chef and co-owner of davidburke & donatella. He is author, with Carmel Reingold, of *Cooking with David Burke.* He lives in Fort Lee, New Jersey.

JUDITH CHOATE is the award-winning author of more than twenty-five cookbooks and the coauthor of *The Tribeca Grill Cookbook* and *The Art of Aureole,* among many others. She works as a consultant to the food industry through her company, Custom Cuisine. She lives in New York City.

A Note on the Type

This book was set in Minion, a typeface produced by
the Adobe Corporation specifically for the Macintosh
personal computer, and released in 1990. Designed by
Robert Slimbach, Minion combines the classic characteristics of old style faces with the full complement
of weights required for modern typesetting.

Composed by North Market Street Graphics,
Lancaster, Pennsylvania

Printed and bound by R.R. Donnelley & Sons,
Crawfordsville, Indiana

Designed by Anthea Lingeman